Quality Through Access,
Access with Quality

William H. Bergquist

Written in association with
Connie Arburua, Jason Bergquist,
Katherine Bergquist, Hattie Bishop, and
Barbara Leigh Smith

Quality Through Access, Access with Quality

The New Imperative for Higher Education

Jossey-Bass Publishers • San Francisco

Substantial discounts on bulk quantities of Jossey-Bass books are
available to corporations, professional associations, and other
organizations. For details and discount information, contact the
special sales department at Jossey-Bass Inc., Publishers.
(415) 433–1740; Fax (800) 605–2665.

For sales outside the United States, please contact your local
Paramount Publishing International Office.

TCF Manufactured in the United States of America on Lyons Falls
Pathfinder Tradebook. This paper is acid-free and 100 percent
totally chlorine-free.

Library of Congress Cataloging-in-Publication Data

Bergquist, William H.
    Quality through access, access with quality : the new imperative
for higher education / William H. Bergquist.
        p.   cm.   (The Jossey-Bass higher and adult education series)
    Includes bibliographical references (p.   ) and index.
    ISBN 0-7879-0071-0
    1. Education, Higher–United States–Aims and objectives.
2. College choice–United States.   3. Quality (Philosophy)
I. Title
LA227.4.B47   1995
378.73–dc20
                                                                    94-41600
                                                                    CIP

FIRST EDITION
HB Printing   10 9 8 7 6 5 4 3 2 1

The Jossey-Bass

Higher and Adult Education Series

Contents

Preface

During the past century, considerable attention has been given to two overarching goals in American higher education: quality and access. Polls of senior academic leaders are conducted each year to identify the highest-quality academic departments in the United States, the best colleges, and the most prestigious universities. Jencks and Riesman (1968) suggested more than twenty-five years ago that the academic departments and institutions that are inevitably rated as being of highest quality (such as Harvard, Yale, Stanford, the University of Michigan, and the University of California) offer a model of quality that most other colleges and universities in the United States strive to emulate, no matter how inappropriate or how unlikely it is that any upstart college or university will ever be "the Harvard of Southeast X State," "the Berkeley of Southwest Y State," or "the Stanford of Central Z State" (Kerr, 1991, pp. 8–15). These exemplars of quality rely on enormous consumption of public funds and private philanthropy to sustain their quality, not to mention severe restrictions on the enrollment of students from underserved populations; only sporadic use of senior faculty in undergraduate courses; limited diversity in student and faculty characteristics; and reduced public accountability.

At the same time, American educators also extol the virtues of access to higher education. In keeping with the nation's democratic and populist values and traditions, the American dream has always included upward social and economic mobility. The central message is that social and economic gains are achieved through education.

Small community colleges and large state university systems were built on this dream. They were to be institutions that enabled young men and women of humble origins and means to apply themselves so that they might do better in life than their parents. Ethnic and racial groups that had known the debilitating effects of discrimination were to obtain an education so that their own rising expectations, as well as the newly optimistic expectations of their parents and communities, might be fully realized.

My book *The Four Cultures of the Academy* (1992) provides one perspective on the seemingly conflicting commitments to both quality and access in American higher education. In it, I identified and described four cultures that prevail in contemporary colleges and universities: the collegial, managerial, developmental, and negotiating cultures. Each has its own set of assumptions and criteria regarding both quality and access in institutions of higher education. Furthermore, these four cultures pervade not only individual colleges and universities but also licensing and accrediting associations, state and federal legislative bodies, and other higher education leadership groups that strongly influence the nature and purpose of these colleges and universities. These various constituencies are often unaware of their own assumptions and biases and hence are unable to perceive the ways in which they confine and distort the nature and purposes of the institutions they are supposed to serve.

Quality Through Access, Access with Quality is likely to be controversial. I was reluctant to write it, given my own biases and personal experiences; however, I took the advice I often give to my own doctoral students when they are considering dissertation topics. I urge them to "enter the mouth of the dragon"—to write about something that is of deep personal concern to them, even if it means that they must struggle with the issues of objectivity and bias. Other books I have written have been descriptive or have provided tools to help educators solve organizational or professional development problems. This book was much more difficult to write, for

I am advocating for a specific set of values rather than trying to describe a situation or solve a problem.

I offer my potentially biased observations, however, from a base of extensive consultation with more than four hundred colleges and universities in North America, some traditional and others not. I am fortunate in having a very broad perspective on American higher education, having consulted in prestigious American and Canadian colleges and universities and influential state, provincial, and national educational associations in the United States and Canada, as well as having consulted, taught, and served in a leadership role at several institutions that are at the bottom of the pecking order. In other words, I have seen higher education from the top, from the bottom, and at many levels in between. I hope that readers will find that my analyses reflect the reality of higher education and that insights gained from the analyses and from my experiences at each level of the system will prove to be of value in addressing the issues of quality and access in their own college or university.

Audience

Given that the issues of quality and access are central to any collegiate institution and that the frequent tensions between quality and access affect all aspects of collegiate life, this book should be of interest and concern to members of the different segments of the higher education community, including administrators, faculty members, alumni, and especially members of governing boards for individual schools and participants in various higher education regulatory and accrediting agencies.

Fortunately, on the issues of quality and access I have been given many opportunities to interact with many different people involved in many different kinds of collegiate institutions. I have found just as much interest in these issues among administrators and faculty members at major research universities as at two-year community colleges. I am particularly pleased that trustees of both two- and four-year colleges and universities have expressed interest in these issues and my perspectives on them. Strong interest in my analyses of quality and access has been expressed also by educators who have been struggling for reform on their own campuses. They are often not fully aware or fully appreciative of the deep roots of resistance to their reform; this book should provide some insight and guidance. In addition, I have found that faculty members who have been teaching and seeking improvement in their institutions for many years are particularly intrigued by the historical perspectives as well as the hope I offer. Many of these men and women share with me a long history of teaching, a record of occasional leadership at their institution, and a commitment to ongoing dialogue (within the institution and among colleagues) regarding the nature and purpose of higher education. They welcome the opportunity to reflect more deeply on the central issues of quality and access in our collegiate institutions.

Organization of the Book

Part One frames the basic premises of *Quality Through Access* . . . regarding the environment in which contemporary colleges and universities operate, the need for integration of quality and access in such an environment, the central role played by access in any commitment to quality in such an environment, and the central role played by quality in any initiative directed toward increasing access.

Chapter One specifically focuses on the nature of our emerging postmodern world, especially as it affects collegiate institutions. In Chapter Two, I introduce several premises regarding the interdependence of quality and access—values in higher education that are usually considered incompatible. Chapter Three focuses on the issue of mission and more specifically on ways in which particular criteria of quality contribute to or block the unification of quality and access. In Chapter Four, I approach the unification issue—particularly from the access side—and identify four prevalent perspectives in American higher education that tend to identify quality and access as either incompatible or at the very least difficult to integrate.

Part Two focuses on these four perspectives. In Chapter Five, I discuss the first perspective, elitism, which is founded on a commitment to quality, often at the expense of access. Chapter Six focuses on the other end of the continuum, the populist perspective, which is built on a commitment to access, often at the expense of quality. The beleaguered perspective is discussed in Chapter Seven; because of internal and external forces, this perspective is oriented toward neither quality nor access but rather toward survival. In Chapter Eight, I turn to the expedient perspective, which tends to value quality and access inconsistently—primarily as they relate to the quest for funds and student enrollment. In each of these chapters, I describe a hypothetical educational institution, which I call Exemplar College/University, from the perspective under consideration in that chapter.

Part Three, which concerns strategies for the achievement and integration of quality and access, provides a fifth, unified perspective on these two institutional commitments. I identify three basic strategies for integrating quality and access in Chapter Nine. The first concerns creative ways of meeting the needs of diverse student populations, the second concerns a sustained commitment to both quality and access, and the third strategy is based on an orientation toward cooperation with other institutions. Chapter Ten focuses in more detail on specific institutional initiatives that can affect both quality and access: assessment, benchmarking, clarification of values, development of professional competencies, empowerment, and feedback, as they contribute to the unification of quality and access. Finally, in Chapter Eleven, I focus on issues of leadership and ways in which leaders can influence both quality and access.

Acknowledgments

I wish first of all to thank my coauthors for their valuable contributions to this book. The reports prepared by Connie Arburua, Katherine Bergquist, and Jason Bergquist are evident in the wonderful insights offered about quality and access by students in three case study institutions (The Evergreen State College, John F. Kennedy University, and the Professional School of Psychology). Jason Bergquist's work is also evident in other discussions regarding the experiences of nontraditional students in contemporary colleges and universities. Barbara Leigh Smith not only prepared a thorough case study of The Evergreen State College but also provided material on nontraditional schools and changes in American higher education over the past twenty years. In addition, Barbara offered many helpful suggestions regarding the entire book at several times during its preparation. I feel fortunate to have had an opportunity to work with this insightful and articulate colleague.

Throughout the book, I have made use of the thoughtful analysis of curriculum and organizational life prepared by my colleague Hattie Bishop for a book that she and I were writing several years ago with three other colleagues—Joanne Gainen, Robert Shukraft, and Bruce Willats. I wish not only to acknowledge the rich contributions made by Hattie (including parts of the hypothetical Exemplar case study) but also those made by our three colleagues.

Many other colleagues have contributed to this book by participating actively and sometimes critically in seminars that I have conducted regarding the concepts advanced in this book. I am particularly appreciative of the contributions made by my colleagues from across the Canadian border. I find that much of my best work occurs when I am invited to consult for Canadian colleges and universities and when I have the opportunity to engage openly and creatively with faculty members and administrators in the Potlatch and Pacific Management Institute programs that are held each summer in British Columbia. I thank Diane Morrison and Judy Wilbee for their continuing leadership in making these events happen each year.

Finally, I want to express my deep appreciation for the support offered by four other people in my life. First, I wish to thank Gale Erlandson, senior editor of the Higher and Adult Education Series at Jossey-Bass. This is the fourth book she has edited for me, and I'm sure that it has been the hardest for her to guide, given the personal nature of its contents for me. Thank you, Gale, for your patience and your competence. I also acknowledge the contributions of Lori McMahan, interim president of the Professional School of Psychology. In the final stages of preparing this book, I stepped down as president of PSP; Lori has done a superb job of managing the transition so that I might complete this book. Thank you, Lori, for your talent and your commitment to PSP.

Third, I wish, as always, to express my love and appreciation to Kathleen O'Donnell, my wife, for her constant support of my work and her encouragement when times have gotten hard over the past twelve years. How does one ever adequately acknowledge the central role played by someone so close and dear? Finally, I acknowledge the indispensable role played by Eunice Kelly in my personal and professional life over the past eight years. She has been the finest colleague I have ever had. Thank you, Eunice, for your unwavering commitment to Kathleen and me over these many years. In recognition of this commitment, Eunice, I dedicate this book to you.

Gualala, California   William Bergquist
February 1995

The Author

William H. Bergquist has been a consultant for thirty years to more than six hundred corporations, collegiate institutions, and human service agencies throughout the United States, Canada, Eastern Europe, and Asia. He has written or coauthored more than two dozen books on postsecondary education, adult development, organizational behavior, and the nature of our postmodern era. Bergquist received his B.A. degree in psychology (1962) from Occidental College and his M.A. and Ph.D. degrees (1965 and 1969, respectively), also in psychology, from the University of Oregon.

Bergquist served for eight years (1986–1994) as president of the Professional School of Psychology in San Francisco and Sacramento. His books on the psychological adaptation to strokes and on the experiences of freedom in Eastern Europe were published in 1994. A book on partnerships, which he coauthored with David Meuel and Juli Betwee, is coming out in 1995, and he is now writing a book on the role of sanctuaries in the personal and professional lives of people living in our turbulent postmodern world.

Quality Through Access, Access with Quality

Part One

---

*Quality, Access,
and the Postmodern
Condition*

Chapter One

Higher Education in the Postmodern Environment

To the extent that my work is known in the higher education community, most people will identify me as an author or a consultant. However, for eight years I also served as president of the Professional School of Psychology, an institution that specializes in providing master's and doctoral level education to mature, accomplished human service professionals. The mean age of my students was forty-four. The school is also committed to being affordable, offering a guaranteed tuition plan that costs less than half as much as most similar institutions. As of fall 1994, master's-level tuition was lower than that of the local state universities.

I mention this because PSP is an institution that is strongly committed to access (in terms of cost, location, scheduling of classes, and so on) as well as quality (small classes, highly qualified faculty, strong student services, and so forth). Yet it is also grappling with issues of accreditation, acceptance, and respectability in the local professional community and even struggling for acceptance among its own student body, faculty, and staff ("We don't look like a traditional graduate school. Are we really any good?"). Readers who come from other educational institutions that are nontraditional or are marginal in other ways will recognize this deep underlying sense of uneasiness about one's personal and institutional respectability. I find myself frequently reflecting on the nature of quality and how it relates to the strong commitment to access that is at the heart of my school.

Three recent experiences have convinced me that such a deliberation would be of value not only to myself and other leaders of nontraditional institutions but also to the leaders of more traditional institutions, who have considerable influence over the nature of higher education. The first experience was a meeting several years ago with a man whose power in deciding the fate of my school with regard to credentialing in the higher education community caused me to think long and hard about the issues of quality and access. Commenting on my own school, this man remarked, "You certainly don't want it to end up being like John F. Kennedy University." I was taken aback both because the comment seemed inappropriate coming from a person in his position and because nothing in my fifteen years of involvement with JFK University could explain why his impression of it was so negative. Furthermore, my son was attending that very school and was receiving an excellent education. I mentioned these facts to the man who made the comment and suggested that he had chosen the wrong person to whom to demean the university.

I had assumed that this person's attitude toward John F. Kennedy University (and perhaps schools like my own) was rare. I was soon rudely awakened, however, by a second experience: the words of Mayhew, Ford, and Hubbard in their book *The Quest for Quality* (1990). I had long respected the work of Lewis Mayhew, a distinguished professor emeritus of higher education at Stanford University, and was therefore quite shocked to read the negative statements that he and his coauthors (who are also leaders in the field) make regarding "relatively new, privately supported, tuition-driven institutions created since about 1970." They identify John F. Kennedy University by name when noting that "in aggregate, [the] practices and processes [of these institutions] leave considerable concern for the quality of education received by their students" (p. 44). They also include the California School of Professional Psychology on this list, and I'm certain that by their standards, my own school would also give these writers qualms.

Although I appreciate their concern for the quality achieved by financially unstable, tuition-driven schools (be they new graduate schools serving adult learners or small church-related liberal arts colleges serving young men and women), I do not appreciate the ease with which they dismiss the exceptional accomplishments of the nontraditional schools over a period of two decades, nor do I appreciate the dated critique they offer (for example, the conclusion that "considerable credit is given for prior experience" in these institutions, which is simply no longer true at most of them).

I am perhaps most disturbed by the complacency and self-satisfaction in their dismissal of the many valuable higher education reforms of the 1960s, 1970s, and 1980s. Mayhew and colleagues note that "the names of established private colleges and universities and flagship state universities almost never appear on the lists of institutions that are seriously and comprehensively participating in radical reform" such as the proposals for lifelong learning and new models of educational access offered by the Commission on Nontraditional Study in 1973. They further suggest that "in many respects, the best reaction of institutions to these cries for reform . . . is benign neglect. . . . Quality-conscious colleges and universities will very likely continue to perform as they have in the past and pay little attention to the rhetoric of the reformers" (Mayhew, Ford, and Hubbard, 1990, p. 18). It is remarkable to read of such complacency in a world that is changing so profoundly.

Though I was pleased to read several critiques of the Mayhew, Ford, and Hubbard book, I found myself concerned that in none of these critiques was there a reflection on the broad-based support for the perspectives being offered. I believe that Mayhew, Ford, and Hubbard have articulated a widespread perception and perhaps have done the field of higher education a real favor by bringing these perspectives out into the open, to be examined and critiqued. As Bogue and Saunders (1992) state in their own recent examination of quality in American higher education, "certain . . . assumptions are widely held by academics and laypersons concerning collegiate quality: only high-cost colleges have quality; only large and comprehensive colleges have quality; only highly selective colleges have quality; only nationally recognized colleges have quality; only a few colleges have quality; only colleges with impressive resources have quality" (p. 7).

The central questions for me became these: Do many people automatically accept the complacent conclusions reached by Mayhew, Ford, and Hubbard regarding the welcomed demise of nontraditional higher education in the United States? Are Bogue and Saunders correct regarding the breadth of these traditional assumptions about quality? During the past year, I have personally come to the conclusion that the opinions expressed by Mayhew and his colleagues are widespread.

A third experience furthered my concern about the loss of support for nontraditional higher education. The leader of a major accrediting agency in the United States suggested to me in a private conversation that innovation was the clarion call in higher education during the 1970s and early 1980s. He observed, however, that it is no longer in vogue, nor is it needed. According to this leader, the late 1980s and the 1990s are primarily a time for consolidation and the clearing out of substandard, nontraditional institutions that now litter the postsecondary landscape. I cannot imagine a statement like Mayhew and colleagues' or the accreditation leader's coming from leaders of the corporate, health care, nonprofit human service, governmental, or religious communities in the United States. In a sector of society that is supposedly preparing men and women for a changing world, the absence of calls for reform is startling.

These three disturbing encounters made me wonder what influences in the higher education community would cause these leaders to opt for the status quo. John F. Kennedy University has existed for more than two decades. My own experiences at the school have convinced me that it does an outstanding job of educating men and women who are holding down jobs, are raising families, and have assumed leadership roles in their local communities. I should think that such a school would be admired as a distinctive addition to the higher education community and as an exemplar of a new amalgamation of quality and access. Yet such is not often the case.

Unfortunately, I know that JFK University is not particularly admired by many leaders in the higher education community who should know better. What seems to be the reason for the failure to appreciate and support this unique institution? More than twenty years ago, Frank Newman and colleagues (1971) wrote about the absence of diversity in American higher education; Jencks and Riesman (1968) similarly described the homogenizing tendencies among colleges and universities in the United States. Have we made no progress over the past twenty years?

My daughter decided two years ago to attend The Evergreen State College in Olympia, Washington, a distinctive public undergraduate institution that offers a thematic interdisciplinary curriculum organized around yearlong programs and extensive faculty-student contact. Though the school is now widely known among educators, having been written about extensively, in many ways it is still on the margin of the higher education community. High school counselors, friends of mine who are college and university faculty members, and other members of our extended family tried to dissuade my daughter from attending Evergreen, describing it as nothing more than a throwback to the 1960s. My daughter decided to enroll nevertheless. She loves her experience at Evergreen and confirms my impressions (from previous consulting experiences at the college) that this is a special school. It blends high quality (in terms of faculty qualifications, faculty accessibility to students and interdisciplinarity, and curricular diversity and flexibility) with accessibility (affordable tuition—Evergreen is a public institution).

Yet my daughter also reports that Evergreen is constantly being criticized by people in local Washington communities. Furthermore, I know that the college struggled for years to build public support and continued funding. It is an institution that never seems to have been fully accepted in the state of Washington, or elsewhere, although dozens of colleges are now adopting features of the Evergreen "learning community" approach to curriculum design. The school would probably make Mayhew, Ford, and Hubbard's list of "institutions at risk"—or, at the very least, they would place its interdisciplinary faculty in the category of educators who "had left—for one reason or another—the established reference group of their chosen academic disciplines or professions to establish new reference groups and reputations" (Mayhew, Ford, and Hubbard, 1990, p. 14).

What keeps Evergreen marginal? Why is the school the butt of so many jokes? Why did so many people want my daughter to go anywhere but Evergreen? What's wrong with a faculty made up of men and women who have left their traditional disciplinary reference group to join with colleagues from other disciplines to tackle important, complex interdisciplinary issues? Answers to these questions might shed some light on the nature of contemporary higher education, particularly with regard to issues of quality and access.

The Postmodern Condition

In setting the context for a discussion of these questions, it is essential to look carefully and systematically at the conditions now faced by institutions of higher education. The conditions go far beyond the confines of our collegiate institutions. They are part of the economic, political, social, and human value shifts that are occurring in our world. At a profound level, these shifts affect the very way in which we conceive of knowledge and the process of knowing (Berger and Luckmann, 1967). Though no word or phrase adequately captures the richness and complexity of any one era in the history of our world, the term *postmodern* has often been used to denote the constellation of conditions that we now face (Lyotard, 1984; W. Anderson, 1990; Gergen, 1991; Jameson, 1991; Bergquist, 1993). I will therefore set the context for my discussion of quality and access by first identifying some of the major characteristics of postmodernity, especially as it relates to institutional life inside and outside collegiate institutions.

Our postmodern world is still being born. It does not yet have clear definition, other than its origins in and differences from the modern era; hence the name *postmodern*. It is still defined with reference to its precursor (modernism) rather than having split off as a free and independent movement or set of ideas and images with a separate and distinctive name. In many ways, postmodernism is both a fad and, at the same time, about fads. Even though postmodernism is filled with superficial, facile, and often internally contradictory analyses, it should not be dismissed, for these analyses offer insightful and valuable—even essential—perspectives and critiques of our emerging era (Huyssen, 1987; Jameson, 1991).

To make sense of the diverse and turbulent postmodern changes that are taking place, I have focused on five dimensions of institutional life: (1) size and complexity, (2) mission and boundaries, (3) leadership, (4) communication, and (5) capital and worker values. I suggest that major shifts have occurred in each of these dimensions as our world has moved from the premodern era (primarily agricultural and trade-based) to the modern era (industrial and service-based). Shifts of a similar magnitude are now occurring throughout the world as we move into a temporary or relatively long-lasting era that is information-based and turbulent.

Size and Complexity

We find in the premodern era the dominance of simple organizational structures (usually based in the family unit) and an emphasis on gradual growth. By contrast, during the modern era emphasis was placed not on the process of growth itself or on the gradual expansion in organizational capacity but rather on the outcomes of growth—large size and an accompanying increase in organizational efficiency and market share. Organizational structures were no longer simple in the modern era. However, these structures were usually uniform within and between organizations (being of a bureaucratic nature). Furthermore, these structures were compatible with hierarchically based forms of leadership and authority and with the energy-intensive and technologically driven processes of mass production.

In moving to the postmodern era, emphasis tends to be placed not on growth and largeness but instead on keeping things small or moderate in size (Schumacher, 1973). Structures are neither simple nor uniform, despite the emphasis on smallness. Rather, the postmodern organization is typified by fragmentation, inconsistency, and a mix of organizational structures, policies, and procedures (Clegg, 1990). Whereas many people view this fragmentation and inconsistency as transitional, between the modern era and some new, as yet undetermined era, there is reason to believe that this will be a much longer lasting condition of postmodern organizations.

Mission and Boundaries

Premodern organizations typically had unclear boundaries (particularly between work and family life) and an unclear mission. There was little need for defined organizational purposes because the work of the premodern organization was primarily done by family members to provide sufficient food and shelter. Furthermore, even among people working in the trades, a mission statement was unnecessary because the product spoke for itself. A system of bartering and exchange of goods and services (for example, the farmer's market) eliminated the need for an elaborate monetary system.

During the modern era, boundaries were quite clear, whereas mission statements tended to remain vague or inconsistent. In modern organizations, clear distinctions were made between the places where employees worked and where they lived, relaxed, and worshiped. We knew when we were entering and leaving a modern organization, and we often defined the organization by its mere existence rather than its specific mission or purpose.

Postmodern conditions have precipitated a crisis with regard to both mission and boundaries. To survive, most postmodern organizations have had to formulate clearer mission statements, in part because they can no longer retain clear boundaries (Jameson, 1991). In the modern world, boundaries (and identities defined by roles and rules) served as "containers" of anxiety (Kets de Vries, 1984; Kets de Vries and Miller, 1984; Zaleznick, 1989; Zaleznick and Kets de Vries, 1985). In the postmodern world, we must look to a clear sense of mission and purpose (both organizational and personal) to overcome this boundariless anxiety, the sense of living on the edge (Lasch, 1984; Gergen, 1991).

As specialty shops in the postmodern malls of corporate and human service life, these organizations must find their own distinctive niches and become more adaptive in the manner in which they produce, market, and deliver products and services (Peters, 1987). Furthermore, organizations in the postmodern world must repeatedly reexamine their purposes and values, for the world in which they operate is constantly changing and demanding new and different products and services. Without a clear sense of purpose and values, these organizations soon splinter or become aimless vagabonds or scavengers that feed destructively on other organizations and segments of our society (Bergquist, 1993).

Leadership

Leaders in the premodern era tended to be "great" men or women selected for their character and education. Great leaders not only controlled organizations but also influenced history and set values. Leaders were either born to greatness or provided with an elitist program of liberal arts and mentorship. They tended to exert authority through a paternalistic concern for the welfare and proper education of those who depended on them (Sennett, 1981). By contrast, the more democratic modern era tended to emphasize structures, processes, and procedures that ensured the appropriate expression of leadership and influence. Events—not great men or women—determined the course of modern history, and values were identified as products of the system and of bureaucracy rather than as products of any specific individual or individuals (Weber, 1947). Modern authority was expressed through the autonomy of rules and regulations, roles, and organizational structures (Foucault, 1965). Leadership in the modern world was equated with management (Sennett, 1981).

The postmodern world has called both the premodern and modern notions of leadership into question (Waldrop, 1992). The postmodern leader is neither inherently great nor merely a product of a system or bureaucracy. Individual leadership can be effectively exerted and will be influential if applied at the right time, in the right place, in the right manner, with regard to the right product, service, problem, or goal (Woodward, 1958; Fiedler, 1967; Vroom and Yetton, 1973; Hershey and Blanchard, 1977). This contingent or situational model of leadership requires careful consideration of both individual and organizational character and style. It also requires a tolerance for ambiguity, a recognition of the need for one to learn from one's mistakes (Schön, 1983), and a clear sense of personal mission and purpose (Greenleaf, 1970; Palmer, 1990).

Leaders of the postmodern world must navigate a treacherous "white-water" environment (Vaill, 1989), filled with unpredictability and the need for short-term survival tactics, as well as long-term strategies based on broad visions and deeply embedded values. Much as in the case of white-water rapids, there are eddies and swirls as well as quiet but powerful flows. We must navigate these white-water conditions as leaders, inventors, visionaries, and workers. What skills are needed to navigate the rapids? Some postmodernists would suggest that leadership requires a spiritual center (Vaill, 1989)—an internal coherence—to navigate the white water. Others would suggest that leaders must be able to reflect on their own practices and learn from their mistakes rather than repeat them (Argyris and Schön, 1978; Senge, 1990).

Communication

Oral forms of communication were dominant in the premodern world. Small, simple organizations allowed men and women to communicate freely with one another. A strong sense of community and homogeneity of interests and values minimized the need for written documents. With the emergence of industrialized and highly specialized modern organizations came an increasing need for written communication (contracts, agreements, records of transactions, and so forth) as a substitute for direct interpersonal contact (Weber, 1947). Rather than seeing and listening to other persons, one read their memoranda or written proposals. Other visual modes of communication also prevailed: television, film, graphics, and icon-based computer programs.

The postmodern world, by contrast, tends again to be more orally based. We call each other and leave voice messages rather than write letters. We eliminate secretaries and clerks and seek to reduce paperwork. Short-term face-to-face meetings, adhocracies, task forces, and temporary systems (Miles, 1964) have replaced long-standing bureaucratic structures that were dependent on written rules and the documentation of policies, procedures, and program ideas (Toffler, 1971, 1980). In this orally oriented world, members of organizations must learn how to bond together in temporary groups (Bennis and Slater, 1968). They must also learn how to detach from one another in order to move on to other groups or projects.

Communication is considered in a unique and provocative manner by various postmodern theorists (including Bateson, 1979). They suggest that organizations are to be distinguished from many other systems because of their primary reliance on the flow of information. Information flow is in turn embedded in a complex network of relationships and conversations. Some postmodernists— especially those who identify themselves as "deconstructionists" (Dews, 1987)—are likely to consider organizations as nothing other than relationships and extended conversations (Lyotard, 1984).

Even the structures and products of an organization are secondary in most contemporary organizations to conversations about these structures and products. Gossip is finally acknowledged as the glue that holds organizations together and provides the means for effective, informal internal communication (Belenky, Clinchy, Goldberger, and Tarule, 1986). Storytelling and narration become effective change strategies in the postmodern era. If organizations are extended conversations, stories are their lifeblood and maintenance system. The elaboration of stories about organizations may be critical to both personal and organizational transformation.

Capital and Worker Values

Land was one of the dominant and most tangible forms of capital in the premodern era. Ancestry and reputation were two less tangible but equally important forms. The divine right of kings prevailed. The Catholic church emphasized property and prohibited the use of money to make money (usury). Workers tended to focus on security and conformity. They sought paternalistic care and asked little in return.

The modern forms of capital, by contrast, were money and buildings. Reputation and ancestry became less important. New wealth was more liquid—and more volatile: "Rich men come and go." This new form of capitalism, supported by Calvinistic doctrine and Protestant churches, became dominant and highly influential (at least in the middle and upper classes) during the modern era (Tawney, 1921; Weber, 1958; Boulding, 1952). One's worldly success (as manifest in the inconspicuous accumulation of monetary wealth) was a sign of one's worth. Poverty was considered in some very basic sense sinful and a sign of inadequacy or laziness.

The new capital of the postmodern era consists of information and expertise (Cleveland, 1982; Drucker, 1989). Approval and its inverse, shame, are central components of the new capital (Sennett, 1981; Hochschild, 1983). Values of the postmodern worker complement this new capital. Emphasis is placed on motivational rather than security factors (Herzberg, 1966). Increasing attention is given to the meaning of work and to the recognition derived from colleagues and supervisors about the quality of one's work. Quality-of-work-life programs and sociotechnical systems dramatically increase worker involvement in the design of production systems and even in daily decision making regarding purchases of equipment, the composition of work teams, and increased worker safety and security (Lawler, 1986). The new values of postmodern workers border on the spiritual as greater meaning, purpose, and involvement are sought in work and affiliation with an organization.

Living in the Postmodern Era

The postmodern world is filled with incomplete and incoherent images of the future (Polak, 1972), as well as fragmented images of art, politics, and the sciences. One cannot help but wonder if the fragmentation and inconsistency—and the accompanying edginess—are temporary. Are we in a major transition between modern society and something new but still unclear? Or have we already moved into a long-lasting postmodern phase, a fragmented world that will not readily change? We may never be able to return to a world of greater simplicity, coherence, and consistency.

From our postmodern vantage point, the premodern world seems to have moved at a leisurely and considered pace. Change tended to be gradual. By contrast, in the modern era, change occurred at an ever-accelerating pace (Toffler, 1971, 1980). The future was closing in on the present at breakneck speed, and modern humans braced themselves for the shock. Preparation for accelerated modern change took place primarily through effective planning and anticipation of impending events and shifting environmental conditions. Analyses of trends and cause-and-effect relationships enabled modern managers to lead by looking ahead and by setting up for any of a number of contingencies.

What, then, of the postmodern world? Change in our newly emerging era will continue to accelerate—sometimes. At other times, change is likely to be gradual. Frequently, we will be unable to predict with accuracy what the rate of change will be at any point in time. Thus we must learn to cope not just with accelerated change but also with reduced rates of change and with uncertainty (Gleick, 1987). Cause and effect is no longer linear (Prigogine and Stengers, 1984; Briggs and Peat, 1989). Rather, everything seems to affect everything else at the same time. Such is the turbulence of our emerging postmodern world (Loye and Eisler, 1987).

Postmodernity and Collegiate Institutions

Higher education is certainly not immune to the postmodern conditions just identified. In collegiate institutions, specifically, the same themes are playing out with regard to the premodern, modern, and postmodern eras. I will look at each of these eras from the perspective of the organizational dimensions just discussed.

The Premodern Collegiate Era

During the premodern era (before the twentieth century in North America and Western Europe, later in other cultures), collegiate institutions remained relatively stable in size. Premodern colleges and universities (especially liberal arts colleges) did not grow, due primarily to selective enrollment. Either the institution was committed to a specific student population (Presbyterian males, Catholic females, Mennonites), or it set high enrollment standards. These restrictions enabled a school's student and faculty populations to remain homogeneous; hence it could easily establish and maintain an informal "collegiate way" (residential-based education and extracurricular activities; Rudolph, 1962). The leaders of these institutions paid little attention to the issues of quality or access, for these institutions (building on the agrarian character of the premodern era) were assumed to be in the business of "raising" proper young men and women, either as parental surrogates (*in loco parentis*) or as educationally oriented representatives of the church (*in loco ecclesiae*).

Leadership in the premodern college and university, as in other institutions of the time, was equated with the "great" man or woman. Presidents led their institutions by dint of charisma, wisdom, courage, and vision (Rudolph, 1962). Faculty were respected as intellectual leaders by their students, and the students were in turn trained to assume leadership roles in their newly formed communities and nation-states. Verbal interaction was encouraged among administrators, faculty, and students in the often small, homogeneous colleges and universities of the premodern era. Everyone knew everyone else, and no firm boundaries existed between the families of administrators and faculty and the daily lives of students on campus. Lively interactions between the faculty and students were encouraged through tutorials, seminars, group projects, and extracurricular activities.

Capital in the premodern college or university was based primarily on land (the campus grounds often resembled premodern estates) and the reputation of the school. In this quasi-familial setting, faculty acted as moral guardians and tutors for students. The leaders of these institutions served as lords of the estate, overseeing the educational operations of their institution. The maturation and full development ("finishing") of the student were identified as the primary goals of the premodern college or university.

The Modern Collegiate Era

With movement of many colleges and universities into the modern era (from the late nineteenth century through the 1960s in North America and Western Europe, later in most other societies), emphasis shifted to institutional growth and the expansion of education into all sectors of society. As colleges and universities (especially comprehensive state universities and community colleges) grew rapidly, big came to be viewed as better. The goal became maintaining stable and explicit organizational structures and processes and establishing statewide postsecondary educational systems. Increasingly, students during the modern era commuted to school instead of living on campus, and faculty members moved from a primary commitment to their college or university to allegiance to their academic discipline or profession. Clear standards were set for the admission of students, and formal programs for the evaluation of student performance were established.

Leadership in the modern college and university was offered by educational managers who properly and efficiently ran well-oiled educational systems. Faculty taught in an efficient manner (often large lecture-based courses), and students prepared for positions in the growing corporate world. Standardization of policies and procedures provided for equitable treatment while discouraging deviations from the norms and certain forms of creativity and spontaneity. Relationships between administrators and faculty became more formal and hierarchical as textbooks and formal lectures replaced the informality of premodern instruction. Administrative staffs grew in size as more paperwork and bureaucracy invaded the collegiate environment. Uniformity of practice was emphasized, in part because the student bodies of these institutions became more heterogeneous with regard to precollege preparation and academic competencies, as well as social and cultural background.

In modern colleges and universities, capital was based primarily on financial assets, buildings, and research facilities. In these quasi-corporate settings, faculty were viewed as employees, instruction was defined as a "cost center," and students were often defined as "income centers" (in independent colleges and universities) or as additional "cost centers" (in state-supported schools). Preparation for career and citizenship was identified as the primary goal of the modern postsecondary institution.

The Postmodern Collegiate Era

As we move into the postmodern era, collegiate institutions are becoming increasingly complex and fragmented. Units of the college or university are likely to be established off-campus. Consortia, cooperatives, and alliances are formed, bringing collegiate institutions into close working relationships with other institutions (collegiate and noncollegiate), thus breaking the traditional boundaries between these institutions (Boulding, 1973). Whereas modern colleges and universities emphasized size and uniformity, the postmodern institution tends to thrive on diversity of form and function (Peters, 1987; Clegg, 1990; Jameson, 1991). With the postmodern diffusion of boundaries, greater attention must be given to mission and purpose if a college or university is to retain its coherence and compete as a distinctive institution with unique curricular offerings in a competitive and volatile student market.

In keeping with the complexity and fragmentation of postmodern colleges and universities, leadership in these institutions is often situational. Successful leadership styles change as men and women in formal leadership roles confront shifting institutional forms and functions. Presidents of postmodern institutions often more closely resemble mayors of politically volatile towns and cities than chief executives of corporations (Cohen and Marsh, 1974). Leadership is exhibited through such roles as learner, servant, visionary, and community builder. Faculty are valued not for their formal status or their disciplinary knowledge but rather for their capacity (and willingness) to help students, colleagues, and themselves find meaning in complex, relativistic settings and interdisciplinary solutions to complicated postmodern problems. Students are prepared not for formal leadership roles but rather for a diversity of roles and responsibilities as lifelong learners, relativistic and contextual thinkers, and committed, ethically responsible citizens (Bellah and others, 1985, 1991).

Capital in postmodern colleges and universities, as in other postmodern institutions, resides primarily in the knowledge that is held by students, faculty, administrators, staff, and other participants in the institution. Given frequent and unpredictable shifts in the knowledge base of postmodern society, the foundation of each postmodern collegiate institution is inherently unstable; the status of the institution is often in jeopardy or at least subject to reconsideration, based on the capacity of the institution to find, absorb, analyze, and communicate new knowledge and information (Argyris and Schön, 1978). In this turbulent environment, faculty are viewed as stimulators, clarifiers, and brokers of information and knowledge. Students are perceived as customers, be they tuition-paying consumers of education (in an independent institution) or voting and taxpaying members of society (in a state-supported institution).

Learning is identified as the primary product of the postmodern collegiate institution (Argyris and Schön, 1978; Senge, 1990). The recipient of this learning can be any member of the community (or communities) formed by this institution. Put more broadly, the most important product that a postmodern collegiate institution can offer both inside and outside the classroom is knowledge. The postmodern collegiate institution is defined not as a static source of knowledge but rather as a brokerage house—a central, nodal point in a complex, nonhierarchical informational network (Schön, 1971)—for self-motivated students, faculty members, administrators, alumni, community members, and others. Our society is increasingly in need of knowledge workers who gain credibility not because they have property, money, or reputation but because they have knowledge of some rapidly changing condition in the world (Bell, 1976; Drucker, 1989). Faculty members, students, administrators, and other members of the higher education community similarly become credible because of either direct knowledge of something or, increasingly, direct knowledge of the source of specific knowledge. The central issue with regard to capital in a postmodern college or university is thus knowledge or, more precisely, the capacity of the institution to generate and make effective use of valid information.

With regard to educational values, the postmodern college or university has little need for motivating factors, for education is directly related to the ongoing concerns and problems of the community. With traditional boundaries falling away, the areas selected for study by students, faculty, administrators, and other learners are directly related to their immediate concerns, though the college or university is also in the business of setting a historical, interdisciplinary context for fuller understanding and effectively addressing the long-term (as well as short-term) aspects of the problem being addressed. Society is the ultimate customer, and learning is the primary product—as in any successful postmodern organization.

If institutional capacity for the generation and application of valid and useful information is the major source of capital in the postmodern collegiate institution and if learning is the primary product and source of educational value, the central question is, how does one build that capacity and sustain those values? This book is devoted to answering that question.

Key Points

1. The postmodern condition is typified by fragmented, inconsistent, and highly complex forms and functions.

2. Given this ambiguity, the postmodern condition is also associated with unclear boundaries and the necessity for a clear mission.

3. Given the postmodern condition, flexible and situationally based leadership is required.

4. A critical role is played by face-to-face communication and storytelling in our new world.

5. Information is the capital of the postmodern era, in keeping with the high levels of involvement that are expected of postmodern knowledge workers in their organizations and institutions.

Chapter Two

Challenges to Contemporary Colleges and Universities

If the analysis of the postmodern condition in Chapter One is valid, institutions of higher education that have historically been known for excellence suddenly find themselves being reexamined and their basic philosophies being rethought. Unfortunately, in response to emerging postmodern conditions, many older collegiate institutions seem to be reverting to a premodern emphasis on the recruitment of traditional students, those who have proved adept at jumping through the hoops of high school and can afford the increasing costs of tuition and housing. Efforts begun in the 1960s and 1970s to extend postsecondary education to underserved populations seem to be losing steam. Maintaining traditional notions about quality exacts a very high price. Public two-year and four-year institutions, long the open door for the underprivileged, can no longer afford to maintain any semblance of excellence in the face of deficit budgets and scarce funding. In a futile attempt to keep up, even these institutions have begun to raise tuition beyond the reach of the majority of potential students.

Where, then, do American students find themselves? Those who manage to find their way into the traditional schools of excellence—Harvard, the University of California, Oberlin, and their ilk—often encounter a narrow range of orthodox methods of education, despite the fact that these institutions have been portrayed as leaders in educational reform in the United States. These centers of excellence have long been in the forefront with regard to ethnic and cultural diversity, yet their students often indicate that they don't really have much contact with anyone who is truly different from themselves. The diversity in these institutions is often a sham, given that their students tend to come from homes and communities that support and encourage education and learning.

Conversely, those who attend state universities, less prestigious liberal arts colleges, or large impersonal private universities encounter diversity among their fellow students but few opportunities and little encouragement to explore and learn from it. They often leave these institutions with the feeling that they have simply survived an endurance test of no practical applicability. They have received an education, but has it really made a difference, given that they didn't learn much of value and can't get a good job without even more education?

Basic Premises of this Book

Is it possible in the postmodern era for a school to maintain both high quality and accessibility? Those that do must abandon traditional modes of education. They must be responsive to changing times and evolving student needs. Above all else, they must rediscover the individual and cease to view their students as statistics. These colleges and universities, few and far between, are on the cutting edge of American higher education and are positioned for effective leadership in the emerging postmodern era.

Premise One

Changes in the nature and dynamics of contemporary society (the "postmodern condition") and of collegiate institutions necessitate a reconsideration of the basic purposes and functions of these institutions. At the heart of this reconsideration are the issues of quality and access.

In a speech given more than twenty-five years ago at Texas Tech, Nevitt Sanford (1973) urged Texas Tech to find its own ideal for making plans for the future, to let its own heritage determine how to deal with the problems it faced rather than try to identify and replicate what everyone else was doing. He stated that the overall aim of education is the full, rounded development of each individual citizen and pointed out that many academic departments, specialties within departments, centers, and programs act more like independent entities than parts of a single, unified institution. According to Sanford, "No one is to blame for this. It is not due to blind passion for separatism, specialization, or empire building. It derives in large part, I think, from the sensational success of the analytical methods of science" (p. 3).

Sanford identified the scientists who break things apart for analysis as "splitters" and contrasted them with scientists who study how things work together as a unit, the "lumpers." According to Sanford, the splitters seem to have the advantage; they have received more federal funds, starting in the 1940s, and seem more important, somehow, than the lumpers. In the social sciences, he observes, the splitters have virtually eliminated the concept of person. "In its place we have 'researchable man'—an aggregate of separable part-functions—which can be studied by existing methods in ways that lead to quick publication" (pp. 4–5).

Sanford observed that when a child is having difficulties in school, a host of experts or professionals gets involved in treating this child. "We have reached a place," he concludes, "where no one, except the patient's or client's mother, connects what is done by one specialist with what is done by another and interprets those actions in the light of knowledge of the whole person" (p. 5). Sanford believes that we have accepted this assumption of compartmentalizing information and of analyzing wholes into manageable parts in our colleges and universities. As a result, departments are concerned only with departments, and knowledge is divided into disciplines, each with its own group of experts.

Is this twenty-five-year-old observation still true today? I believe that it is. Sanford's call for a return from analysis and dissection (splitting) to synthesis and unification (lumping) is even more relevant to the postmodern collegiate institution's attempts to reintegrate disparate and fragmented ideas and forces.

I offer a pair of premises concerning the interdependence of quality and access. One concerns the reliance of quality on access.

Premise Two

> In a successful postmodern collegiate institution, quality is enhanced through increased access. The more diversified the people and resources of an educational institution are and the more accessible differing perspectives, communities, contexts, and paradigms are, the greater is the potential quality of education, research, scholarship, and community service at the institution.

In a postmodern world that requires flexibility of perspective and breadth of knowledge about our globalized community, it is indefensible for any educational institution in the United States to remain cloistered.

Conversely, access is dependent on quality.

Premise Three

> An institution that increases access to its resources but provides resources that are of less than primary quality is not providing access at all. In the successful postmodern institution, access is legitimized through the enhancement of quality, and quality is in turn improved by increasing access.

The need for quality in any commitment to access is rarely discussed by leaders of contemporary institutions, yet it is crucial. Improved quality makes an institution more reputable. Reputation, in turn, is a critical factor when increasing access, given that men and women who are usually ignored by higher education already have one or two strikes against them. A low-quality education will do nothing more than reinforce stereotypes and shatter the self-images of people who often already have a fragile sense of self-esteem.

Case Studies

Throughout the remainder of this book, I expand on these three basic premises and describe ways in which contemporary colleges and universities have confronted the postmodern condition by defining and achieving quality while also sustaining access and, even more important, attaining quality through access. In so doing, I offer both a hypothetical case study (Exemplar College/University) and case studies of three real institutions that have attempted to be successful in this regard: The Evergreen State College (Olympia, Washington), John F. Kennedy University (Orinda, California), and the Professional School of Psychology (San Francisco and Sacramento, California). These three case studies are based on reports prepared by Barbara Leigh Smith and Katherine Bergquist at Evergreen, by Jason Bergquist and myself at JFK, and by Connie Arburua and myself at PSP.

Some readers might wonder why I have focused on these three institutions rather than picking ones from the mainstream of American higher education. I have done so because I firmly believe that these institutions and others like them represent the future of American higher education. This does not mean that traditional liberal arts colleges or large, traditional universities will become extinct, but it does mean that new institutional forms and new modes of interaction between quality and access are more likely to come from these "fringe" institutions. The older, more traditional institutions can learn from the younger schools and, in consortial arrangements, interact with and participate with them in experimenting to achieve both quality and access.

Four Stages of Institutional Development and Acceptance

I also offer these specific case studies because they show collegiate institutions at different stages of development in terms of accreditation and public acceptance. The issues of quality and access are confronted differently by schools at different stages of development and community acceptance. Such variables as accreditation and public image have a profound impact on a collegiate institution's capacity and willingness to integrate quality and access effectively.

In general, all collegiate institutions fall into one of four stages of development and acceptance. The stage one institution is neither regionally accredited nor, as a rule, publicly accepted. As a result, it is usually financially unstable or vulnerable. The stage two institution has regional accreditation but still has marginal public support or appreciation in the higher education community. It is typically still struggling with accreditation issues (it may be on probation or on a short-term review cycle) and is rarely financially secure. The stage three institution has a stable accreditation status but is still considered a marginal institution and is vulnerable in terms of long-term financial support (public or private). The stage four institution is stable with regard to both accreditation and finances. It is widely respected by the higher education community and by the general public.

Examples of stage four nontraditional institutions that seek to provide both quality and access include the British Open University, Berea College (Kentucky), and the University of Waterloo (Canada), along with such venerable institutions as the University of Chicago (Illinois) and Antioch College (Ohio). The Evergreen State College (Washington), along with another public institution, Empire State College (New York), and two private institutions, Alverno College (Wisconsin) and Goddard College (Vermont), exemplify stage three.

Stage two institutions are exemplified by such nontraditional private schools as John F. Kennedy University (California), Nova

University (Florida), Flaming Rainbow University (Oklahoma), and Columbia College (Illinois), as well as a few public institutions such as Yukon College (Canada) and the new San Marcos campus of the California State University system. Finally, stage one status is exemplified by many little-known institutions. I would point specifically to two private graduate schools in California with which I am acquainted, the Professional School of Psychology and Pacifica Graduate School.

As you may have noted, one of the institutions on which I intend to focus is at stage one, one is at stage two, and one is at stage three. Nontraditional colleges and universities such as Evergreen, JFK, and PSP find the integration of quality and access particularly challenging because they are swimming against the tide with regard to acceptance and support both from their colleagues at more traditional institutions and from the general public. As I trace the three schools throughout this book, I will reflect on these developmental issues as they relate to the issues of quality and access.

Methodology

The information I use in these analyses comes from several sources. First, Barbara Leigh Smith, provost and long-term leader at The Evergreen State College, produced a case study for her institution. I prepared a case study of John F. Kennedy University based on interviews with the current president, Charles Glasser, and a long-term past president, Robert Fisher, and on reviews of university documents. I also made use of my own experiences as a consultant to and instructor at the university and a dissertation on the university completed by Elinor Fisher (1982), wife of Robert Fisher, then president of the university. My case study of the Professional School of Psychology was both the easiest and the most difficult to prepare, given my role as president of the school. I built my case study not only on my own experiences as faculty member (for ten years) and president (eight years) but also on reports prepared for both the state of California (state authorization) and the Western Association of Schools and Colleges (regional accreditation).

In addition, forty interviews were conducted with diverse sets of students from each of the three institutions. These one- to two-hour interviews were conducted and analyzed by Jason Bergquist (a student at JFK), Katherine Bergquist (a student at Evergreen), and Connie Arburua (a student at PSP) over a three-month period (October 1 to December 31, 1993).

The Evergreen State College

In this case study, I focus on the experiences of students in an educational institution that is highly flexible, student-centered, and oriented toward integration of the various disciplines. Evergreen is a relatively small state-supported four-year college located on the outskirts of Olympia, Washington. It is particularly well known for its ad hoc curricular planning structure and the participation of students and faculty in intensive, interdisciplinary seminars that often last an entire year.

While Evergreen, as a state-supported college, builds on a firm populist foundation and accepts students at low in-state and nominal out-of-state tuition rates, it also in many ways operates like a traditional high-status liberal arts institution. One would usually expect to find such a curricular structure and close student-faculty interactions only at an exclusive liberal arts college (such as Hampshire College).

Furthermore, the whole ambience of the college—including its unique campus, spacious and beautiful, set in a thick evergreen forest—bespeaks high status and wealth. It is a far cry from the typical commuter college or university, situated in a major urban area and accessed by public transportation. Like many traditional liberal arts institutions, Evergreen is located near a major city, and many of its students (called Greenies) live with other Greenies in student housing on or near the campus.

Yet Evergreen also feels very much like a high-access public institution. Many of its students hold jobs, and many come from families that could not afford private colleges or universities. A large number of students attend simply because of geographic proximity; yet there is a much higher percentage of out-of-state students than at other Washington schools, who are attracted to Evergreen by its curriculum and close student-faculty interactions. Evergreen is distinctively attempting to integrate quality and access, to blend traditionally elitist curricular and pedagogical models with populist goals and admission criteria. In sum, Evergreen attempts to offer a high-quality liberal arts education at very low cost to students from a variety of socioeconomic backgrounds.

John F. Kennedy University

John F. Kennedy University was one of the first in the United States to be founded specifically to serve an adult population. It is a small private nonprofit university located in Orinda, California. Founded in 1964, JFK offers programs in liberal studies, graduate psychology, management, holistic studies, and law. Most JFK students work full-time and have families to support. They bring with them maturity and the practical skills of having had a career. They approach their commitment to a new education with seriousness and intensity.

Like Evergreen, JFK was founded with mixed roots. On the one hand, it was begun specifically to serve working adults—a clear access-oriented mission. The university first held classes in a defunct mortuary and relied heavily on part-time instructors and over-worked and underpaid but highly committed administrators. On the other hand, JFK has always prided itself on its "blue-blood" origins. Many of the early faculty and administrators came from prestigious universities (such as Harvard, Columbia, and the University of California). Robert Fisher (JFK's second and longest-tenured president) came with academic credentials from Harvard and the London School of Economics, as well as a major teaching position at the University of California. In my 1993 interview, Fisher still spoke with great pride about the academic credentials of the early administrators and deans of the university. JFK tried from the first to provide an accessible education without in any way compromising on traditional criteria of quality.

The Professional School of Psychology

The Professional School of Psychology is a postgraduate institution that offers master's- and doctoral-level education on two California campuses (San Francisco and Sacramento). PSP is a selective graduate institution, accepting only the "best" students who are qualified to achieve high academic standards. Yet PSP is also accessible, for the "best and brightest" students being served by the school are not those traditionally served by graduate schools. PSP's students are older adults (average age is forty-four), working primarily in the human services, who can afford neither the time nor the money required by many other graduate schools in Northern California.

The academically traditional origins of PSP are reflected in the credentials of the first leader of the school, Michael Cohen (doctorate from the University of Wisconsin) and of many early faculty members, who were not only clinical practitioners but also, in several instances, interdisciplinary scholars. PSP's nontraditional, access-oriented origins are similarly evident in the people who started the school. PSP was founded by three professionals affiliated with Huckleberry House in San Francisco, one of the first halfway houses in America for runaway youth (primarily serving "flower children" left over from the Haight-Ashbury days of the late 1960s). The founders observed that many of the men and women working at Huckleberry House and other social service agencies in the area had many years of experience in the field and were very bright and curious about the work they were doing. However, they were often blocked in their career because they held only a bachelor's or master's degree. They were unable to return for a more advanced degree because they worked at least eight hours a day, received low wages, and found that traditional educational institutions in the area tended to ignore or devalue their rich human service background.

PSP was founded to serve these accomplished human service professionals by offering a low-cost, high-quality master's and doctoral program for working adults. Classes were scheduled during evenings and weekends, a monthly tuition payment plan was inaugurated, and small classes were conducted by seasoned professionals to ensure an educational environment that was both challenging and supportive. This unique way of providing graduate education to mature adult learners was balanced by a more traditional emphasis on demanding coursework, high entrance standards (focusing on previous life accomplishments and extensive field experience rather than school grades), and (as at JFK) strong academic credentials among PSP faculty.

Throughout this book, I will refer to these case studies when describing ways in which collegiate institutions attempt to unite quality and access. I identify the characteristics and strategies of postmodern educational institutions that have learned how to achieve the critical integration of quality and access.

Key Points

1. Institutions of higher education must reconsider their basic purposes and functions. At the heart of this reconsideration are the issues of quality and access.

2. Quality and access, often considered mutually exclusive, must be brought together in the postmodern era. They are in fact interdependent. This book serves to elucidate the inextricable relationship between them in the emerging postmodern world.

3. In a successful postmodern collegiate institution, quality is enhanced through increased access. The more diversified the

people and resources of an educational institution are and the more accessible differing perspectives, communities, contexts, and paradigms are, the greater will be the potential quality of education, research, scholarship, and community service in the institution.

4. An institution that increases access to its resources but provides resources that are of inferior quality is not providing access at all. In such an institution, access has become a sham. Access is legitimized by enhancing quality, and quality is improved by increasing access.

5. In a postmodern world that requires flexibility of perspective and breadth of knowledge, it is indefensible for any educational institution to remain closed to the diversity of perspectives that access can bring.

6. A commitment to quality makes an institution more reputable. Reputation is crucial when increasing access. A low-quality education will do nothing to boost the fragile self-esteem of people traditionally denied access.

Chapter Three

Redefining Quality
in the Context of Access

In the successful postmodern institution, quality is enhanced through increased access. This is critical to the success of the institution, for if the two must compete, one or the other will lose out. And when either quality or access must be sacrificed, quality is particularly vulnerable, for access can be increased by means of certain basic structural and legalistic means (such as quotas), whereas quality must be achieved and sustained through improvements and changes not only in structures but also in processes and attitudes (Watson and Johnson, 1972).

What exactly does it mean to say that quality is enhanced through increased access? It may have been possible during the premodern and modern eras for superior quality to be achieved and maintained in a high-status, traditional setting, despite or even because of the isolation of the institutions and their students from much of the surrounding world. This is no longer the case. Today a successful education of the highest quality requires that students be exposed to many different aspects of the world around them, for the world can no longer be kept at bay. We are all part of a complex and turbulent world, regardless of our class, economic status, upbringing, nationality, race, or gender. None of us can be disengaged. Regardless of our definition of quality, diversity and complexity of perspective are critical in some way. Students must be exposed to diversity and complexity if for no other reason than to move beyond a simplistic, dualistic frame of reference to a more complex and relativistic one (Perry, 1970).

Typically, diversity and complexity are achieved by increasing access—by opening the doors of a college or university to differing perspectives and value systems. This increased diversity in turn requires a reexamination of traditional notions about quality. Some of these traditional notions seem to block the acceptance and integration of diversity in our colleges and universities, while others discourage the integration of quality and access. Four criteria of quality can either encourage or discourage diversity and integration. In discussing these issues, I will refer to the three schools introduced in Chapter Two: The Evergreen State College, John F. Kennedy University, and the Professional School of Psychology.

Four Criteria of Quality

Quality has usually been defined and assessed according to one of four sets of criteria:

1. *Input criteria:* nature and extent of resources available to the institution, including characteristics of incoming students, faculty credentials, size of library, physical facilities, and financial reserves

2. *Output criteria:* nature and extent of institutional products, including graduating student characteristics, alumni success, research and scholarly publications, and public service

3. *Value-added criteria:* differences that the institution has made in the growth of all members of the institution, including intellectual, moral, social, vocational, physical, and spiritual development

4. *Process-oriented criteria:* level and manner of participation by all appropriate constituencies in the educational, administrative, and governance processes of the institution, including the definition and assessment of quality

Each of the four approaches provides valuable insights into the nature of quality in our contemporary colleges and universities.

Input Criteria

Input criteria have been the most commonly identified measures of quality for many years. Astin (1985) notes that reputation is commonly equated with quality and is based primarily on such input-oriented variables as selectivity of students (acceptance-rejection ratio), educational cost per student (tuition, room and board, and so forth), and number of doctorate-granting departments. While Astin identified one output-oriented measure as a significant reputation variable—number of doctoral degrees awarded—he also pointed to a second measure of quality that is input-based—extent of resources in the institution (endowment, mean salary of faculty, research funds available).

Many contemporary authors (and most accrediting agencies) have focused on input measures: quality of entering students, number of books in the library, quality of graduate degrees held by faculty, number of square feet of classroom space, student-faculty ratio, and so forth. Mayhew, Ford, and Hubbard (1990) note that any time a service-oriented organization is being evaluated, "the assessment of quality will probably be shaped by the knowledge, skill, attitude, appearance, and timeliness of the providers as they interface with the needs and expectations of the receiver of the service" (p. 27).

Many members of the higher education community (as well as other members of society) quite rightly assume that if you put good things together, you will get something of value. This concept of education and the assessment of its quality is closely associated with traditional high-status institutions. It can also inspire innovation: faculty members, students, and administrators can explore new modes of teaching and learning without being constrained by prespecified educational objectives. Faculty, students, and administrators are selected for their excellence and their potential and are then left alone to make something wonderful happen.

Output Criteria

Output-based criteria of quality build on the assumption that we are accountable for what is produced in our colleges and universities. Input measures tend to be institutionally based and are often self-serving ("We know what is best and don't have to specify the outcomes"); output measures, by contrast, are society-based ("We do what society wants us to do and are accountable for demonstrating that"). Whereas input measures tend to be associated with more traditional educational perspectives, output measures tend to be of more contemporary origin. In many instances, the output criteria match with the "product-based" and "user-based" definitions of quality found in many corporations and human service agencies (Garvin, 1988, pp. 39–46; see also Mayhew, Ford, and Hubbard, 1990). As Astin (1985) notes, educational quality and reputation are being determined today on the basis of demonstrated outcomes more often than in the past. Institutions tend to be rated as excellent in his survey if they have low dropout rates, if their graduates achieve high levels of success in being admitted to graduate education programs, and if their graduates are ultimately successful in their careers (in terms of salary and recognition).

Ironically, Mayhew, Ford, and Hubbard (1990) arrive at an output-oriented criterion of quality in their own pursuit of an adequate definition of quality, even though much of their discussion seems to be based on more traditional standards. They conclude that quality undergraduate education "consists of preparing learners through the use of words, numbers, and abstract concepts to understand, cope with, and positively influence the environment in which they find themselves" (p. 29). Unfortunately, this is a restrictive and dated perspective on the skills and knowledge needed by young men and women as they prepare for the postmodern era. Whereas some colleges and universities should focus specifically on words, numbers, and abstract concepts, that should not represent the full range of purposes regarding undergraduate education. We must be respectful not only of the vocational and professional preparation programs in our undergraduate (and graduate) institutions that focus on additional skill sets but also of alternative institutions that offer programs with non-Western, postmodern, or social-critical knowledge bases.

Bogue and Saunders (1992) also offer an output-based definition of quality that relates closely to that offered by many of the advocates of total quality management in the corporate sector: "Quality is conformance to mission specification and goal achievement—within publicly accepted standards of accountability and integrity" (p. 20). This definition, unlike that offered by Mayhew and colleagues, allows for more diversity of institution type and is responsive to changing social needs and values. Bogue and Saunders themselves suggest that one advantage of such a definition is that "it respects and affirms diversity of institutional missions and their historical and environmental settings" (p. 20)—a critical factor in any postmodern collegiate institution.

Second, Bogue and Saunders's (1992, pp. 20–21) output-oriented definition "requires an operational expression of mission and goals," answering the question, "What difference did we make?"—a more value-added approach. This definition also holds a third advantage: it "focuses debate on purpose" and encourages the building of consensus around ends (outputs) rather than means—a more process-oriented approach. Fourth, according to Bogue and Saunders, their definition "encourages public disclosure of institutional mission, goals and performance results"—a strong selling point for output-oriented criteria, given that input and value-added measures are more internally oriented and that the process-oriented criteria are usually much more ambiguous and less convincing to the general public. Finally, Bogue and Saunders suggest that their definition "contains an ethical test" in that it encourages broad-based involvement in the identification and monitoring of institutional mission.

Value-Added Criteria

The value-added criteria of quality are based on the assumption that it is the *difference* achieved in students between the start and end of an educational process that is important, not just the start (input) or the end (output) itself. These value-added criteria provide a healthy corrective against the excessive emphasis of input criteria on traditional resource bases and high admission standards. A collegiate institution that is oriented toward value-added criteria focuses primarily on using the school's existing resources rather than on acquiring additional resources.

Garvin (1988) speaks of this orientation as "values-based," suggesting that quality is defined (from this orientation) in terms of the interplay between certain output measures and the other given commitments of the institution (for example, affordable programs). As I will note in my examinations of the Professional School of Psychology and John F. Kennedy University, the quality of an institution is often determined at least in part by its commitment to a particular mission, even if this commitment may mean a compromise in the quality of input (money, land, student enrollment standards, and so forth). Ironically, these "values-based" institutions often do at least as well as other institutions with fewer mission-based restrictions in resources with regard to output measures of quality (for example, performance on state licensing exams or admission to graduate school).

In an institution that is oriented toward value-added criteria, the poorly prepared or learning-disabled entering student is likely to be perceived as challenging rather than handicapped. In many ways, high-status colleges and universities are more vulnerable to value-added criteria of quality than less selective institutions, for it is usually harder to improve the performance of students who are already well educated and trained than it is to improve the performance of poorly prepared and undereducated students. This "ceiling effect," however, provides no greater bias in determining the quality of an institution than the input criteria (with a bias toward reputation and tradition) that favor highly selective, high-status colleges and universities. As Alexander Astin (1990), a long-term champion of the value-added model, has noted, if the quality of an institution was determined not by its selectivity (or some other input measure) but rather by the extent to which it is effective in developing the talents of its students from whatever level they are at when entering, then institutions would have a chance to be judged excellent. The unchanging hierarchy of status (Kerr, 1991) would be superseded by a responsiveness to the need of society for the development of all people at all ability levels.

The value-added criteria provide an equally healthy corrective against the myopia of output-based notions of educational quality, given that output criteria fail to take into account the entry-level skills and preparation of students. Simply showing that alumni of one school are more likely to be accepted into a graduate program than alumni of another school does not provide convincing evidence of superior quality unless the entry-level competencies of the students in these programs are comparable. Research into student development conducted by Astin and his colleagues amply illustrates the fallacy of a purely output-oriented mode of assessing value and attests to the effective use of these value-added criteria of quality. Astin (1985) himself strongly advocates what he calls a "talent-development" concept of educational quality: "Its basic premise is that true excellence lies in the institution's ability to affect its students and faculty favorably, to enhance their intellectual and scholarly development, and to make a positive difference in their lives" (pp. 60–61). Although the first part of this definition would suggest a more output-oriented definition of quality, the key phrase that transforms it into a value-added definition is "make a positive difference."

Process-Oriented Criteria

The fourth set of criteria focus on the process of achieving quality. Among corporate gurus of quality, process-oriented criteria often take the form of a commitment to "continuous improvement" or an abiding concern for "conformance to standards" (Crosby, 1979, p. 15). In higher education, a commitment to or an abiding concern for a particular process is more likely to focus not only on the process of production (in the case of higher education, the process of instruction) but also on decision-making, planning, and problem-solving processes associated with educational matters inside the institution. This approach suggests that it is the process of education that is most important, not the resources (input) or outcomes (output). It is not what we do or what we accomplish that makes for quality; rather it is the way in which we do what we do and how we decide what to do that differentiate a high-quality education from a process-oriented approach to quality.

One of Astin's (1985) four variables of quality in higher education tends to conform to process-oriented criteria: the "curricular content" variable. In many instances, it is the process whereby a curriculum is formulated that determines quality, not the actual product of these curricular deliberations. In many instances (as I will note with regard to The Evergreen State College), the deliberations about and construction of curricular offerings are the lifeblood of the institution and are themselves an important source of new learning for faculty, administrators, and students.

The Carnegie Foundation for the Advancement of Teaching (1990a) offers an even more encompassing statement regarding quality as a process. The writers of this report suggest that the quality of higher education is defined in part by the quality of the community that is formed in and by the college or university. They identify this first as an "educationally purposeful community" (p. 9) in which faculty and students work together toward a common goal and then as an "open community" (p. 17) characterized by freedom of expression and civility. Third, the community of quality embodies justice: "a place where the sacredness of each person is honored and where diversity is aggressively pursued" (p. 25).

The Carnegie Foundation also suggested that the community of quality is disciplined. It is "a place where individuals accept their obligations to the group and where well-defined governance procedures guide behavior for the common good" (p. 47). It is also a "caring community" (p. 47) in which the welfare of and service provided by each of its members are paramount. Finally, this community is celebratory, one where "the heritage of the institution is remembered and where rituals affirming both tradition and change are widely shared" (p. 55). These six criteria beautifully summarize the heart of a process-oriented approach to quality and could readily serve as central guidelines for any college or university that seeks to achieve a high quality of process in its operations.

A Multidimensional Definition of Quality

Each of the four approaches to quality is critical when assessing the overall effectiveness of a collegiate institution and when relating quality to access. I propose, therefore, that a comprehensive and useful definition of quality must include all four sets of criteria, and I offer the following as one such definition:

> Quality exists in a college or university to the extent that adequate and appropriate resources are being directed successfully toward the accomplishment of mission-related institutional outcomes and that programs in the college or university make a significant and positive mission-related difference in the lives of people affiliated with the

college or university and are created, conducted, and modified in a
manner that is consistent with the mission (and values) of the
institution.

Each of the four sets of criteria regarding educational quality must
be accepted as viable and important. They can all contribute to an
effective postmodern vision of quality and access. When only input
or output measures are used, access and quality become incompatible
goals. Institutions are unable to achieve their mission or to sustain
quality in part because they tend to focus on only one or two of these
definitions of quality—typically the input and output definitions.

I will expand on this definition by exploring the four criteria of
quality in more depth and describing how they play out in the three
case study institutions.

Input Criteria

The successful postmodern institution enhances quality through
access by making efficient use of existing resources. Efficiency results
from the mission-driven allocation of these resources, the mission
being linked to both quality and access. The institution can achieve
efficiency by answering a series of central questions regarding input
criteria: Which resources are needed to ensure quality? Which traditional resources, if any, are no longer needed by our student population? Which resources must we provide ourselves, and which can
be obtained through consortial or other cooperative arrangements?
And finally, which resources of the state or national government
should be available to us?

These questions concerning the efficient and appropriate use of
resources are not asked in a vacuum. They are influenced and often
distorted by the dominant bias toward defining quality primarily in
terms of input and, more specifically, by very traditional and indiscriminate notions about the kind of inputs (resources) that produce
high quality. Regarding the decline of undergraduate education in

the United States, Mayhew, Ford, and Hubbard (1990) present a traditional (and highly distorted) view on the use of resources in nontraditional institutions: "The secret (or not so secret) ingredients for these programs consist of part-time cheap labor in the form of adjunct professors; many self-education services, labeled 'independent study'; and low-cost or free physical facilities, such as a grade school building on Saturdays, an office building, or even the homes of students or adjunct faculty." They go on to note that these nontraditional uses of resources are justified through the "rhetoric of need fulfillment, service, democracy, or breaking the rigidity of traditional academic programs" (p. 34). An examination of their list of ingredients finds, first, a fairly close match with two of the three case institutions: John F. Kennedy University and the Professional School of Psychology. Both schools rely on "cheap labor" in terms of adjunct (part-time) professors. Both make some (sparing) use of independent studies, and both schools have been set up in nontraditional physical facilities rather than on lovely, tree-shrouded campuses.

Both schools have chosen to embrace these ingredients because they make sense when working with mature, employed adults. Why, for instance, should faculty be appointed full-time when the students they serve are working adults who typically come to school during evenings and weekends? It is absurd for schools such as JFK and PSP to hire faculty who sit in their office eight hours each day without any students to serve. This is not an issue of "cheap labor" as Mayhew and colleagues suggest; rather it is an issue of using resources efficiently.

Similarly, independent study programs are appropriate for many adult students because these men and women have complex lives and may often do better under a more flexible format. Furthermore, these adults often have greater access to sources for new learning on the job and in the community than traditionally aged students who neither work nor have extensive community ties. Why shouldn't independent study programs be made available to these students?

After all, independent study and tutorial programs hold a revered place in the history of Western higher education, and they are common in Europe among scholars at even the most traditional universities.

What about the use of physical facilities that are not traditional (office buildings, elementary schools, and so forth)? If a school can save money on its facilities and as a result direct a greater proportion of its financial resources to instruction or keep tuition costs low, why must traditional campus facilities be used? Why not return to the ancient and once respected Socratic tradition of the itinerant scholar and the primacy of teaching and learning over grounds and buildings?

Adult students, in particular, do not need elaborate physical facilities. They typically don't spend much time on campus anyway, and when they are on campus, they are usually in class or meeting with their professors. Furthermore, is there anything wrong with being innovative in the use of nontraditional facilities for classroom education (see Bergquist, Gould, and Greenberg, 1981)? Why should the leaders of a nontraditional school be faulted for being good stewards of their school's funds? Perhaps more traditional schools with large overhead expenses could learn a lesson from their more visionary and flexible colleagues.

Basically, the issue is one of being sensible in the use of scarce resources. What a foolish waste of resources (and inexcusable use of tuition dollars) to hire full-time faculty, ban independent study, and purchase expensive physical facilities to comply with inappropriate and outdated notions of quality! Unfortunately, many schools such as JFK and PSP are now being forced to move in traditional, costly directions to build or maintain their image, reputation, and accreditation.

For instance, schools that primarily serve adult students are compelled to hire full-time faculty who dutifully hold office hours each day (or several times a week) doing non-school-related work because their students are at work and cannot make appointments.

I have personally been a faculty member at two schools that were caught in this dilemma and know the experience of being paid to do nothing. I vividly remember spending many hours sitting in my office waiting for students to come in, knowing full well that few could break free to see me during my (required) office hours. Typically, I would do some work on a manuscript during my office hours and meet with students at nearby restaurants for an early-morning breakfast or late-afternoon coffee.

What, then, are the appropriate resources that a school needs if it is to maintain both quality and access for nontraditional students? When students at the Professional School of Psychology are asked about resources that are of particular value, add quality, and relate specifically to the school's mission, they speak of committed teachers, teachers who are also actively engaged as clinicians, small classes, high academic standards, older students, and teachers and students who are roughly the same age. Given that many of the students are already successful professionals, instructors at PSP must be particularly gifted, for such students tend to keep teachers on their toes. A second-year doctoral student at PSP indicated that she particularly appreciated the selection of faculty who are at the same time challenging and supportive: the faculty at PSP, she says, "have superior minds, but they encourage me at the same time." She likes the fact "that we [students] are treated like colleagues" and that "there is a lot of interaction between students and teachers."

Fellow students are a distinctive resource that is valued highly by PSP students. Students who were interviewed spoke frequently of the unique expertise provided by other students: "I think that there are people of real value here. It is so nice that the student body is made up of older, more mature people with lots of life experience. I admire many of my classmates, what they have done." Students commented on the diversity of the PSP student body, deeming it a particularly valuable resource. When speaking of the administrative staff as a resource, PSP students usually focused on the caring attitude of these men and women: "PSP is unique in the way it is supportive of its students. . . . I really experience a sincere interest in the welfare of students. People have gone out of their way for me, and I won't forget it."

Ironically, PSP students often mentioned the fact that the school is not regionally or APA (American Psychological Association) accredited as a distinctive resource. One doctoral student noted that PSP "is like one's poor relations, in a way. It makes us unique. I guess not being accredited is part of that, being the poor relation." Another commented that the school's philosophy and its orientation toward mature professionals would probably not be possible if PSP were accredited by the American Psychological Association: "We can be so much more flexible because we're not APA-accredited. That has been very important to me. I think it helps attract working people, particularly those of us who work full-time. I don't think schools that are APA-accredited want people like me in their programs. I don't think they value older learners."

In examining the input-criteria-of-quality perspective at John F. Kennedy University, similar themes were discovered. This is not surprising, given that this university also caters primarily to adult learners. Student populations at both PSP and JFK are composed mostly of working adults who are returning to school to further a career or seek personal development. Some of these students have had their learning stunted or seriously impaired by terrible schooling experiences. Many had enrolled at a four-year state university immediately after high school, unsure of their goals and already feeling disenchanted by the high school experience. Others graduated from a four-year institution but now find themselves in need of a career change. JFK and PSP offer students the unique possibility of training for a new career while continuing to working full-time.

PSP and JFK students clearly need experienced teachers and student service personnel who are sensitive to their past experiences of failure, frustration, and disenchantment. Large classes, impersonal teaching, and a greater emphasis on social life than on education were all elements that drove many PSP and JFK students

away from other schools; hence those things should not be replicated at PSP or JFK. Both schools must provide a different kind of
faculty member and staff member and a different kind of classroom
experience. Given that students at PSP and JFK (and other commuter schools, for that matter) have primary contact with the
school through classes, the resources of these schools must be
directed primarily toward this setting.

Classes should be kept small so that students can interact with
one another as well as with the instructor. Faculty development,
instructional technology, and instructional support services become
particularly important. Students who have previously experienced
failure or disillusionment in a collegiate setting or are experiencing
the vulnerability associated with career transitions are challenging
to teach and to support with student services. This can be a heavy
burden, but instructors and administrators must be aware of these
factors and do as much as possible to facilitate the difficult processes
of teaching and learning.

As I noted with regard to the observations made by Mayhew,
Ford, and Hubbard (1990), many of the traditional input-oriented
resources that typically define quality are not appropriate at either
PSP or JFK. The library at both schools, for instance, may not have
to be as big as those found at colleges and universities that serve traditional student populations, considering that students at both PSP
and JFK often have easy access to excellent existing libraries (both
public and university). The dimension of technology is also relevant here. Libraries are now much more technology-driven than
they were even ten years ago. Information is stored on compact
disks or is readily available via modems. Must libraries replicate
holdings when they are so readily available through interlibrary
exchange? Shouldn't the limited resources of libraries at most
schools—especially schools such as PSP and JFK that serve primarily mature, commuting learners—be devoted to information
retrieval rather than the collection and storage of expensive print
media?

What about traditional student services? Do the mature students at JFK and PSP really need assigned advisers? Does a university like JFK or a graduate school like PSP need recreational facilities or a student union, given that their students usually come to class and then go home, like commuter students at other universities? They already have access to many other recreational facilities and meeting places as firmly established taxpaying residents in the local community.

What about full-time core faculty? This is a particularly important issue. Why does JFK need a full-time faculty when the students are not around for the faculty to assist anyway? Yes, curriculum development should involve faculty. Furthermore, some faculty members should be available to meet with students every evening or weekend. However, this work can just as easily and often more easily be done by part-time faculty, given that these men and women (like the students they serve) are likely to be free during the evenings and weekends. It is not uncommon for full-time faculty in many collegiate institutions to be on campus during the day and part-time faculty to be on campus during the evenings. Hence an institution that primarily serves evening students can probably serve its students better with either part-time faculty or a full-time faculty that is uniquely committed to evening work hours.

What about other colleges and universities? Which of the many traditional resources can they forgo or reduce? Reductions in full-time faculty at Evergreen are probably not appropriate, given the key role of curriculum development in this institution of adhocracy. Substantial library holdings also make some sense, given that students and faculty are moving rapidly across disciplines in their thematic course offerings and need immediate access to books and journals from many different fields. Furthermore, Evergreen is located in a community where there are not many other institutions with large libraries. However, Evergreen recognizes that it needs a library organized and delivered in new ways. One aspect of addressing this need is rethinking the status of reference librarians, who at Evergreen rotate into the curriculum one quarter of every nine in exchange for a faculty member who rotates into the library.

All of this movement helps bridge the gap that frequently exists between the information services and resources and the faculty. What about a smaller administrative staff, in light of the key role of faculty governance at Evergreen? Couldn't faculty (and students) assume greater responsibility for the ongoing operations of the institution, given that small student-faculty project groups are at the heart of the school?

Another input-oriented question that postmodern colleges and universities should ask concerns the use of externally based resources: Can't some of an institution's resource needs be met through consortial arrangements that help keep costs down? Like many small collegiate institutions, JFK is involved in several consortia. For instance, faculty at JFK participate in faculty development programs focused on adult learning with colleagues from other regional schools that primarily serve adults. JFK is also in a library consortium, involving various graduate schools of psychology in the San Francisco Bay Area (of which PSP is also a member). Yet the full extent of interinstitutional activities has never been fully explored by the leaders of JFK. What about joint interinstitutional administrative development programs that focus on adult students? Couldn't the psychology library consortium be replicated in other areas (particularly liberal studies, law, and management)? What about consortia involving not just other educational institutions but also corporations and various training and educational groups that are working closely with JFK's School of Management?

Such an arrangement existed for several years between JFK and the NTL Institute (one of the most prestigious and longest-standing programs in organizational training and development in the world). Students enrolled in a joint master's degree program sponsored by JFK and NTL. (A similar program had been established between NTL and American University, in Washington, D.C.) The exceptional faculty participating in this program were recruited from both schools. As a result, students availed themselves of insights offered by academicians and local practitioners (from JFK) and internationally known consultants and trainers (from NTL). The eighteen-month program featured not only coursework but also NTL-oriented training experiences and internships.

Several reasons have been given for the demise of the JFK-NTL agreement. One seems to have been pressure from the regional accrediting agency. This body opposes the selection of faculty in any program by an outside agency—in this case, NTL. Sadly, the strength associated with diversified perspectives and cultures in partnerships, consortia, and various other cooperative agreements, such as with JFK and NTL, often is also the weakness of these agreements (see Bergquist, Betwee, and Meuel, 1995). A school such as JFK, with limited resources and unique student demands, cannot afford to let these cooperative efforts fail.

A final input-oriented question concerns governmental resources. At Evergreen, arrangements are being made to forge collaborative relationships between the college and state agencies located in Olympia. One current effort envisions a collaboration based on "emerging technologies" between Evergreen and ten agencies concerned with environmental issues. The collaboration would involve networking the partners to share resources as well as joint training and research activities. What could be done at JFK or PSP to increase the use of governmental resources?

Perhaps cooperative agreements could be hammered out between private schools such as PSP and JFK, on the one hand, and public university libraries, on the other. At present, leaders of many public universities are complaining that too many students from private colleges and universities are making use of the public university libraries instead of their own. These complaints are understandable, given the struggle in even the most prestigious university to provide adequate library services for its own students. Yet isn't publicly supported education intended to serve the educational needs of all taxpaying citizens, including those attending other schools? Furthermore, without these private institutions, the prestigious universities (and their libraries) would be inundated with an even greater demand for access and service. In the future, educational institutions such as PSP and JFK will survive to provide valuable services to distinct populations of students only if public resources are defined in more accessible and populist terms.

What about other public resources? As a privately owned school, PSP is not eligible for public dollars and is in fact required to pay taxes (becoming an income center rather than a cost center for public higher education). Like most private institutions, JFK makes extensive use of student loan programs that are guaranteed by the state or federal government. Many Evergreen students are also supported at least in part by state and federal dollars. Both schools have also participated in various federal and state funding programs for innovation. Unfortunately, like most schools that serve primarily adult learners, JFK is not typically defined by the federal funding agencies as a school that serves underserved populations; hence it has never even considered applying for government funds associated with federal "developing institutions" mandates. Given the aging nature of the American population, the need for multiple-career preparation, and the consequent need for more institutions to provide education to mature adults, it is surprising that there has been so little discussion at the federal level about funds for schools like JFK, which are at the forefront of innovation in adult education.

Output Criteria

We can make a particularly important contribution to the integration of quality and access by influencing how output measures are defined and employed. Quality and access can be brought together through much broader and less self-serving definitions of successful output. An institution can be of high quality if its graduates serve underserved populations in society. In this way, the institution not only provides greater access to potential students but also provides its graduates with greater access to potential clients, patients, or customers. The quality of output is in this way closely related to an expanded notion of access. Institutional quality can be measured by an even broader perspective on output, namely, the extent to which graduates and other products and services of the institution contribute to an institutionally shared vision of the "good society" (Bellah and others, 1991).

In light of this challenge, one major question should be posed with regard to output measures of quality: What are appropriate criteria for assessing the ultimate social value of an education? For example, should attention be given to employment, salary, contributions to society, admissions to graduate school, licensing exam scores? A school such as the Professional School of Psychology, for instance, like many schools that serve primarily working adults, looks very strong when both personal and social outcome measures are applied in assessing its quality. Three of the most common personally oriented output measures, for instance, are job placement rates, mean salary a certain number of years after graduation, and pass rate on standardized postgraduate licensing or certification examinations. PSP graduates do very well on all three criteria.

These postgraduate achievements are deceptive, however. Virtually all PSP graduates are employed in excellent jobs within six months after completing their degrees, but this exceptional placement record has little to do with the school. Most of the graduates were holding down good jobs even before they received their degrees and, in many instances, kept the same jobs that they had held down throughout their involvement in the graduate program.

Similarly, the salaries of PSP graduates one to two years after degree completion also look impressive, as do the rates at which PSP graduates pass the California state examinations for marriage, family, and child counselors (master's-level license) and psychologists (doctoral-level license). But as mature, accomplished adults, many PSP students were making a good salary even before they entered graduate school, and their rich life experiences certainly help them with the examinations (particularly the oral exams for both licenses, which are based on real-life cases). Should PSP take any credit for these outcomes, considering that the school has little to do with the salary levels of students while they are in school (other than a few instances when students get raises because they are enrolled in a graduate program) or with the students' accumulation of experiences on the job?

In some instances, PSP students actually accept lower-paying positions after graduation, having shifted from corporate careers to the less well paid human services. Is that an indication that the school has failed them? This is where the social-oriented criteria become relevant. Given the need in the human services for mature men and women with rich life experiences, perhaps the shift to lower-paying human service positions should be considered a benefit to our society. Clearly, output criteria such as employment and salary can be deceptive and must be analyzed cautiously and wisely.

Another complexity concerning socially based output criteria must be added to the equation for PSP. Given that the school charges a much lower tuition than virtually any other school of psychology in Northern California and offers its own distinctive loan program that enables students to graduate without any debt, the salary levels of graduates must be set against the absence of postgraduate debt. Graduates of other schools of psychology (or medicine, dentistry, law, or architecture, for that matter) often owe $50,000 to $100,000 on student loans. In obtaining a job, therefore, they must make a good salary if for no other reason than to pay off their loans.

PSP graduates, by contrast, owe nothing when they graduate. As a result, they can pick and choose among jobs without concern about loan repayment. Many PSP graduates choose to work in jobs that do not pay much but are personally satisfying and of great social benefit. The leaders of PSP are proud of the fact that some of their graduates earn more than $120,000 per year while others make less than $30,000. The latter graduates have been able to choose a career of low-paid service in part because PSP has not burdened them with a large student debt.

Unfortunately, outside agencies (such as state and regional accrediting boards) sometimes seem either to overlook or to care little about this significant accomplishment by PSP and its graduates—as well as such accomplishments by other schools that support low tuition costs. Fortunately, the general public is starting to pay attention to these cost factors. *Money* magazine now ranks one hundred four-year undergraduate schools on a combination of sixteen factors that combine cost and quality (based on traditional input measures of quality such as faculty and library resources and student entrance exam scores). The New College of the University of South Florida ranked first for two years (1993 and 1994) with a low tuition of $2,030 for Floridians and $7,943 for out-of-state students and high input measures of quality (*Money*, Sept. 6, 1994). Others ranked high were Rice University (Texas), Trenton State College (New Jersey), and the State University of New York, Binghamton.

In an era when our society is trying to control the costs of medical and mental health services, schools such as PSP and those mentioned by *Money* are contributing by keeping down educational costs and student debt. Yet the leaders of these schools often experience subtle (or even overt) pressure from other schools and outside agencies to increase tuition levels and shift the student's tuition-paying burden to loan programs that initiate payback after graduation. Perhaps output measures of postgraduate salary should be modified such that student educational debts are subtracted from salary level to obtain a net income figure. Thus the salaries of alumni who owe $100,000 in student loans might be reduced by the amount being paid on that loan per year (including interest) when income-oriented output measures are calculated. We might even take a further step, adding social debt to this output-based measure of quality. After all, due to large outstanding loans, alumni of many expensive undergraduate and graduate institutions are not free to serve the most important unmet needs of our society.

Value-Added Criteria

In recent years, many nontraditional educational institutions (and some accrediting agencies) have begun to look at quality in a new way by defining it in value-added terms. The major question that must be addressed from this perspective is, how does one determine and measure the critical value-added dimensions of a student's life in a collegiate institution? Gregory Bateson (1979) wrote about "differences that make a difference" in our world. Which differences make a difference in an institution of higher education, and which are trivial or ephemeral? And at how many points along the way should measurements be taken?

Typically, a value-added definition of quality focuses on the experiences of the student while enrolled in the college or university. This perspective concentrates specifically on what the institution contributed to the student's life. As a result of this internally oriented perspective, value-added criteria are often aligned with student development and with other values of the developmental culture (see Bergquist, 1992). At present, student development theory has not yet realized its potential—though this theoretical perspective has played an important role in such areas as the fostering of critical thinking and writing across the curriculum. The central question appears to be, how can the theory be applied in the typical classroom? As Knefelkamp, Widick, and Parker (1978) asked a while ago, what is the relationship between student development theory and real-life practice? There is still no clear answer. In the case of criteria of quality, the specific question becomes, how can student development theory help articulate and direct the measurement of value-added student development? If we had an overall theory of student development that encompasses all parts of the college, how would we apply this theory to the measurement of quality?

The first major problem concerns boundaries (this seems to be the case with many postmodern problems). What are the appropriate criteria for assessing student development, and in what areas (for example, personality development or moral development) are we crossing the boundaries? When are we no longer in the appropriate domain of a collegiate institution? As soon as we look at many dimensions of student development, we are in areas that most faculty members prefer to ignore: social development, value clarification, concern for the whole person, and spiritual development.

A second major problem concerns the implications of student development measurements for the curricular and extracurricular activities of the institution. Should the faculty and administration be held responsible for the full development of their students? This may be legitimate if value-added development is being equated with quality. Is student development something that can be planned, or does it usually occur independent of any specific actions taken by either faculty or administration?

For instance, does development tend to occur in formal educational settings, or is it more likely to take place in the informal bull sessions of the college dormitory or on "the playing fields of Eton"? Like many developmental theorists, Riker (1981) suggests that student development is not only broad-based but also rather elusive:

> A critical factor in several areas of development, including cognitive, ethical, moral, and ego as well as interpersonal development, seems to be a growing awareness of self in relation to others. Important learning about oneself—about one's identity, interest, hopes and self-worth—can occur in conversation between roommates or within the context of a congenial group. Within such a group, students can clarify their values, identify their strengths and limitations, test new ideas, try new roles, and on the basis of these experiences, review and perhaps refocus their goals [p. 673].

A third major problem concerns the incorporation of student development objectives in the mission of a college or university. In the preface to *The Modern American College*, Sanford (1981) quotes Chickering as stating that the "overarching purpose of our colleges and universities should be to encourage and enable intentional developmental change throughout the life cycle" (p. xvii). Sanford and many other developmental theorists would agree with this purpose, yet other developmentalists suggest that developmental theory should steer clear of application and be considered descriptive rather than prescriptive. Many of the most successful developmental theorists—Erik Erikson and Lawrence Kohlberg being the most prominent—have been roundly criticized for identifying specific modes and stages of development as somehow universally better than other stages.

Knefelkamp, Widick, and Parker (1978) are among those who question the belief that we should foster developmental change: "Students often experience a move from dependence on parents to independence in decision making and value choices. Whether or not it is good to move from such dependence to independence is another problem. Similarly, one might observe that many students experience an identity crisis and infer that it would be good for all students to do so" (p. xiii). Knefelkamp and colleagues also mention the homogeneity fallacy of developmental theories. Students differ from one another in many ways, and rarely can we group them on important variables. Our theories do not account for individual differences, nor do they help an administrator or faculty member deal with an individual.

Given that our student development theories do not deal very effectively with the case of one, we are walking on very thin ice when we set up criteria of quality based on the assumptions of uniformity of development. In applying student development theory to the assessment of quality we may—as Knefelkamp, Widick, and Parker (1978) warn us—be applying this theory "as though students were an inert substance much like projectiles that can be twisted, turned, and thrust in [specific] directions. . . . Do we have the *right* to bring about our purposes? . . . We must recognize in our theory that students are alive, make choices, are as aware of us as we are of them, that they act as well as are acted upon. In fact, they are deciding, choosing, interacting persons whose nature changes as we work with them" (p. xiv).

With all of these warnings, we can still make use of student development theory when defining quality in terms of the value that is added by a college or university, provided that we are careful about both the criteria and their use. The following points may serve as guidelines in this regard. First, student development tends to be holistic. It usually combines thoughts, feelings, and behavior. Often development seems to be associated with surprise and with a shifting of perspectives. After a critical developmental episode, one can rarely "go home again." Frequently, students' major developmental breakthroughs involve their own growing sense of self-confidence and competency. They feel more skillful and are a bit wiser while overcoming their fears about being students again and being judged by other people.

A third-year student at Evergreen originally expected that college would be one big beer blast and that being a college student would take up all of his time, between studying and going to fraternity parties. At Evergreen, however, he soon discovered that he had to "deal with who I was" at that particular time in his life: "Evergreen makes you come to terms with things. You have to come to terms with yourself before anything else. . . . I realized that it's really hard. Learning academically and learning about life are very different things, but you do both at Evergreen. The learning is self-generated. [Evergreen] has made me come to a better understanding of myself, . . . dealing more with making things happen for myself—not just making it in college, but things to help me in my life."

A much older student in PSP master's program similarly commented on her developmental surprises:

I was afraid that I wouldn't be as good as the other [students at PSP].
I don't write as well as I should. Never wrote very much in my other
programs. I was scared I would not measure up. It's not different than
I thought—lots of reading, lots of writing, small classes. I went to
undergraduate school at a [University of California] campus. I had
classes with over a hundred students, and in one class I never saw
the professor even once. . . . I was just afraid of looking like I didn't
belong there. I had a friend who went to PSP, and he said the standards were pretty high. I was afraid I wouldn't get in. I have to work
hard but I do all right.

In her case—and in the case of many other PSP, JFK, and Evergreen
students—the answer to their anxiety about performance is not the
lowering of standards, for this only confirms their sense of inadequacy. Rather, as this student indicated, development occurs when
students approach the hard work as a challenge and look for the
support of their fellow students and faculty in helping them meet
it. Quality is achieved when there is a balance between cognitive
and affective challenge and support and when a student overcomes
the fear of inadequacy by overcoming real obstacles established to
ensure high quality of student performance (Sanford, 1980).

Many of the students interviewed at JFK expressed similar initial fears about their ability to perform at an undergraduate or graduate level. They braced themselves in entering the university,
expecting once again to be considered not much more than a number or a nameless face in the class, despite what they had heard to
the contrary. Often, even though the students had chosen JFK
specifically because of its reputation for being different, they had to
live it to believe it. They came to JFK assuming that teachers would
be unapproachable and that any questions or problems with the
material would be confronted in private, hoping that they have at
last matured enough to succeed. They came viewing higher education as an obstacle course that they could work through, if tena-
cious enough, and receive a degree at the other end.

In almost all of the interviews, JFK students expressed a pleasant, if slightly uneasy, surprise upon starting their first quarter. The maximum class size at Kennedy is usually twenty-five, and classes as small as ten or twelve are common. Instructors are addressed by their first name and often meet outside of class with students, as both counselors and friends. Each class is structured as a colloquium, in which the input of the students is as important as that of the teacher. These are people with considerable background in the real world, and the philosophy at JFK is that this must be respected and honored.

Similarly, at PSP, "differences that make a difference" often center on shifting perspectives regarding the nature of teaching and learning itself. As in the case of JFK students, many of the mature learners who come to PSP have had negative experiences in other educational institutions and come to PSP with substantial emotional baggage. A fifty-year-old female physician who recently returned to school at PSP stated it this way:

> I have gone to so many schools. I went to medical school about fifteen years ago. It was cutthroat. Very male. I mean very competitive. Everyone looked out for *numero uno*. Period. There was little contact with teachers. There was a strict hierarchy. Teachers were addressed formally as "Doctor So-and-So." So were students during class. They would refer to us as "Doctor So-and-So." It felt so pretentious. There were only eleven women students out of a class of one hundred and twenty. It was tough to be a woman. . . . During anatomy class, there would be female nudes interspersed among the slides. Each one would bring a barrage of catcalls. So I wasn't looking forward to graduate school. I thought of it as a means to something I wanted to do. I thought maybe of getting a master's in history or foreign policy. I thought I was going to have to dig out my old suit of armor. I have lots of friends with graduate degrees, but it never occurred to me to ask them about school. I thought everyone's experiences would be similar to mine. What a surprise!

A second component of student development that seems relevant when defining quality concerns the students' discovery of their own talents as learners and as people who are capable of thought, judgment, and persuasion. The students and faculty at Evergreen are, according to a senior there, "totally interested in learning and want to get down to the basics. . . . There are people at Evergreen who think that what they do here is the most important part of their lives. They are learning things they will take away and use with a dedication to bettering the world."

This young woman offers a wonderful image of how elitism and populism can be effectively blended. The all-encompassing nature of education at Evergreen is classic elitism. Typically, only the full-time residential college student who need worry about nothing else in life has the luxury of becoming totally absorbed in the college experience. Certainly, students who must also hold down a job and raise a family cannot focus exclusively or even primarily on their collegiate experience. Yet students at Evergreen do hold jobs and raise families. College can still be a deeply enriching experience for these students, however, because while enrolled at Evergreen, they focus on one program and one theme at a time. Students at most other schools take courses in several different areas and hence have few opportunities for integration of material—campus and dormitory bull sessions notwithstanding. The students at Evergreen, by contrast, have a much greater opportunity for integrative experiences in their seminars and work projects. Furthermore, the Evergreen students can take their own commitment to creating a better world—a classic populist value—back out into their personal life and community through their work, their families, and local volunteer activities.

Our Evergreen student goes on to observe that her seminar experiences at the college have taught her to "keep my mouth shut. Before I was exposed to peers who got into my face, I would say something as soon as I thought it. Now I keep my mouth shut until I have thought through my ideas. I've gotten a lot from hearing more viewpoints. I like listening to people and then going back to my ideas to see how the two can mix. Its fascinating how the same piece of material—a book or movie or whatever—can affect two people in totally different ways. I think Evergreen encourages the sharing of different ideas and respecting others' opinions." Whereas many female students—especially those returning to schools after many years—need the support of faculty and fellow students in finding their voices, other women and men (like the young woman from Evergreen) need the challenge of refining their own voices as well as listening more carefully to other people in their lives—especially those with divergent perspectives.

Students at JFK similarly find that learning is derived more from dialogue than from lectures when educational quality is high. They must also learn how to listen, as well as to express their own ideas. There is a constant give-and-take between students and teacher, creating an energy of sharing. There is not much of a social scene at JFK; the classes serve as intense forums for personal contact in and of themselves. Students often experience the classes at JFK as small capsules, unique experiences that are sheltered from the outside world—learning sanctuaries.

Finally, student development seemingly relates to value-added-criteria quality when all aspects of the institution contribute to the development of the students' competencies and sense of self-worth. One PSP student commented that there is "a sense of mastery" at the school. "I have come to realize that I am capable of mastering an unfamiliar discipline. Education is really just applying yourself—just get down and do the work that is assigned. There's nothing else quite like doing the work itself."

Process-Oriented Criteria

A partial answer to the dilemmas posed by a value-added, developmentally oriented definition of quality is to be found in the emphasis on process. From this perspective, what is learned in the classroom becomes less important than the way in which learning takes place. How the college or university is run is emphasized more than particular educational outcomes. From a process-oriented perspective, all aspects of a college or university become grist for the mill and sources of new learning for everyone involved—students, faculty, and administrators. A student at PSP put it this way: "You are ninety percent responsible for what you get out of an education, but the ten percent that is the institution's part is vital. All my effort would be in vain if it were not for what the school provides. . . . Regarding institutions, I think I am even more aware that each institution has its own character, that the character of the school may not be what gets people to come, but it sure has a lot to do with whether people stay and what feelings they develop toward the school—affection, loyalty, commitment, and so forth."

Given this perspective, we need to take an entirely different approach to community life than most colleges and universities have taken. In essence, learning moves to center stage for all members of an institution. This, as Sanford (1973) notes, places students back in first place. Every activity, every action, every resource is directed toward students and, more generally, toward maximization of learning for every constituency. This type of change means integrating the curriculum and cocurriculum. This approach means acquiring control over auxiliary activities (such as competitive sports, the student bookstore, and research contracts) in order to bring them back into the arena of learning.

In essence, from a process perspective, the cocurriculum (or "hidden curriculum") of a college or university will have to be brought explicitly into the learning community. Administrators and faculty will have to become more aware of the lessons being learned by the students about the organization and operation of their own institution (Barber, 1984). Students learn other lessons about teaching and learning from the way they occur in the classroom. At an even deeper level, students learn about values and aspirations from the dominant, though often unacknowledged, cultures of the institution (Bergquist, 1992). A collegial culture teaches certain things about the nature of tradition, heritage, and status that are quite different from those taught by a managerial, developmental, or negotiating culture.

At their best, teaching and learning at all three of the institutions being studied here convey something about the exciting and nurturing nature of new ideas. Students often come to these nontraditional institutions because they are afraid of learning in a formal setting. Interviews revealed that seminars can provide valuable opportunities for growth in both mind and spirit. Students often identified seminar-based classes that changed their lives in one way or another. They also pointed to interdisciplinary courses as being particularly valuable from a process perspective. These courses offered new insights even in areas with which the students were already familiar. The real-life experiences and expertise brought into the classroom by students from many different settings and socioeconomic levels further enriched the dialogue.

The silence that many students have taken for granted as their natural response to being in a classroom often comes to an end in JFK, PSP, and Evergreen seminars and interdisciplinary courses. Many students—particularly women (Belenky, Clinchy, Goldberger, and Tarule, 1986)—see attending class at one of these schools as a chance to free a voice that they long ago suppressed. Their voices are respected, and they are free from hypercritical inspection. The experience of finally being heard can be life-changing and often opens the door to learning in a whole new way, with new confidence and courage.

The Evergreen, JFK, and PSP student interviews revealed yet another dimension of process-oriented quality. When learning is taking place, everything seems to glow. Learning becomes an exciting opportunity rather than a chore. There is an intensity among the students at these schools. Dedication to and excitement about learning are infectious. This spirit emanates from the student body and infuses the institution with purpose. The fact that all students have made the decision to return to school and to effect great change in their lives results in the sense that everyone at the school is there to learn, not just to mark time. This atmosphere frees the discussion to focus on the task at hand—pursuing knowledge and pushing one's personal growth to the limit. "This experience has been by far the best education of my life," notes a PSP student. "I have gone to many schools. This is the first place where I have seen students treated more as colleagues than as underlings. I have been particularly impressed with the school's maintaining high standards and at the same time not being individually competitive. I could really tell you stories from other places. . . . What a relief this place has been."

A final dimension of the process-oriented perspective on quality concerns interactions between students and faculty. Frequently, the process of engagement between student and faculty when high-quality teaching is occurring takes on the characteristics of a warm, lasting friendship—particularly when the student is older than the average college-age learner. One PSP student recalled just such a relationship with her family therapy instructor, Nancy:

I had a real attitude. I thought that family therapy functioned as a whitewash for perpetrators [of crimes], . . . that it diluted the concept of personal responsibility. At any rate, I wanted no part of it—but it was a requirement. So, anyway, I said something like that to [Nancy] at the first class. Well, the class [turned out] great. Systems theory . . . was a new way of thinking for me, a new way to look at things. I could see what a radical shift it was from more traditional ways of knowing. So I ended up putting a lot of time and effort into that class. By the end of the class, [Nancy] and I had developed a real affection for each other, and she . . . provides me with recommendations when I need them for internships. I am still not a family therapy devotee, but I appreciate the contribution [of those theoreticians] to the field, and I like the boundaries that they pushed.

Instruction at all three institutions is often uniquely personal. Faculty and students see each other as people, and the individual interests of both can be addressed as fully as possible. Students interviewed at all three schools often described classroom format and requirements as negotiable. The general feeling in a class is only what the students and teacher collectively make it. The instructors respect students and understand that they are serious about their studies; students' ideas about alternatives to assignments are therefore usually considered. Teachers also expect that students will push themselves as far as possible. Instructors at all three schools are not afraid to tell students that they can and should strive for even higher goals.

In many of the interviews, students expressed anxiety about embarking on or returning to higher education. The thought of interaction between students and faculty often elicits fear as well as excitement. A large number of students are led to these schools through word of mouth, so they know to expect a certain difference in the education that they will receive. However, the wounds of past experiences are often too deep to make the return to school entirely comfortable.

Learners are drawn to all three schools because they feel that dialogue is as important to the learning process as the input of information. Students often observed that they gained the most through the teaching and learning process itself. JFK, PSP, and Evergreen do not embrace traditional input-output means of teaching, expecting the student to regurgitate the teacher's words verbatim. Unfortunately, most of the students interviewed had received just that kind of education in the past and found it hard to adjust to a different mode of teaching and learning.

Typically, at the heart of the matter for many students—and for many faculty and administrators as well—is the issue of authority in a process-oriented educational institution. From a process perspective, there must be a shift in the nature and source of authority in the institution. Sanford (1980) draws a distinction between authority as status or position and authority as relationship. When authority is seen as a relationship, the institution is aware that authority is possible only when the students (or faculty or administrators) react with respect or confidence in it. This kind of authority gives guidance and support. It is a social process.

A student at PSP defined this important index of quality in relationship to others, citing the "egalitarian relationship between students and faculty" as one of the most important factors at PSP.

There are none of those ridiculous "rights of passage" requirements. Students are treated just as respectfully as faculty and administration. I'm not saying that there are not role differences, and I am very aware that I am a student, but there is no intrinsic feeling of operating in a hierarchy with me at the bottom. I think the maturity of the students attracts a certain kind of faculty. I happen to think that this school attracts outstanding faculty. . . . We have a lot of diversity: old, gay, gifted, not so gifted, business types, rich bored housewives, poor struggling single mothers, administrators, lawyers, ministers, nurses, podiatrists, chiropractors, teachers, jocks, and on and on, and I love it. I think that having a tuition that is affordable to more people is part of what makes this place fly. I think that focusing primarily on older second- and third-career adults makes this place unique and special.

As Sanford (1981) points out, the broader participation by students and faculty in the governance processes of institutions like PSP, Evergreen, or JFK does not mean giving students what they want, but it does mean considering decisions and their impact on students. This approach also means considering how the decisions are made and the messages sent through the administrative structure. The assumption is of responsibility, not control. Although students (and faculty) often ask for greater control, they may be hesitant to assume the responsibility that comes with it. In that narrow space between the challenge of increased responsibility and the support associated with building a collaborative community lies a rich potential for new learning by everyone involved in the school.

Key Points

1. Quality in American colleges and universities has been defined in four ways: according to input criteria, output criteria, value-added criteria, and process-oriented criteria.

2. Each definition of quality is critical when assessing the overall effectiveness of a collegiate institution and when relating quality to access. The following definition of quality incorporates all four sets of criteria: Quality exists when adequate and appropriate resources are being directed successfully toward the accomplishment of mission-related institutional outcomes and when programs make a significant and positive mission-related difference in the lives of people affiliated with the college or university and are created, conducted, and modified in a manner that is consistent with the mission (and values) of the institution.

3. Each of the four approaches to quality contributes to an effective postmodern vision of quality and access.

Chapter Four

Myths and Concerns About Integrating Quality and Access

Regardless of the type of American postsecondary educational institution being considered, all have evolved in close conjunction with the United States' unique historical development. The concepts of quality and access are intimately related to several basic social forces that have operated throughout the history of this country. A first historical theme concerns the long-standing American preoccupation with demonstrating quality—with "keeping up with the Joneses." Beginning with the first colonial colleges, there was an abiding concern for showing that American collegiate institutions are as good as their European counterparts. Later, a pecking order evolved in American higher education.

The quality of European collegiate institutions was defined primarily by the class of their students: the higher the class of the students attending, the better the quality of the institution. But in America, there were no overt social class distinctions (beyond race, an important but indirect class marker). American educators therefore had to look for other standards of quality. They didn't have to look very far. They borrowed from their European colleagues not the concept of social class but rather one specific aspect of class, the style of life that students are trained to lead. This "collegial way" (Rudolph, 1962) was replicated in many institutions, leading to uniformity of practices in American colleges and universities (Jencks and Riesman, 1968).

A second theme in the growth of the United States has been "the American dream." This dream has taken economic, political, social, and religious forms. One aspect of it is the right of every

American to move from the lowest to the highest levels of society. One major route to fulfillment of the American dream was believed to be higher education. The desire to provide access to higher education to most citizens was inherent in the Morrill Act of 1862 with the establishment of land-grant universities. A later example was the Servicemen's Readjustment Act of 1944, known as the GI Bill of Rights (Vaughan, 1985). Although the American dream was never fully realized through postsecondary education (see Jencks and Riesman, 1968), many mission statements in American colleges and universities speak of the role of higher education in promoting upward social and economic mobility.

Higher education needed to be not only more inclusive but also more selective. Many educators believed that the only way to provide quality education was by accepting only top students. The growth of sophisticated assessment techniques and large testing institutions (such as the Educational Testing Service and the American College Testing Program) to find these highly qualified students documents the importance of selectivity in American colleges and universities. As Astin (1985) notes, many prestigious colleges and universities produce very successful graduates not primarily because of the education and training that the students receive while in college but rather because of the remarkable talents and contacts that the students bring to the institution. These students would be highly successful graduates of any institution they choose to attend.

Many collegiate mission statements reflect these seemingly opposite notions about quality and access as the chief ingredients of the American dream. On the one hand, we wish to open our arms to men and women from all sectors of society. On the other hand, we wish to select only the very best from these sectors and must ignore some sectors if this would require a lowering of admission standards or diminish in any other way the traditional standards of quality in our institutions.

Recent history has also influenced the mission statements of colleges and universities. The impact of the late 1960s and early

1970s has greatly affected the governance structure and the role of presidents in educational institutions. The turmoil of the 1960s in higher education toppled the president from the perch of academic leader (Cohen and Marsh, 1974). Nason (1981) suggests that today "some presidents see themselves as managers of the store, labor union negotiators, mediators among competing factions, budget balancers, glorified office boys. They clearly view themselves as expendable" (p. 267). College and university presidents bemoan their loss of power and the constraints imposed on them—legal constraints, administrative regulations, and participatory power of faculty and students (Riesman and Fuller, 1985).

After the turmoil of the 1960s and the expansion of the 1970s come the difficult financial times of the mid and late 1980s and early 1990s. Enrollments have plateaued, inflation has caused tuition to skyrocket, and cutbacks in private, state, and federal funding have made balancing the budget difficult. In addition, the demands on educational institutions have changed. The skill levels of undergraduate students have declined steadily since the 1960s (Levine, 1980). Average scores on the College Board's Scholastic Aptitude (now Assessment) Test and the American College Testing Program have declined steadily. Students have been arriving at colleges without having taken the traditional high school courses. According to Levine, "Thirty-five percent have not taken second-year algebra, 28 percent have not had even one year of a foreign language, 27 percent have not taken junior- or senior-year English, 22 percent have missed geometry, and 20 percent have not had a year of any specific science, such as biology or chemistry" (p. 74).

Three major reports in the 1980s—*Involvement in Learning: Realizing the Potential of American Higher Education* by the National Institute of Education (1984), *To Reclaim a Legacy: A Report on the Humanities in Higher Education* by William Bennett (1984), and *The Closing of the American Mind* by Allan Bloom (1987)—called attention to the problems in postsecondary institutions. All three seemed to be asking for stronger leadership from all administrators, especially presidents, with clearer statements of purpose regarding where educational institutions are going.

Unfortunately, these reports also called for a return to some very traditional educational values and in many cases a retreat from our national commitment to access. Leaders were urged to reassert traditional standards, reintroduce the classic Western-oriented curriculum, and, in essence, shut the doors to nontraditional student populations who are underprepared for this classical education. These same attitudes are being perpetuated in the work of Mayhew, Ford, and Hubbard (1990). Similarly, many public colleges and universities have begun to restrict access on the part of nontraditional students—usually by reviving traditional admission standards (English literacy, formal high school preparatory program, and so forth), less vigorously pursuing student aid packages, and adding additional tuition fees for mature adult learners who already have degrees (see, for example, Gill, 1991).

Given these trends, we cannot assume that these concerns or perspectives are simply a short-term manifestation of 1980s conservatism. Furthermore, the same nostalgic return to earlier forms is a central ingredient in virtually all sectors of postmodern society, whether we are talking about motion pictures, churches, or political rhetoric. At the heart of the matter is an inherent belief that quality and access are incompatible goals for any collegiate institution.

Current Status of Access in American Higher Education

In 1968, Jencks and Riesman wrote of the unrealistic status of the American dream of access, much as they wrote of unrealistic academic models of quality. Like many other higher education historians, Jencks and Riesman noted at the time that there was little evidence to suggest that American higher education had served as a consistently and broadly effective vehicle for upward social and economic mobility. Though there have been many noteworthy examples of institutional excellence with regard to access and many remarkable individual stories concerning the impact of higher education on underprivileged youth, there is also a long history of disappointing results in this area.

In his more general and more challenging study of inequity in America, Jencks (1972) concluded a few years later that educational attainment is clearly related to family background, especially family economic status, thus suggesting that American education in general and higher education in particular had not been notably successful as a vehicle for social mobility, given that students were more likely to attend and remain in school if they came from higher socioeconomic backgrounds. Whereas primary and secondary education did help first- and second-generation Americans learn the language and culture of this country, postsecondary education led not so much to upward socioeconomic mobility as to the raising of entry-level qualifications for jobs in America (see O'Toole, 1977).

What about today? Is the assumption of upward social mobility's being propelled by education still a myth? In a late 1980s survey of "demographic realities," Levine and Associates (1989) concluded that American higher education has done no better job of fulfilling the American dream in recent years than Jencks suggested was the case in earlier eras. Although the enrollment of some underserved populations in higher educational institutions has increased over the past two decades, in most cases this increase has occurred as a result of major increases in the size of this specific population rather than because of any success in increasing this population's access to American colleges and universities.

We can look specifically at each of the major groups of underserved, nontraditional student populations to see the breadth and depth of this failure. With regard to racial and ethnic minorities, Levine and Associates (1989) note, first, that African Americans "made substantial progress in higher education enrollment and participation in the early to mid 1970s" but "lost ground in the 1980s.

In fact the 1980s have been called the years of lost opportunity for blacks" (p. 64). A more recent report by the Office of Educational Research and Improvement (1990) notes that the enrollment of African-American men actually decreased by 2 percent from 1978 to 1988—though there was a 14 percent increase for African-American women. Authors of a 1992 *Postsecondary Education Opportunity* report similarly recorded a drop in the rate of college enrollment among African-American high school graduates in 1992, down to the rate of 1975 ("College Entrance Rates," 1992). In 1993, they again reported no progress. Comparisons between bachelor's degree attainment records from 1980 through 1991 revealed a downturn for African-American women and very little change for African-American men ("No Progress," 1993).

With regard to Hispanics, Levine and Associates (1989) conclude that although this is a rapidly growing segment of the American population, "access to college has declined even more sharply for Hispanic high school graduates than for their black counterparts." Furthermore, "there has been a notable decline in degree attainment ratios among Hispanics enrolled in four-year colleges [in the Los Angeles, Chicago, Houston, and Philadelphia] areas between 1980 and 1984" (p. 57). *Postsecondary Education Opportunity* noted that the rates for college enrollment of Hispanic high school graduates increased in 1992; however, this increase only brought the rate back to its 1976 level ("College Entrance Rates," 1992). In 1993, it again reported no progress. Comparisons between bachelor's degree attainment records from 1980 through 1991 revealed a negative change for Hispanic men but a positive change for Hispanic women ("No Progress," 1993).

Asian-American student populations have consistently grown in American higher education as the number of immigrants from Asia have increased in recent years. However, Levine and Associates (1989) note that the current tendency for Asian-American families to value and promote education flies in the face of racial discrimination: "Although Asian Americans . . . invested heavily in education, this did not appear to result in nearly as much earning power for them as it did for whites. This disparity was largely attributed to the persistence of racial discrimination" (p. 99).

Levine and Associates did not specifically focus on Native American students; however, a recent report from the U.S. Office of Education (Carnegie Foundation, 1990b) reveals a very stable and very low rate of enrollment of Native Americans in American colleges and universities since 1976, despite increases in their population in the United States. In 1990, only 9 percent of Native American adults had completed four years of college, compared to 20 percent for the total population (O'Brien, 1992).

A second major underserved population in the United States is older students. Levine and Associates (1989) note that the number of adults (aged twenty-five to fifty-five) attending college "peaked in 1988. It will probably decline throughout the rest of this century because the baby boomers who dominate the nation's population are zooming past the peak adult enrollment ages." Charles Anderson (1990) similarly noted the 1988 peak and the subsequent decline, though he is more optimistic about enrollment throughout the rest of the century. *Postsecondary Education Opportunity* offered a rather negative portrait of access for mature adults. It indicated that college enrollment rates in general between 1960 and 1980 increased significantly for persons aged eighteen to twenty-four years but remained fairly constant for persons aged twenty-five to twenty-nine and decreased for persons aged thirty to thirty-four. By 1990, the rates for the twenty-two to twenty-four age group had dropped to 21 percent, less than 10 percent for persons aged twenty-five to twenty-nine, and about 5 percent for those aged thirty to thirty-four ("Growth in College Enrollment Rates," 1992).

Finally, we can examine the least visible but perhaps most important underserved population in the United States, people at the lower socioeconomic levels. Levine and Associates do not focus on socioeconomic level, though obviously this factor is intertwined with issues of racial and ethnic discrimination. In 1993, college freshmen identified financing their college education as a major concern; only 30 percent of college freshmen reported no concern about college finances, the lowest percentage since 1966 ("Affordability Concerns," 1993). Whereas 86 percent of eighteen-to twenty-four-year-old students from the top quartile in terms of family income are enrolled in college, only 75 percent of those from the third quartile, 64 percent from the second quartile, and 52 percent from the lowest quartile are enrolled ("Family Income Backgrounds," 1993). Finally, whereas students from families in the top quartile have a 65 percent chance of obtaining a baccalaureate degree by age twenty-four, only about 5 percent of students from families in the bottom quartile are likely to complete college by that age ("Disparities," 1993).

Clearly, the American dream that has propelled so many of the goals and aspirations of American higher education and has at times distinguished postsecondary education in the United States from the more class-bound educational structures of other countries is found wanting in the 1990s. Though our country made some significant advances during the 1960s and 1970s, we have fallen back in terms of commitment to access since then and have actually lost ground, given expansion in the size of many underserved populations. Why has this occurred? How do we deal with this central issue of access? What role does quality play?

Quality and Access: Five Institutional Perspectives

To move higher education beyond its current dilemma regarding quality and access, I propose that quality can be achieved in our emerging postmodern world only when complemented by diversified resources, which in turn depend on access. Furthermore, access to educational programs that are of low quality is not really access. Efforts to integrate quality and access rarely reach fruition, in part because of four dominant perspectives in American higher education on the inherent contradictions between a commitment to quality and a commitment to access. A fifth perspective—what I have termed the unified perspective—is required if the integration of quality and access that I think is crucial to the survival and flourishing of postmodern collegiate institutions is to be achieved.

Borrowing from the two-factor theories of Blake and Mouton (1984) and Hershey and Blanchard (1977), the five perspectives can be positioned along two axes, one representing quality and the other access (see Figure 4.1).

Elitist Perspective

The elitist perspective is characterized by high concern for quality and low concern for access. From the elitist perspective, the primary role of postsecondary education is the preparation of the people who

Figure 4.1. The Five Institutional Perspectives in Terms of Quality and Access.

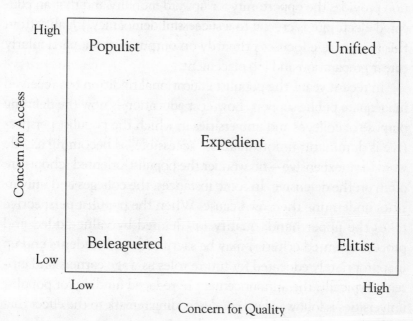

will assume leadership roles in our society. It is assumed that these people should receive the highest-quality education so that society might improve. Quality from this perspective is defined primarily in terms of input criteria. This may mean that people who are underserved in our society will be denied access; however, over the long haul, highest-quality education for the people deemed best qualified to lead is of greatest importance. The elitist perspective is associated primarily with the collegial culture (Bergquist, 1992). The future of this perspective is potentially in doubt, and changes are likely in institutions in which it thrives if they are to survive, considering that philanthropic and public financial support for elitist-oriented educational institutions seems to be waning.

Populist Perspective

Access is of primary concern from the populist perspective. Populism has a long and distinguished history in American society, especially in higher education. The tradition is built on the belief that education provides the opportunity for upward mobility and that an educated electorate is crucial to a successful democracy. Quality from this perspective focuses primarily on output criteria, particularly career preparation and job placement.

In recent years, the populist educational tradition has received inadequate public support. Low-cost education is now the defining purpose of colleges and universities in which the populist perspective is dominant; unfortunately, "accessible" is becoming a code word for inexpensive—no wonder the populist-oriented schools are often on the defensive. In some instances, the colleges and universities undermine their own cause. When the populist perspective takes the upper hand, quality (as defined by value-added and process-oriented criteria) may be sacrificed, and students end up inappropriately educated for future roles as wage earners and citizens. Typically, the announcement of reduced funding for populist universities is followed by a condescending remark to the effect that "at least they have received *something*."

Typically, the managerial culture is closely related to this perspective, and public funds are often the primary sources of tenuous support. Not all public institutions can be defined as populist; many large state universities are elitist, research-oriented, and highly selective with regard to student enrollment. However, even these elitist state universities were initially founded with a commitment to public access, and in some instances, they have remained committed to both quality and access.

Beleaguered Perspective

The leaders of colleges and universities never start out with a beleaguered perspective, characterized by low concern for both quality and access. Rather, they end up there when their institutions abandon the commitment to any specific purpose or vision other than survival. Quality is ill-defined or treated skeptically by faculty, staff, and administrators, who are simply trying to get by for one more day. If quality is defined at all, attention usually focuses primarily on process, especially how decisions on the allocation of scarce resources are made.

In the beleaguered college or university, access is considered a burden rather than a challenge, given that funding is usually dependent on the whim of a state legislature, board of regents or trustees, or donor rather than on enrollment figures. Decision making from this perspective is so irrational or inconsistent that systematic concern for either quality or access would be a waste of time.

Frequently, institutions that fall into the beleaguered perspective have failed in their efforts to become either elitist or populist. Efforts to become elite may have come too late—strong financial support for elite universities was available only for a brief time after *Sputnik* and the ensuing short-lived American interest in basic research and scientific exploration. Institutions that tried to move toward traditional definitions of quality in the 1970s and 1980s offered too little too late. Similarly, the civil rights movement and the surge of the baby boomers into colleges and universities during the 1960s sparked a short-term interest in populist colleges and universities that welcomed underserved populations. Institutions that were not in a position to benefit from this public support in the 1960s were simply too late in the 1970s and 1980s to gain a foothold in American higher education. They soon became marginalized, and there many remain.

Expedient Perspective

The expedient perspective, widely encountered in postmodern colleges and universities in the United States, is characterized by moderate concern for both quality and access. From this perspective, the two goals are regarded as inherently incompatible and subject to conflicting pressures. Leaders of institutions in which the expedient perspective is dominant typically feel that they must accommodate each of these pressures, even though compromise is always the result. The focus of these leaders is often on finding funds to support school operations, whether these funds support elitist or populist purposes. Quality may be defined in many different ways from the expedient perspective, depending on the program, the students being served, and the funding source.

Although this perspective and the institutional strategies that accompany it may have some survival value, it will not serve postmodern collegiate institutions effectively in the long run.

Unified Perspective

The unified perspective is characterized by high concern for both quality and access. From the unified perspective, as has been noted several times, access becomes genuine through the enhancement of quality, and quality is in turn improved by increased access. Improved quality makes an institution more reputable—a critical factor when increasing access for men and women who are usually ignored by higher education. Greater access improves quality by encouraging a diversity of resources and worldviews.

From the unified perspective, quality is enhanced through increased access by making efficient use of existing resources. Efficiency is in turn dependent on mission-driven allocation of these resources. With regard to output measures, one can make a particularly important contribution to the union of quality and access by influencing the ways in which output measures are defined and employed. Quality and access can be brought together through much broader and less self-serving definitions of successful output. Institutional quality can be measured by an even broader perspective on output, namely, the extent to which the graduates and other products and services of the institution contribute to an institutionally shared vision of the "good society." An institution can be of high quality if its graduates serve underserved populations in society. In this way, the institution provides greater access not only to potential students but also to the clients, patients, or customers of its graduates. The quality of output is in this way closely related to an expanded notion of access. This in turn sets the stage for a multidimensional definition of quality that incorporates value-added and process-oriented criteria along with input and output measures.

Five Perspectives in Action

In Part Two, I describe each of the four traditional perspectives on quality and access. I propose that the elitist perspective is embedded in a premodern set of experiences and constructs, whereas the populist perspective is embedded in a more modern set of experiences and constructs. The beleaguered and expedient perspectives have few historical roots and are being buffeted by many postmodern forces.

In some instances, these perspectives are chosen by the people who founded or now lead the institution; in other instances, they are adopted out of necessity or lack of other options (at least in the minds of the leaders). Even though in many instances I will be discussing the role of these perspectives in two- and four-year colleges and universities, the same perspectives are articulated in many different institutional settings—not just higher education. These perspectives resemble the notion of paradigms first articulated by Thomas Kuhn (1962). Typically, advocates of a specific perspective (especially the elitist and populist perspectives) have never considered any other assumptions about quality or access. The stances from which they see the world have become deeply ingrained and even fully institutionalized.

Quality, Access, and the Four Cultures of the Academy

To gain a better sense of the interplay between quality and access in postmodern institutions and the potential barriers to be found in collegiate institutions wishing to move toward unification of quality and access, I turn again to my 1992 analysis of academic cultures and identify how each culture relates to the issues of quality and access.

Collegial Culture

The collegial culture typically defines access primarily in terms of ethnicity and physical disabilities (but not learning disabilities). These initiatives are rarely considered when identifying the sources of quality in these institutions. Many elitist institutions—to which members of the collegial culture aspire—have impressive programs for recruiting and providing scholarships for young men and women from underrepresented populations, though they often embrace selective accessibility, recruiting only the best and brightest from among these populations. Though elitist and collegially oriented faculty and administrators typically do not put access high on the agenda, much can be learned from these faculty and administrators, particularly with regard to curricular issues and the recruitment of minority faculty.

Schools like PSP and JFK have not been as successful as the elitist schools in recruiting ethnically diverse students, hiring minority faculty, or establishing rich and diverse curricular offerings. Less financially secure institutions like PSP and JFK must rely on the diversity of socioeconomic level, age, and occupation among students to make up for a lack of ethnic diversity. For instance, one PSP student commented during his interview:

> You don't see much color here. That doesn't mean that this is your basic white middle-class WASP school either. For that you can go to the Big Two [Stanford and California State] or you can go to "little Harvard" [a prestigious nearby graduate school of psychology]. . . . My classes are represented by quite a cross section of people. We have rich and poor, gay and straight, bored housewives and career professionals. We have people who went to Ivy League undergraduate schools and people who went to Podunk U. We have working people in their thirties and retirees in their sixties. I think we even have a few students in their seventies. To recruit more minorities, I think there would have to be scholarships.

Another PSP student was even more emphatic about the complexity and difficulty of trying to compete with elitist neighbors in building an ethnically diverse student body and faculty and about the richness of the diversity that already exists at PSP:

> For a graduate school, [PSP] is pretty diverse. It certainly is more diverse than anything I have been around previously. I don't see how a school this size can recruit and keep minority faculty. Every school around is wanting to do the same thing, and most have more resources than we do. I suppose the best opportunity would be through the adjunct [part-time] faculty. Maybe we would be able to attract more diversity through limited contracts. I know this isn't an easy problem to solve. Given the financial realities, I think this school does quite well. Even though the tuition is the lowest in the Bay Area, it still takes a pretty good paying job to be able to afford it. I have really enjoyed going to school with [people of] so many different professional backgrounds.

This student was particularly struck by the nurses in his classes. He admitted to a prejudice toward nurses that he wasn't aware of until he confronted these students in class: "I must have thought that nurses were not particularly academically gifted, or I wouldn't have been so surprised to find them so." He recognized that certain competing institutions, with much higher tuitions and stronger financial resources, probably have a more diverse faculty; however, he finds PSP to be a school that frequently shatters his own stereotypes about occupation, age, and gender.

Managerial Culture

Administrators and faculty who are deeply imbued with the managerial culture and hope to create a populist institution tend to focus on affordability when seeking to increase access and often exhibit less concern with quality than with access. Representatives of the populist tradition and managerial culture often try to keep costs down in order for less wealthy students to gain access to a postsecondary education.

All three case study institutions have an interesting mixture of elitism and populism. On the one hand, emphasis is placed on individual attention and flexibility. Elitist schools with substantial resources have typically had the luxury of providing ample opportunity for students to get extensive faculty and administrative attention and have adapted school regulations to the distinctive needs of the exceptional students being carefully and thoughtfully served in the elite environment. On the other hand, JFK, PSP, and Evergreen are populist institutions that must face many problems associated with being outside the inner circle of elite schools in American higher education. As schools with limited financial resources, JFK, PSP, and Evergreen must be much more efficient. They must be effectively managed if students are to get an adequate education and the school is to remain truly accessible in terms of cost, course scheduling, and so forth.

Furthermore, JFK and PSP are among the schools classed at the lower levels identified in Chapter Two. The leaders of both schools must always look over their shoulders at the regional accrediting standards, given that these institutions are considered marginal in terms of influence and reputation in the higher education community. The pressures of financial viability and accreditation have produced a growing mountain of paperwork and regulations at both PSP and JFK, which reduces the capacity of faculty and students at these schools to attend to individual student needs or to be flexible in applying the rules of the university to distinctive student concerns.

Developmental Culture

The developmental culture typically differs from both the collegial and managerial culture in its emphasis on serving learning-disabled and culturally disadvantaged student populations. For representatives of this culture, quality is often closely related to achievement in the education of disabled and disadvantaged students. This academic culture also tends to emphasize multicultural and gender-sensitive curricular reforms as a way of promoting not only greater access but also greater diversity of perspectives and hence quality.

JFK is an excellent example of an institution that retains a strong populist tradition in its commitment to serving adult learners while embracing a developmental culture and perspective. Compared to other universities, JFK is swift to change and reconfigure its vision with the times. Because of its small size and liberal approach, the university remains relatively flexible and fairly quick to respond to crisis. However, the school is struggling with the important issue of diversity. As at Evergreen and PSP, the student body at JFK is predominantly white and middle- to upper-class. The tuition, though not high compared to most private institutions, is nonetheless formidable, and the school is located in the predominantly white city of Orinda, one of California's wealthiest communities.

Even though the university is putting great effort into increasing student diversity through community outreach programs and diversity committees, the financial aid office has actually had more minority grant funds available than there were students to accept them. Students repeatedly expressed during their interviews that although they felt they were being exposed to a vast array of new experiences at the university, it lacked the richness that ethnic diversity can provide. Though a few of the interviewees did say that they were being exposed to more diverse people than normally would be the case in other domains of their lives, the consensus at all three schools was that more minorities should be recruited.

Many of the students at all three schools feel that, more than location and high tuition, the main problem in attracting minority or underprivileged students seems to be a lack of awareness in the surrounding communities. One of the solutions may therefore lie in more focused recruiting strategies aimed at letting the local community know about the opportunities available at these institutions. Many of the interviewees felt that theirs is primarily a school that one "stumbles upon." Members of the community do not know much about the school's philosophy regarding high quality and accessibility; they only hear about cost and location. In addition, at all three schools, the faculty, though balanced by gender, is primarily white. Many of the students interviewed felt that this may also be a deterrent both to ethnically diverse students wanting to enter and to the diversity of education that current students seek.

Although JFK has become more traditional over the years, ghosts from the past still linger. People in the local community still talk about the school's starting up in a mortuary and for many years offering a degree in parapsychology. It consequently has always suffered among the more conservative from a certain image of eccentricity. Similar image problems were experienced at both Evergreen in the 1970s and PSP in the 1980s. At all three schools, strong efforts have been made to leave this image behind. Though a certain portion of the students at JFK, PSP, and Evergreen were attracted by the innovative spirit of the school, there is a trend toward "respectability" at these schools that may alienate these very students in the future.

For better or worse, JFK, Evergreen, and PSP have become schools for middle- to upper-class white professionals and their children. Whether this is a cause or an effect of the conservative bent is difficult to say, but it has become a strong influence. In many ways, the current administrations at all three schools seem bound to ignore certain aspects or departments that may appear odd to the general public (such as the Graduate School for Holistic Studies at JFK or many of the independent study projects at Evergreen). Furthermore, many of the people interviewed feel that various programs at all three schools are being slowly but surely standardized to attain some elusive image of legitimacy. These moves may open the doors for greater institutional respectability and eventually even greater diversity in the student population, but a certain feeling of loss often accompanies such a move. In short, conflicting visions seem to be doing quiet battle at all three schools.

Perhaps it is the energy generated where these visions cross that makes schools like JFK, PSP, and Evergreen special. The interplay between an appeal to the middle class and the insistence on alternative modes of learning and experiencing the self may be satisfying a need for quality in this often overlooked segment of the population. Students who come to JFK, PSP, or Evergreen are not looking for Cal Berkeley or the University of Washington, nor are they looking for a fringe school. They are looking for an atmosphere of support and intimacy that will encourage their personal and intellectual growth. A common thread in the interviews was that these students had finally found a place where they felt they belonged. Students at each of these schools feel that they are being treated as individuals, and that is one of the most important services that any collegiate institution can provide. Students feel that the classroom and the administrative offices are places where they are respected and where their voices will be heard.

The three case study institutions are relatively small and versatile yet remarkably stable with regard to mission and educational process. These schools provide grounding points for their students: quiet and personal places in which to learn. Perhaps JFK, PSP, and Evergreen are developmentally oriented models for the future of higher education. They are intensely and uniquely committed to a specialized portion of a diversifying culture. The needs of the people have become increasingly complex, thereby making it impossible for the large, traditional institutions to meet the demands for both quality and access. It is time that the many who have slipped through the cracks of higher education get their needs met, and it will be institutions like JFK, PSP, and Evergreen that rise to this challenge. Through such schools, learners can once again find themselves appreciated, respected, and treated as individuals.

Negotiating Culture

This fourth culture is often prominent at many of the nontraditional institutions formed during the 1960s and early 1970s (such as Evergreen) that have established and vigorously maintained a strong populist tradition. More than the other three cultures, a negotiating culture tends to be strongly associated with increasing access for all populations that have been victims of social or institutional discrimination over the years. Quality is often dismissed by representatives of this culture unless it is achieved for all members of the collegiate community.

Representatives from the negotiating culture tend not to focus on specific groups, as the other three cultures do. They are often deeply committed to affirmative action in the recruitment of all underrepresented and underserved groups and may at times move indiscriminately from one such group to the next. Their concerns for affirmative action are typically not confined to students but also apply to faculty, administrators, and staff—though their commitments are at times countered by equally strong union-based commitments to seniority and academically based commitments to tenure. Though a commitment to affirmative action sometimes seems to contradict a concern for the welfare of current employees in a college or university, it is in keeping with the liberal, social-activist leanings of many leaders of faculty and staff unions.

The Evergreen State College is filled with men and women who are deeply imbued with the norms and values of the negotiating culture. These committed members of the Evergreen community are greatly concerned with access—though they usually lack the zeal for order and managerial accountability that accompanies many forms of American populism. "Greenies" seem to be more inclined toward a variant on American populism, the American anarchistic tradition.

The Evergreen State College was founded to fulfill a commitment to unite quality and access, and by the late 1980s, it had succeeded in many ways. The founding faculty believed that quality in a progressive, forward-looking institution required diversity and access and that access without quality was academically indefensible. Nonetheless, thinking in the college about the relationship between quality and access was never simple, never uniform, and seldom prescribed. It continues to be debated around individual cases and largely ensured through the hiring process and the shared values and commitments of the faculty. Anyone in the community will admit that a gap remains between the community's aspirations and the reality of the institution's grasp. The relationship between access and quality at Evergreen—as in most collegiate institutions that are strongly oriented toward negotiation—is probably best understood as a dynamic one, a long-term conversation and debate played out against the backdrop of the constraints and opportunities of an evolving institution. These debates and negotiations inevitably center on the dual identity of Evergreen as an increasingly confident nontraditional institution and a public liberal arts college.

From the beginning, *access* and *diversity* had multiple meanings at Evergreen. The founding faculty at the school—like many representatives of the negotiating culture—believed that there were many things wrong with the way these terms were defined at traditional institutions. Evergreen's founders were concerned with process (as is true in all negotiating cultures): Who participates as a student and as a faculty member? How is the teaching and learning process structured? How are quality and access defined and assessed? The fourth process-oriented approach to quality (see Chapter Three) finds fertile ground at Evergreen, as it does at other highly interactive, nontraditional schools (such as Antioch). With their broad latitude to experiment, the founding faculty at Evergreen tried to design a teaching and learning environment that was both more challenging and more appropriate to diverse learners and the contemporary world than that found at more traditional schools.

The protracted negotiations over notions of access and quality at Evergreen led to new and evolving approaches to the concept of faculty. From the beginning, Evergreen had unconventional notions about who might be a teacher and what constituted appropriate credentials. At the same time, these unconventional notions were often accompanied by a certain element of disagreement and ambivalence. Despite some quibbling, a doctoral degree has never been a hard-and-fast requirement for faculty hiring. In the early years, a number of people were hired with minimal academic credentials. As it turned out, this decision cut both ways: a number of these teachers left, but others stayed and thrived at Evergreen. The capacity to individualize decision making, maintain appropriate standards, and resolve tensions between elitist and populist values continues to be one of the greatest challenges for any organization that is imbued with the negotiating culture.

Early in Evergreen's development, a decision was also made to broaden the concept of faculty to encompass others in the college community. In a largely successful attempt to bridge the gulf that often exists between academic faculty and library staff, reference librarians were hired with faculty status and routinely rotated into full-time team-teaching responsibilities. Regular full-time teaching faculty, in turn, rotated into the library. Other Evergreen staff could acquire faculty status to sponsor a limited number of individual contract students in their areas of expertise, a valuable notion that became less frequently exercised in the wake of workload increases in the mid 1980s. Notions of the faculty also included the larger community through the vehicle of intern sponsorship and field supervision. Nearly half of the students serve internships at some time during their education at Evergreen. Almost from the start, Evergreen invested heavily in a highly professional cooperative education office, a crucial element in maintaining quality. In 1992, with federal funding support, Evergreen further broadened its relationships with the community and brought community studies faculty into full-time programs.

Differing notions about access and quality also influenced admission policy and curriculum offerings. From the beginning, Evergreen had to straddle the fence between public institution and nontraditional college. This played out in a lengthy debate about the mix between in-state and out-of-state students and the desirable balance of students from Washington high schools and community colleges. Nonetheless, for most of its history, the college did not actually have the luxury of picking and choosing among student applicants, a circumstance that has only recently changed. Also, as a public institution, access is heavily influenced by state policy on tuition levels, admission standards, and off-campus programs.

The Evergreen College tried to provide access and attract diverse students along a number of dimensions but had definite limits in terms of its programmatic boundaries. The college was always quite inflexible about accommodating large numbers of part-time students, and students who were not interested in the full-time coordinated-studies programs found few alternatives. When the college became overenrolled in the late 1980s, part-time options were cut even further. Individualized study options were also constrained by both faculty preference and the limited number of faculty sponsors.

Many at Evergreen believe that it is a place where nontraditional students can succeed, and they feel that these students should have first preference. At the same time, faculty remain rather firmly committed to an admission process that stands against predicting student success at Evergreen and selecting students through traditional measures such as the SAT. Even prior academic performance is regarded with skepticism as an adequate measure of match with the institution. The feeling is that what came before matters less than what someone can do now. There is some irony in the fact that the college is becoming increasingly selective by traditional measures such as the SAT even though it tries not to be. As the state has become more prescriptive about legislating access through admission requirements, the college has had to become even more creative in adjusting the formulas to take account of nontraditional factors.

At the same time, many of Evergreen's reform efforts have now come full circle as colleges across the nation are adopting traditional Evergreen practices such as teaching portfolios, narrative evaluations, and student self-assessment. There is talk at Evergreen about this being a period of "refounding." As dozens of new faculty join Evergreen and new students enter, academic practices that had vitality in earlier times need to be reborn and revitalized lest they atrophy and become tiresome bureaucratic requirements. The challenge remains to integrate continuity with core values, to maintain a sense of rooted identity and vitality in the face of critical transitions.

Key Points

1. The dream of equity and opportunity that propelled American higher education is found wanting in the 1990s. Despite the significant advances of the 1960s and 1970s, we have since fallen back in terms of commitment to access and have actually lost ground.

2. The failure of American colleges and universities to fulfill the American dream can be attributed in part to the assumption that quality and access are opposites. We want to open our arms to people from all sectors of society, yet we want to select only the very best from these sectors and even rule out some sectors if including them would require a lowering of standards or would otherwise diminish quality.

3. That assumption is being challenged. Greater access actually improves quality by encouraging diversity of resources and perspectives. The postmodern era requires complex and relativistic thought; this in turn requires exposure to diverse experiences among faculty, administrators, and students. Whereas attention has often focused on the value that postsecondary education has for students from underrepresented and underserved populations, it should be redirected in the postmodern era to the value that these populations contribute to other members of the collegiate community.

4. Collegiate institutions must be responsive to new student populations by changing the basic culture of the institution and by acknowledging the unique contributions to be made by each of these diverse populations. For such changes to occur, we must understand and reexamine the various perspectives on quality and access in contemporary colleges and universities: elitist, populist, beleaguered, expedient, and unified.

Part Two

Four Perspectives
on Quality and Access

Chapter Five

The Elitist Perspective

The origins of American higher education are closely associated with elitism. Colonial American educators always felt like second-class citizens as they looked with admiration and envy across the Atlantic Ocean to long-established colleges and universities in England, Scotland, France, and Germany. Although they may have left these countries precisely because of the rigidity of their class systems, religious orders, and even educational institutions, they nevertheless sought to emulate many of these despised forms—perhaps out of a desire for continuity with their past, as well as grudging admiration for the quality and reputation of these revered institutions.

Thus, from the first, an attempt was made to emulate the European institution of higher learning and to establish a comparable pecking order among American colleges and universities that tended also to subsume the elitist criteria of quality of the European educational system, reflecting such premodern values as reputation, continuity, ancestry, and a life of contemplation free of both physical labor and commerce. These institutions would produce elite graduates who were to lead the new country with all of the distinguishing characteristics of their more class-oriented peers in Europe.

Today, of course, we live in a quite different world. However, many of the same criteria of quality persist not only in the minds of the people who lead contemporary colleges and universities in America but also those who judge the quality of all educational institutions (state legislators, members of accreditation teams, journalists and other writers about higher education), whether these institutions were initially established on an elitist foundation or not. The elitist perspective is particularly influential with regard to input criteria of quality (see Chapter Three). Highest quality is defined by the amount and superiority of resources at the institution as well as its selectivity in the admission of students and the hiring of faculty. Barron's Measures of College Selectivity, for instance, are often used as a measuring stick of quality, at least among members of the general public. Institutions defined as "most competitive" by Barron's are among the elite in the United States, almost by definition.

During the past thirty years, some high-status institutions—including Harvard, Yale, Stanford, and the University of California—have tried to combine the populist and elitist perspectives. They have introduced extensive student aid and scholarship programs for minority students or have even (in the case of the University of California, for instance) transformed the basic curriculum of the institution in response to the need for multicultural diversity. These efforts are to be commended, and programs created by these elite institutions should be emulated (usually on a smaller and less costly scale) in lower-status colleges and universities.

Yet it would be naive to assume that the elitist perspective is fading at these institutions. Lewis and Kingston (1989) report that nearly one-quarter of all freshmen at private, highly selective colleges and universities report family incomes of $100,000 or more; only 7 percent of entering freshmen at all American colleges and universities come from families at this income level. Even a high-status university such as Harvard, which has for many years tried to recruit for diversity as well as merit, is constantly being influenced in admission decisions by both internal and external forces that push for entrance of members of the elite classes in our society (Karen, 1990). Furthermore, the high-status colleges and universities of the United States tend to attract students (from all socioeconomic levels) precisely because they ensure graduates high-status positions in society (Kingston and Lewis, 1990).

What role does the elitist perspective play in our contemporary colleges and universities, and how does this perspective influence the ways in which we are all inclined to view both quality and access? I will first address these questions by turning not to a high-status institution but rather to a lower-status school in which the elitist perspective exists alongside the other four perspectives. I turn specifically to Exemplar College/University, a hypothetical composite of many colleges and universities of my acquaintance. I will describe in concrete terms the ways in which elitism influences our institutions of higher education by describing a typical day in the life of Exemplar as its leaders confront elitist standards that may no longer be (or may never have been) appropriate to this struggling postsecondary institution.

Exemplar College/University from the Elitist Perspective

Exemplar is a hypothetical postsecondary institution that is now, like many other contemporary colleges and universities, slightly on the decline with regard to both reputation and funds. At its peak in the late 1960s, Exemplar achieved such an admirable reputation and level of enrollment that leaders on campus and in the local community were proclaiming Exemplar "the Princeton of the West," "the University of Michigan of the South," or "the Harvard of the Valley" (take your pick). Since then, however, Exemplar has struggled. Although enrollment in the practical divisions of the institution, as well as in the social and behavioral sciences, has been maintained, traditional liberal arts students have become a vanishing breed. As Exemplar's tuition rises, the admissions staff finds it harder and harder to recruit traditional college students.

From the elitist perspective, Exemplar is in trouble. The school's endowment has never been very large, public support for higher education in the state is declining, and the rising cost of education has made it hard to balance the budget. To appeal to contemporary students, Exemplar continues to offer new majors, each of which adds to the school's administrative complexity and overhead. The price-cost squeeze is unremitting, and no one seems to have a clear or compelling answer to Exemplar's problems.

At one time, Exemplar was known for its interdisciplinary humanities program, a two-year core required of all students. Such a program is directly aligned with the elitist perspective. Exemplar dropped that program in the mid 1970s, replacing it with a distributive program that allowed for more choice and involved courses from all of the Exemplar departments, reflecting the "deterioration in standards" that many elitists decry. A current debate is raging at Exemplar about the reintroduction of a two-year interdisciplinary program. This debate is tempered by difficulties in balancing the budget. During the past five years, losses have been minimized at Exemplar only by deferring major maintenance and delaying raises in faculty salaries. Last year's budget was an unexpected shock. The loss was 30 percent more than anticipated at the start of the year and was not discovered by the comptroller until the year's end. Current projections call for a similar deficit next year, and Exemplar is under pressure to cut costs, including instructional costs, even further. Any major curricular change is likely to be expensive. In setting the stage for the drama of life at Exemplar, I will introduce a brief cast of characters (more will join in subsequent chapters).

Kevin Gravitz, president. President Gravitz is a visionary, a man who had a dream for Exemplar that now seems to be lost. When he came twelve years ago, Gravitz hoped to establish Exemplar as a model of the best kind of interdisciplinary, liberal arts oriented postsecondary institution, an extension of the elitist heritage he experienced as a student. In addition, Gravitz hoped to add to the liberal arts perspective a (very nonelitist) commitment to the pressing social issues of our era, including racism, sexism, poverty, and social conflict. He believes passionately that each of these social problems fit into a broader "social *problématique*" that can be fully understood only from a systematic, cross-disciplinary perspective. Gravitz is now painfully aware that it may not be possible to realize this dream during his presidency. He feels isolated, a bit lost as to what to do next, and burdened by the administrative details of his job.

Dorothy Kirkwood, academic vice president. Vice President Kirkwood is a careful, diligent worker, as befits a former chemistry professor. She is currently committed to developing an orderly and systematic planning process at Exemplar, an achievement that would be in sharp contrast to the school's usual pattern of acting on impulse. She is the first woman to serve in a major administrative office at Exemplar, and in her second year on the job, Kirkwood still feels the pressure to demonstrate her capability and effectiveness. In fine elitist tradition, Exemplar has a reputation for "chewing up" academic administrators. Under the pressure of day-to-day tasks and the currents of chaos and individuality that cause ongoing disorder, Kirkwood is beginning to understand why.

Joseph Chung, parent. Joseph Chung is a sixty-year-old parent of Chinese heritage who recently lost his wife of thirty-five years. His daughter, Catherine, is very important to him, especially since she is his only child. She arrived late in his marriage. Since his wife's death, Chung has been very close to his daughter, and she calls him whenever she needs support (psychological or financial). Her latest call came just yesterday, when through her tears she described problems at registration. Due to a mix-up in her schedule, Cathy is afraid that she will not be able to get into the nursing program next term as she had originally planned. Her father has reacted in his usual direct manner: he has come to Exemplar and expects to see someone who can straighten this out. He comes with a sense of purpose and without an appointment.

Scene One: Exemplar Town and Campus, First Day of School, Fall Term

For President Gravitz, this morning offers a rare moment of reminiscence. He remembers wistfully his expectations when he became Exemplar's president. He now knows that faculty conflicts and economic realities make the realization of such expectations difficult. But he still can feel the lure of his deeply rooted sense of how the academy should work, and he resolves to give his ideals another try.

At this moment, Gravitz is aware that soon he will have exhausted his energy, at least at Exemplar.

By 8:30 in the morning, Vice President Kirkwood is at her desk, trying to digest the latest set of financial and enrollment projections for the current academic year. The picture is worse than the administrators had anticipated. She wonders if some new way of thinking about the curriculum could change this pattern in the future. She hopes so. The report from the regular committee at the end of last year was a disappointment. That draft contained only another rehash of distribution requirements, with every department getting its pound of flesh. She hopes that the new special committee will stir things up, try something daring or exciting.

Her phone rings. Someone in the registrar's office has an irate parent on her hands and cannot find an adviser to help. "Could Dr. Kirkwood see the gentleman?" Kirkwood sighs and reminds herself of the chaos of the first days of any academic year. She hears herself saying, "Send him on down," without too much reflection. Kirkwood puts aside the documents she was working on and prepares to do some interpersonal work.

In a moment, Joseph Chung comes into the office. He starts deferentially, for he is aware that he is in the vice president's office, but his exasperation bursts through. His anger and concern make his story jumbled and disconnected, but the pieces of a familiar pattern soon emerge. A student is unable, for reasons yet unknown, to get into the courses she thinks she needs to enter the nursing program. The parent is frustrated at not finding anyone who knew what he was talking about or finding only staff members who acted as if he was doing something wrong by trying to help his own daughter.

Vice President Kirkwood listens carefully, taking notes all the while. As soon as she can, she breaks into his jumbled narrative. She sympathizes with Chung, pointing out that early on the first day of classes is a particularly awkward time to obtain information from hard-pressed staff members at any school. She indicates the steps she will take to correct the situation and explains why his daughter is enrolled in the courses she is taking. As she talks, Kirkwood writes notes in the margin so that her secretary can start taking the steps to find a suitable faculty adviser, obtain appropriate academic records, and gather other necessary resources. It is clear that Chung would like to keep talking, but Kirkwood smoothly eases him out the door, using her efficiency to good effect.

As Kirkwood walks back to her desk, she is aware of twinges of frustration and anger. Why do the counseling and registration systems always have these loose ends? We say we care about students. Why do we act as if we don't care at all? Why does this kind of problem wind up on my desk, distracting me from other tasks that are my direct responsibility? For Joseph Chung, the conversation leaves a mixture of satisfaction and confusion. Will this vice president really follow through? Will Cathy be able to get into the classes she needs? Chung is not sure what more he can do now, so he heads for his car. At this particular moment, he is not very impressed with Exemplar, though he holds some hope that Vice President Kirkwood will be of assistance.

By 11:30 in the morning, Dorothy Kirkwood is in the middle of her weekly meeting with President Gravitz, in his office. The academic vice president is now arguing the issue that she hoped she would get to in this meeting: the decision to reallocate monies from the Faculty Development Fund to the general operating budget. At first she is quiet and calm, arguing the importance of the fund for Exemplar. As Gravitz brushes aside her arguments, she feels her exasperation rise, and she hears herself asking if this use of the fund is really legitimate, if the donors would be happy if they knew that their money was not being used for the purpose it was intended. The president's response is the practical one, stressing the institution's current needs over less essential programs like faculty development.

Kirkwood leaves the office with a curious mixture of feelings. She feels the power of the president's arguments, his concern with the practicalities of the balance sheet. At the same time, she feels a sense of loss, hearing Gravitz sacrifice dreams and ideals that until recently were his primary motivators. She feels the need to represent the interests of the faculty in such arguments. On this issue there will be some sharp words and feelings with which she will have to deal. At the same time, she wonders whether she is not being too confrontational. Would it be better for Exemplar if she were more sympathetic to Gravitz's dilemmas?

Later, at 5:45, in the parking lot, Kirkwood settles into her car. All day long she has been involved in a host of first-day problems. Now, out of her office, her mind shifts to longer-range issues. Can Exemplar find a new way of organizing general education? Should she support humanistic approaches, or more practical ones? She has the disquieting thought that all of this may be nothing but a big expenditure of time with nothing to show for it. Can this kind of committee really make a dent in the education that goes on at Exemplar?

For Kevin Gravitz, the day is not over. At 7:05 P.M. he is walking to the dining hall for an alumni association reception. This one is for the aging members of Exemplar's championship basketball team of 1956. The walk across campus triggers the hope that he might find a way to duck out of this dinner early. Maybe he could spend a few intimate moments with his wife or chat with his kids about their day. Maybe he could read a few pages in that best-seller on education that everyone has been talking about. Or maybe he could just sit quietly and enjoy a moment without thinking of Exemplar. As he approaches the dining hall, his mind shifts back. What is the name of the league's most valuable player on that 1956 team? Remington? No, Rawlings—that's it! Gravitz puts on his presidential face and enters the building.

Scene Two: Nearby City, Next Day

The more Joseph Chung thinks about his experience at Exemplar, the more concerned he becomes. How does he know that his daughter is really OK? He decides to talk to his secretary about what happened. She has children; maybe she can offer some suggestions. His secretary asks him about the college. Why did he recommend Exemplar to his daughter in the first place? Chung pulls out the new Exemplar catalogue that he received when visiting the campus that morning and reads to his secretary from the Exemplar statement of mission and purpose:

> The educational program at Exemplar is designed to give the student maximum flexibility to find and pursue the student's own path toward competency and mastery. The student is required to select a field of concentration or to develop a cross-disciplinary concentration with faculty approval. At least half of the coursework must be selected, with the help of a faculty adviser, from outside this field.
>
> A mind responsive to a liberal education becomes much more than a repository of knowledge. As it gains that knowledge, it also acquires a sense of the relatedness of its parts, a perspective on its past, a basis for critical judgment, and an ability to bring an informed intelligence to bear on both scholarly and worldly problems.
>
> Through all of the student's work, it is expected that the student will identify the values that have given direction to human conduct and select the ones that have meaning for the student. The student will become increasingly aware of complexity and able to cope with ambiguity. The student will learn to ask important questions, to cut through irrelevance to the heart of an issue. And the student will learn to use innate skills and intelligence to act with meaning and conviction. If the liberal education has been a good one, it will prove itself in long years of increasing strength of mind and spirit and in continued learning throughout a lifetime.
>
> For each student, this liberal education will have provided perspective and insights both within and beyond whatever role the student selects, and it will provide options also for possible future changes in directions.
>
> The liberal arts involve the study of human triumphs in uncovering the unknown, of efforts to assay the unknowable, of formula-

tions of society and value, of the evolution of philosophies and expression. Members of the Exemplar community firmly believe that this is the education that will produce the imagination to build the future.

"That is what I wanted for Catherine. What else can I give her? But that place didn't even answer my questions. How can Catherine get these things? What can I do?" Joseph Chung sadly closes the Exemplar catalogue. He must do something for Catherine now. He decides to visit other colleges, starting tomorrow.

A Premodern Elitist Perspective

The elitist perspective at an institution such as Exemplar is rooted in the premodern era, though these roots are often hidden under the topsoil of modern-day rhetoric and form. The elitist perspective is also typically dominated by the collegial culture (which is also rooted in the premodern era), though there is often a sprinkling of the developmental culture among people who embrace the elitist perspective (in keeping with the colonial college and its Oxbridge origins; Bergquist, 1992). To understand the nature of an institution such as Exemplar that attempts to incorporate the elitist perspective and the strategies that can be used in bringing this type of institution to a new awareness of both quality and access, I will systematically examine its primary organizational characteristics, looking first at size and complexity, then at mission and boundaries, leadership, and communication, and finally at capital and educational values.

Size and Complexity

In general, the most successful collegiate institutions from the elitist perspective, like other high quality premodern organizations, tend to remain relatively stable in size, primarily because they are

highly selective in their admission of students (as well as the selection of faculty and administrative leaders). Although the population of student applicants may rise and fall over time, the number
of accepted applicants remains essentially the same—unless the
institution (like Exemplar) faces enrollment shortfalls, in which
case it is usually in difficult straits and is viewed very negatively from
the elitist perspective. Collegiate institutions that tend toward the
elitist perspective rarely have a well-developed mechanism for student recruitment and often deem the marketing of their institution
distasteful and undignified. As a result, presidents like Gravitz who
are trying to respond to elitist criteria of quality are caught in difficult economic crunches and often have to sacrifice existing programs (such as faculty development) or proposed programs that
make the institution distinctive and even more attractive to a
shrinking elitist student market.

Socioeconomic class tends to serve as the primary criterion for
enrollment from the traditional elitist perspective, though with the
recent push for affirmative action and social responsibility, the
socioeconomic barriers are beginning to fall away. A school like
Exemplar is particularly interested in attracting very bright and
ambitious minority students (such as Catherine Chung) who fully
accept the dominant norms of society and, in truth, offer very little diversity. The enrollment shortfalls, coupled with affirmative
action imperatives, often leave elitist-oriented colleges and universities with high tuition but substantial scholarship and loan programs (often sponsored by federal or state funds) for students from
the lower socioeconomic levels. As a result of these various mechanisms of financial support, there is a bimodal distribution of students in many contemporary colleges and universities that seek an
elitist status. Only the very rich and the very poor can now afford
to go to these colleges and universities.

One consequence is that these elite institutions, which tend to
set the tuition levels for the entire higher education system in the
United States, know no ceiling. Very few of these institutions have

ever lost applicants, let alone enrolled students, because tuition was too high. Wealthy parents, who typically embrace the elitist perspective themselves, will pay whatever it takes to get their sons and daughters into high-status schools. In fact, the higher the tuition, the better the quality and the more selective the institution—at least as perceived by many elitist parents. For the poor students (and their parents) who are able to obtain scholarships or loans, the cost of tuition is also irrelevant, either because they don't have to pay it or because they are willing to pay just about anything if they think it will afford them upward social mobility and will not have to be repaid until they have become wealthy—thanks to their collegiate experience.

As in the case of many organizations that were formed in premodern times, high-status colleges and universities tend to be relatively simple in form. They closely resemble familial and religious organizations—not surprisingly, considering that one of the dominant functions of most traditional, elitist colleges in their early years was to serve as a substitute for the parents and familial system (*in loco parentis*) or as a substitute for the hometown church, providing moral guidance (*in loco ecclesiae*).

Typically, from the elitist perspective, one person should be in charge of a college or university. This person is often the charismatic, wise, courageous, or visionary president. Carefully chosen and revered for thoughtful leadership, the president stands in an elevated position with respect to the "lower" levels of administration and faculty at the institution, much as the institution stands at a higher level than "lower-status" institutions. The president and institution are not to lord it over less fortunate subordinates or institutions; rather, they should display a benevolence and thoughtful concern for the welfare of those less fortunate.

Similarly, the hierarchical relationship between faculty member and student is very clear from the elitist perspective. Faculty should be wise and always right. Students are bright and promising as future leaders of their community. However, they are also young, innocent, and still empty, to be filled by their benevolent teachers, mentors, and senior classmates. Even alumni are treated as second-class citizens when they return to their elitist educational origins. As successful as they may have become, they still treat their professors with almost reverential respect. Success in life for those who embrace the elitist perspective is defined primarily in terms of the quality of one's mind and character. College and university faculty (and other academic leaders who once were faculty) are expected to exemplify these qualities and thus be long-term role models for both current students and alumni.

This simple, uniform elitist perspective tended to pervade many collegiate institutions during the nineteenth and early twentieth centuries. As we move toward the twenty-first, these images from the past continue to haunt the halls of our hallowed colleges and universities. Although images of colonial businesses and human service organizations now seem quaint and profoundly out-of-date, images of collegiate institutions from this same era remain alive and highly influential today—particularly in an institution like Exemplar, which has elitist aspirations but is struggling to find its distinctive character.

President Gravitz and Vice President Kirkwood are fighting over the issue of priorities for their institution in part because they must first meet many of the now outdated criteria of quality in their institution (faculty degrees, elegant buildings, immaculate grounds, large library holdings, a large but heavily encumbered endowment). Once dollars are spent to meet these old, elitist notions about educational quality, there is very little left to satisfy more contemporary notions about quality—for example, meeting community needs in ways that enhance student learning, provide educational access to specific underserved populations, or (Dorothy Kirkwood's wish) provide rich professional development opportunities to all members of the Exemplar community, including faculty. Given the lack of dollars to meet the legitimate contemporary goals of Exemplar, Gravitz and Kirkwood must collude in providing rhetoric for their catalogue (the one that Joseph Chung read) but not in the actions they take in the daily practices of their institution.

Mission and Boundaries

From the elitist perspective, the mission of a college or university is relatively unimportant and can in fact be left unclear. As in many premodern organizations, that lack need not stand in the way of success. The "collegiate way" provides implicit norms and values for elitist institutions and precludes the need for a clearly articulated mission statement. Collegiate life in an elitist school provided for many years not only a formal education but also a more informal socialization or "finishing" process. Colonial colleges were intended for wealthy young men preparing for professions (medicine, law, ministry) or women preparing for marriage to wealthy young men. Attempts were made to homogenize rather than diversify in these elitist institutions (Jencks and Riesman, 1968). More than forty years ago, Parsons (1951; Parsons and Bales, 1955) identified the important role played in any social system by institutions that maintain and preserve the latent patterns (heritage, norms, values, aspirations) of this social system. High-status colleges and universities traditionally provided these latent functions of pattern maintenance in many American communities, and from the elitist perspective, this continues to be the primary role of contemporary colleges and universities.

This conservative perspective was particularly important during the colonial period in America, when citizens were deeply concerned about the loss of their roots in European culture. As we move toward the twenty-first century, there may be less of a perceived need for this pattern maintenance function—at least to the extent that the pattern is primarily produced and maintained by what many critics of Eurocentric education are now calling "dead white guys." Today, there is a growing concern for honoring and investigating non-Western civilizations and even Western civilization from something other than a traditional male perspective.

Heritage-based curricula need not focus exclusively or even primarily on the Western tradition or, for that matter, on traditions that existed for a long period of time primarily because they were supported by a strong and aggressive military regime (Bergquist, 1977). Short-lived (and forgotten long-lived) traditions of a gentler and more collaborative nature might be particularly valuable to honor and study in our turbulent postmodern world (see Eisler, 1987). Given these challenges to traditional curricular offerings and notions about appropriate cultural patterns to maintain, the missions and roles to be fulfilled by elitist institutions are now subject to criticism and in need of profound review.

Thus, despite the traditional lack of a pressing need for a clear mission statement in premodern high-status colleges and universities, contemporary institutions are being driven toward further clarification in this domain. High-status institutions must now attend to their mission statements, as virtually all other colleges and universities do. Most state, regional, and national accrediting associations require such a statement. Hence, if nothing else, elitist colleges and universities must accede (at least superficially) to these accrediting requirements.

Furthermore, a formal mission statement is usually considered critical to effective institutional planning and management and effective student recruitment. Though high-status institutions traditionally have never had to worry about adequate student enrollment and retention, concern is now growing about these matters, and growing concern has often translated into a clarification of mission. As Martin (1985) states, "If we are concerned about the quality of student life on campus, and propose reforms, in all probability our definition of quality and our formulation of changes will be informed by the college's institutional mission" (p. 41). Martin further suggests that if a college is to provide a viable student life program or provide for the development of faculty and staff, this development must be in line with the mission of the college.

Even with all of these pressures on elitist colleges and universities, many of these institutions are guided by a lofty but ambiguous mission statement or by an omnibus statement (like Exemplar's) that simultaneously covers everything and hence nothing. In either case, the mission statement is typically ignored and provides very little direction to faculty in the way they build their curriculum and teach their courses or to administrators in the way they run the school and serve their students. Exemplar resembles many contemporary colleges and universities with elitist aspirations (or at least elitist rhetoric). Joseph Chung, the Exemplar parent, faced a problem that confronts many students and parents of students who are enrolled in financially strapped institutions with strong elitist aspirations. The formal mission statement of the school does not match the actual performance of the faculty and administrators who staff the school. Chung naively and optimistically thought that the mission statement at Exemplar meant something. He took this statement as a "contract" between him (and his daughter) and Exemplar regarding how his daughter would be educated and what was to guide the school's educational philosophy and standards.

Chung was seeing firsthand a major difficulty of elitist colleges and universities: mission statements are rarely used as they were initially intended. Why, Joseph Chung might ask, is there such a discrepancy between the glowing words of the catalogue and his tangible and rather painful experience at the college? "Are the words of the catalogue nothing more than a sales gimmick to get my money?" If so, colleges and universities are nothing more than glorified used-car lots that should be more severely regulated (Marchese, 1991).

Nevertheless, perhaps the people who serve in elitist-oriented institutions have good intentions and mean well in writing these lofty phrases. They are simply not yet able to deliver on their promises, in part because their institution has never had to worry much about either mission or marketing. When Chung reads the current Exemplar mission statement, he is impressed by its vision. When President Gravitz reads the statement, he is more likely to recall the bloody battles that were waged over a particular word or

phrase. He is likely to ask, "Why do I lead this college toward con-
sensually based statements of institutional purpose and belief when
these statements have so little impact on what actually occurs at
the school?"

If mission statements are inevitably difficult to operationalize,
even in resource-rich elitist institutions, we should simply ignore
the catalogue statements and examine what is actually occurring
inside the college or university. Perhaps the next time Joseph
Chung looks for a college that will serve his daughter's needs, he
will sit in on classes and talk to professors and members of the
administrative staff—preferably in the company of his daughter.
Even more important, perhaps Gravitz and Kirkland should sit in
on some classes or live in the dorms for several days (as several college presidents have done in recent years) to get a better sense of
how their school is enacting its mission—where it is succeeding as
well as where it is falling short.

High-status colleges and universities were traditionally noted
for having unclear boundaries. Family connections often influenced
admissions during the early years of these schools and still do at
many high-status colleges and universities (Karen, 1990). The
actual prerequisites for admission to an elitist college or university
are often unclear, even though everyone knows that these institutions' "standards" (whatever they are) are very demanding. Typically, the high standards manifest themselves primarily with regard
to applicants who do not come from the "right" families or do not
have some specific demographic feature (race, ethnicity, geographic
region) or talent deemed desirable by the college or university.

The diffusion of boundaries is perhaps no better exemplified than
in the dominant role played by the extracurriculum from the elitist perspective. According to Rudolph (1962), the original American college was "dedicated to disciplining and furnishing the mind"
(p. 138). Rudolph goes on to say that early colleges were much better at molding character than intellect and better at disciplining
intellect than furnishing the mind. Learning, in the classroom, was

limited to the recitation of memorized materials. However, students gradually wrought changes in the school, beginning quietly with student literary societies, which brought a much needed vitality to learning, in sharp contrast to the dullness of the classroom. These societies maintained their own libraries, which were better equipped than the college libraries in both numbers and scope.

By the late 1820s and 1830s, a new social system had developed in American colleges, based on fraternities, and later sororities, which cropped up at virtually all elitist institutions. Fraternities offered what was not provided in the classrooms: a social community. They became an escape from the "monotony, dreariness, and unpleasantness of collegiate regimen which began with prayers before dawn and ended with prayers after dark; escape from the long winters and ingrown college world, from the dormitory with its lack of privacy" (Rudolph, 1962, pp. 146–147). As fraternities assumed more and more of the roles that had been played by the literary societies, the societies declined and had virtually disappeared by 1870.

Organized athletics started to show up at elite colleges and later at elite universities. At first, athletics were met with some hostility and indifference. After all, the Puritan work ethic was not amenable to play—especially not play out of doors for all to see. However, the German outdoor gymnasium movement, brought over by immigrants, finally became popular. In 1860, Amherst set up a department of hygiene and physical education with the following slogan on the gymnasium: "Keep thyself pure: the body is the temple of the Holy Ghost." Rudolph (1962) explains, "In the extracurriculum the college student stated his case for the human mind, the human personality, and the human body, for all aspects of man that the colleges tended to ignore in their single-minded interest in the salvation of souls" (p. 156).

College leaders were not quite sure that extracurricular activities were a good idea. However, no one knew how to stop what the students had started: "When the students were finished they had planted beside the curriculum an extracurriculum of such dimensions that in time there would develop generations of college students who would not see the curriculum for the extracurriculum; who would not believe that American College had any purpose other than those that could best be served by the vast array of machinery, organizations, and institutions known as student activities. To what had been a curriculum in the 1780s was added a vital extracurriculum by the 1870s" (p. 137).

College students had won their fight to nourish the social, physical, and intellectual being as well as the soul. As the university system grew, the extracurriculum was an important force in maintaining collegiate values among the students. To this day, athletic teams, fraternities, sororities, social clubs, theater groups, newspapers, magazines, and other student activities and organizations keep alive important aspects of student life.

During the colonial era, the extracurriculum was a student reaction against the sterility of the curriculum. During the nineteenth and early twentieth centuries, the extracurriculum was compensation for the rise of professionalism in the academic world and the accompanying intellectuality, impersonality, and fragmentation (the parts and pieces of disciplinary specialization). The extracurriculum, more than coursework, was the area in which to develop skills to be used in one's professional and personal life: "The great extracurricular growth of the 1920's, the remarkable advances made by intercollegiate athletics during these years, were only partially the conscious efforts of young men to learn organization values and to sharpen their other-directedness on the way to success. The extracurriculum was also an agency of the collegiate emphasis on fellowship, on character, on well-roundedness, and as such, it was a powerful instrument during the period of the 1920's in bringing the university ideal into accommodation with the collegiate ideal" (Rudolph, 1962, p. 464).

With the onset of the Great Depression and just after, interest in extracurricular activities waned a bit in high-status American collegiate institutions, at about the same time as populist institutions, which minimized extracurricular activities, began to gain credibility (though little financial support). Populist students, who had no hope of finding a job without diligent preparation, became serious students. These activities enjoyed a resurgence in the early 1940s and then grew rapidly after World War II. By 1960, interest in student activities had again declined in both high-status and populist institutions, but athletics remained strong and grew stronger. By the late 1960s, only political activities and athletics seemed important to students. Today student activities have again become important at elitist colleges and universities. Fraternities and sororities are gaining in strength of numbers, while athletics continue to be more and more of a problem, taking more and more resources (Eble, 1983).

Leadership

From the elitist perspective, collegiate institutions should be led by great men (or, in certain instances, great women). This is a central assumption that operates in most elitist conceptions of the perfect collegiate institution. In a great institution, there are great academic leaders as administrators, there are great faculty, the school has produced great alumni, and the current student body is the cream of the crop. Given this image of singular greatness, especially among the leaders of the institution, it is very difficult to confront the leaders (or the trustees) of such an institution with organizational problems or ineffectiveness. Although few organizational leaders are open to hearing bad news, leaders who take the elitist perspective are particularly resistant, in part because they are colluding in the myth of their greatness. What occurs most often is that the ineffectiveness of elitism-oriented leaders is covered over by the competency and very hard work of a committed administrative staff that supports them. As high-status colleges and universities become more cost-conscious, they are increasingly likely to look not only for leaders with strong administrative skills but also for ones who take on these difficult administrative and managerial chores as their primary task at the school. In my own work as a consultant to institutions led by elitists, however, I still find that staff members are holding the institution together with bureaucratic baling wire—but that is not unique to elitist institutions or even, for that matter, to educational institutions.

What about Kevin Gravitz and Dorothy Kirkland? Are they effective leaders, or has their ineptitude been protected by their diligent staff? Given that Exemplar is experiencing financial problems, the two probably have little staff support. Furthermore, even if they could fund staff positions, they can no longer rely on strong staff support, given that they cannot pay enough in salary to attract high-quality administrators. Even staff assistant positions in many colleges and universities now go unfilled, no longer considered the prestigious plums for new graduates that they once were. Bright young men and women are now more likely to be lured away to graduate school or to a high-paid corporate position. Perhaps Gravitz and Kirkland should look elsewhere for administrators and staff assistants—perhaps to retired men and women who would like to be of service to an institution that benefits society or would like to take courses while working at the school.

Traditionally, in elitist-oriented institutions, the president served as a moral leader and educator. Today, as our colleges and universities have become more secular, we no longer talk about morality or character, though we still address issues of ethics and social justice. In elitist-oriented institutions, it is not unusual for presidents and other major campus leaders to consider these overarching issues. Given that many of these men and women come out of distinguished careers in a specific discipline, their movement into the more interdisciplinary world of ethics and social justice comes, understandably, as something of a shock to themselves and others on campus.

Yet the transition often does occur, and the likes of Derek Bok of Harvard or even a renegade such as Boston University's John Silber can find widespread support for (or at least interest in) personal pronouncements about many social issues. One of the most distinguished and most highly regarded of these articulate elitist presidents was Theodore Hesburgh of Notre Dame University. Perhaps Hesburgh was able to speak and write forcibly and persuasively on such diverse topics as the learning society and American foreign policy because he and many of his colleagues at Notre Dame, with its Catholic heritage, straddled the fence between elitism and populism.

For a president like Kevin Gravitz, who has some elitist leanings and is struggling with the difficult issue of diverting money raised for professional development into the general fund of his institution, the issue of moral leadership may be particularly painful. Right now, he does not feel good about his own actions and is in no mood to tell others how to run their lives. If many of our elitist-oriented college and university presidents similarly face internal financial and enrollment problems, where will the moral leadership in American higher education come from? What if it continues to come from these elitist leaders who themselves face difficult daily issues in the areas of finance and ethics, commitment and morality? They will have struggled with these issues in keeping their own institutions alive and true to their mission. Perhaps these academic leaders, speaking from the context of a more situational ethic, will ultimately have more to say of real importance about moral conduct than elitist leaders who never had to struggle with making payroll.

Capital and Educational Values

From the elitist perspective, collegiate capital is defined in tangible terms, primarily of campus grounds and endowments, and in less tangible (but no less important) terms of reputation. Traditionally, during the premodern era, capital (and quality, for that matter) was defined in terms that were rarely disputed. It was assumed that with sufficient resources, there would be exceptional education. This is one of the most prevalent unchallenged myths of learning in American society.

While populist institutions tend to look like high-rise corporations, elitist colleges and universities tend to look like the homes (and even castles) of landed gentry—perhaps because these institutions were first meant to serve as surrogates for the family homes of the upper-class members of society. High-status, elitist-oriented college and university campuses are maintained like estates. They have large spans of open space (lawns, well-tended gardens), stately buildings tastefully interspersed with small groves of trees, and hillside views of the surrounding community. The campus plan is usually of ancient and revered origins (the ultimate being the University of Virginia campus plan crafted by Thomas Jefferson), and that plan is carefully adhered to, even at great expense.

It is indeed remarkable that leaders of many contemporary colleges and universities who, like Kevin Gravitz at Exemplar, are currently facing difficult financial problems will not even begin to consider selling off some of their institution's extremely valuable real estate. The hesitation is understandable on realistic grounds, for selling off property doesn't solve a problem but merely defers it. Nevertheless, having sat in on several heartrending board discussions concerning the resolution of financial problems, it is remarkable how taboo the topic of a land sale usually is for collegiate leaders who hold the elitist perspective. What would happen if Gravitz suggested that Exemplar sell off some of its campus to pay for Kirkwood's new faculty development program? How long would he be able to retain his job? Two weeks? Ten minutes? The commitment to land (and its relationship to reputation) is deeply rooted in the elitist perspective.

Reputation is the second major form of capital from the elitist perspective. The very notion of elitism conveys something about the importance of reputation. A high-status college or university that is considered elitist typically costs much more than "lesser" institutions of similar quality. However, it can rarely demonstrate that it delivers a better education than less expensive institutions. What the high-status college and university can deliver, by definition, is reputation. This form of personal capital can in turn be quite beneficial to a young man or woman (particularly from a lower socioeconomic level or a minority group) who is seeking employment, marriage into a family "of quality," enrollment in a prestigious graduate school, or simply a "higher station in life" (Kingston and Lewis, 1990).

Typically, the reputation of a school is conveyed and maintained informally through some alumni or referral network. It would be bad form for a high-status college or university to advertise its degree programs. Except for public concerts, lectures, continuing education programs, and the like, advertising is rarely encouraged (or even allowed) in these colleges and universities. Public relations is important, but it must be subtle and reserved for scholarship and research or the thoughtful reflection of a campus leader or scholar on some current event or social problem. Marketing of degree programs and hustling of students is left to the less fortunate and lower-status institutions built on populist or expedient foundations.

With regard to the educational values inherent in the elitist perspective, there is actually very little to say, for assumptions about teaching and learning are quite simple. In an elitist setting, maturation (rather than education per se) is conceived of as the primary product of the elitist institution. This conception of maturation as the primary product potentially opens the elitist faculty member or academic administrator to contemporary concepts of student development, and keeps these faculty members and administrators from falling into the trap of quantifying and ultimately trivializing the educational goals of students (as often occurs from the populist, beleaguered, and expedient perspectives). Faculty and administrators with the elitist perspective, however, typically have done little more than articulate their support for the notion of student development. They have chosen instead to remain vague and passive regarding ways for the college or university to encourage the maturation of its students. Mostly, what a high-quality education does, from the elitist perspective, is inundate carefully selected students with sumptuous resources, assuming that valuable education and cherished leadership positions will automatically ensue.

Key Points

1. The origins of American higher education are closely associated with elitism. Colonial American educators, gazing across the Atlantic at long-established colleges and universities, sought to emulate many European forms—perhaps out of a desire for continuity with the past as well as admiration for the quality and reputation of these institutions.

2. Today we face many problems that were unknown to the people who first formulated the elitist perspective. However, many elitist criteria of quality (particularly input-based criteria) persist in the minds of the leaders of contemporary colleges and universities in America and the arbiters of quality of all educational institutions, whether originally established on an elitist foundation or not.

3. The premodern elitist perspective developed in high-status institutions that were remarkably stable in size (because of selective admissions) and that established simple structures that served as surrogates for family or church. From the elitist perspective, mission was unimportant, or was obvious in light of the rich resources assembled by these institutions. Boundaries were usually unclear, with a close interrelationship between education and the molding of moral character for the sake of family, church, and social class.

4. From the elitist perspective, greatness in both administrative and instructional roles is essential. Leaders rule and faculty teach in elitist settings through face-to-face, informal communication. The formal curriculum is complemented (and at times almost supplanted) by extracurricular activities. The elitist perspective values grounds, status, and reputation, and all members of the elitist community strive to preserve existing social patterns.

Chapter Six

The Populist Perspective

Prior to the American Revolution, only three fields of professional endeavor existed in this country: theology, medicine, and law. The preparation of men (and later women) for these three professions was initially relegated exclusively to high-status colleges. However, these professions soon opened to members at the lower socioeconomic levels, resulting in a broadening of the professions that was unthinkable in colonial times. Furthermore, other professions began to appear (nursing, teaching, engineering, architecture), and new demands were placed on colleges and universities to begin "professionalizing" such renegade areas as agriculture and business management. With each of these expansions in America's sense of what constitutes a profession came a corresponding expansion in the mission to be served by collegiate institutions. High-status institutions simply could not meet all of the emerging educational and certification needs.

While this expansion in the more practical side of American higher education was taking place, recognition of the less practical and more academic side of the educational enterprise was also increasing. Soon after the Revolution, the major religious denominations began requiring a liberal education as a background to enter theology. The same became true for medicine and most entries into law. By the early 1800s, a B.A. degree had become a preprofessional requirement. Rudolph (1984) articulated a widely held commitment in this country at this point in its history "that the American college delivered a nonprofessional and nontechnical education in the arts and sciences, an experience in refinement

125

and intellectual growth" (p. 14). By becoming refined in such a manner, a person was eligible for a leadership role—certifiable as a gentleman or lady in this country. Thus a division in the purpose of higher education appeared. High-status institutions were beginning to serve the academic needs more fully and exclusively, while the newly emerging, more populist-oriented colleges and universities were taking on the more practical needs.

Populism was forged not only in the furnace of practicality but also on the anvil of equity. The values and aspirations of the elitist-oriented institution hark back to the colonial era of American history, whereas populist values and aspirations, particularly those concerned with equity, arose in the expansionist era. Americans were no longer confined, as European surrogates, to the eastern shores of the continent. They discovered a new frontier west of the Allegheny Mountains and gave birth to a new group of rough-hewn national heroes who were conquering these new frontiers not with education and professional training but with practical populist savvy and homespun wisdom.

The Jacksonian era (1828–1868) in particular was characterized by a spirit of egalitarianism and populism. Unlettered clergy served outside of the major religious denominations. These populist ministers were from lower socioeconomic denominations (Baptists and Methodists) rather than from the denominations of the upper classes (Presbyterians and Episcopalians). As Rudolph (1984) notes, state legislatures accused the elitist colleges of being "centers of privilege and purveyors of useless learning." Rudolph explains: "The American liberal arts college was of preindustrial origin. Its concern with the education of gentlemen, its lack of sympathy with many of the egalitarian and exploitive impulses of the age, and its Christian orientation suffused the classical curriculum and the humanistic style of the old colleges. The American university, on the other hand, was child of the new order, a product of the Industrial Revolution eager to play a central role in the refinement and specialization of knowledge and in the training of cadres of experts to keep the machinery of society running" (p. 14).

Thus, changing requirements for professors and the notion that higher education was a requirement to be a gentleman or lady, set against a background of equality for everyone and the growth of the university movement, laid the battleground between these two conflicting ideas—elitism and populism—which concerned the purpose of higher education in the late nineteenth and early twentieth centuries. These battles also involved academic professionals, and the outcomes shaped the role of the contemporary educator.

The American university system, which developed between the Civil War and World War I, combined the idea of the English college with the German research university and added the American idea of a university as a public service. Thus, from the first, most American universities blended elitism and populism. The major impact of the university system was that of a change in viewing vocations and certification; old vocations became professions, and universities provided the certifications. In addition, universities provided social mobility by becoming the route into corporations and business bureaucracies. By emphasizing equality, the clientele of higher education changed, and the different clientele changed the system. Higher education became a meritocratic, bureaucratic system.

The result was a confused vision of purpose with no clear way to set priorities for the educational system (Rudolph, 1962, 1984). Furthermore, individualistic aspirations replaced a shared concern for society or the human community in many populist-oriented colleges and universities. Whereas the high-status elitist-oriented institutions focused on preparing leaders for society (given that these young men and women were usually already well established in a family enterprise), the lower-status, populist-oriented institutions focused on helping graduates achieve individual goals and move up the socioeconomic ladder. The college system had the same kinds of confusion as it tried to copy the growing university system. "In an atmosphere of confused purpose, jumbled priorities, and forgetfulness, the universities and the colleges that aped them had no difficulty in offering a source of study equally confused, jumbled, and forgetful" (Rudolph, 1984, p. 15).

In many ways, the confusion and tension between elitism and populism in American higher education was resolved with the growth and maturation of the community (or junior) college system in America. These new institutions took much of the pressure off four-year undergraduate institutions both public and private. As Brint and Karabel (1989) note, community colleges in the United States have fulfilled the American commitment to equality of opportunity, enabling other institutional types to move back to a more elitist mentality.

Community colleges offered second chances for students with poor academic records in high school or previous college experiences. They also offered two-year programs, which may be more compatible than four-year programs with the unpredictable conditions that many men and women face as they try to fit postsecondary education into complex lives. Only traditional college-age students from the upper socioeconomic levels are able to plan comfortably on four uninterrupted years of education. Community colleges have also broadened access by offering both academic and vocational programs, by allowing part-time enrollment at any point in the student's educational career, by offering programs at community-based sites near students' homes and at times of the day when they can take classes, and by improving the prospects of access to higher-status four-year institutions through the transfer of college credit (Brint and Karabel, 1989).

At an even more basic level, community colleges have sustained the populist and egalitarian ideologies in America by typically being more flexible than four-year institutions in the continuous redesign of educational programs to meet shifting community and student needs (Brint and Karabel, 1989). Not only are students allowed to change their mind and readily shift majors in community colleges, but the colleges themselves are allowed to "change their minds" and shift programs. I am reminded of an incident that occurred twenty years ago at a national conference on educational innovation when one of the key academic leaders at St. John's College (a bastion of the elitist perspective) humorously noted that he wasn't sure why he was invited to speak at this conference, considering that St. John's is not a school that changes its curriculum very often. He noted that the only change over the previous twenty years had been the addition of several books to the college's great books list! St. John's exemplifies the best of high-status, elitist-oriented institutions, yet very few community colleges in the United States could have survived for twenty years without far greater changes than those made at St. John's.

In light of major shifts in the demographics of the United States (Levine and Associates, 1989), increasing concern for the disenfranchisement of many sectors in American society, and evolving roles for women and underserved populations in American politics, the populist commitment in America can no longer be sustained solely by community colleges. When African-American and Hispanic high school graduates are shunted off to vocational training programs offered by community colleges because these are the primary programs being offered by the only postsecondary educational institutions in which they can afford to enroll and for which they are prepared, there are major problems with regard to equity and access in America (Ballesteros, 1988).

When we condemn community colleges and other open-access schools as "deficit" institutions that are "at risk" with regard to quality, and when we malign their students as unqualified to receive a college education (Mayhew, Ford, and Hubbard, 1990, p. 36–37), we have eliminated the tension between elitism and populism. However, we have done so by relegating access to one kind of institution, the community college, and then discrediting or at least isolating this institutional type from the mainstream of American higher education. If the rhetoric of access is confined to the community college while other educational institutions are allowed to provide "high-quality" education only to upper-middle-class, traditional-aged Caucasian students, we have failed as a nation to fulfill our populist vision.

Four-year American colleges and universities must confront the issues of access as well as quality; they can no longer avoid them. Given that most colleges and universities in the United States must embrace an uneasy blend of elitism and populism, it is important that we understand and learn to appreciate the historical interplay between these two forces.

In this chapter I will turn again to the hypothetical institution, Exemplar College/University, introduced in Chapter Five. Chapter Five viewed Exemplar from the elitist perspective, focusing on how its elitism had worn a little thin and its leaders were scrambling in a rather unelitist manner for dollars and students. In this chapter, the perspective shifts to populism. What does a struggling institution like Exemplar look like from the populist perspective? How must it address its problems if it purports to be responsive to the unmet needs for postsecondary education among certain underserved populations in the local community?

Exemplar from the Populist Perspective

In exploring the nature and dynamics of the populist perspective at Exemplar, I will be looking not so much at the interaction between the administrative leaders of the school, as I did in examining the elitist perspective, but rather at the behavior of a small group of faculty and students who hold diverse and sometimes contradictory ideas about the nature and purpose of their institution. Following is the cast of characters for this continuing minidrama.

Gretchen Karpoff, assistant professor of psychology. Gretchen Karpoff is an enthusiastic "newly minted" instructor who returned to school somewhat late in life to complete her undergraduate and graduate degrees. She is strongly motivated by the importance of education in her own life and hence is committed to a populist mission: the education of students, particularly nontraditional students.

Professor Karpoff is oriented to a participatory mode of learning, including active student involvement in class discussions, experiential learning, and assignments that connect ideas presented in class with an individual student's life experiences. She is also deeply committed to her field and sees psychology as an important component in everyone's education.

Burke Deffenbach, professor of history and humane letters. Burke Deffenbach is a curious mixture. He is a respected senior member of the faculty and a noted scholar. He is an elitist who doesn't seem to fit the populist mold very well. Perhaps that is why he is also a burned-out teacher. At times Deffenbach is an inspiring thinker, capable of moving a class with the fire that has made him the most powerful faculty member in Exemplar's recent past. At other times he seems to rely on old notes and lukewarm ideas. He is content to let other scholars explore terrain that once was his. It has been several years since he has published a major paper. His classic textbook is dated and out-of-print. As a populist institution, Exemplar neither encourages nor discourages Deffenbach's scholarship. Many of his colleagues, in fact, seem to be indifferent. Deffenbach has been through many curriculum revisions at Exemplar and is tired of the whole process. At the specific request of President Gravitz, he has agreed to give general education "one more try" and to work on a new vision of education for Exemplar.

Betty Cordell, junior psychology major. Betty Cordell is a reentry student who is completing her education after fifteen years of marriage and motherhood. She came to Exemplar because of publicity about the school's new emphasis on mature students. But then she went through registration. Not only were there the usual lines, forms, and other annoyances, but she also had to deal with "parental approval" forms, fees for campus activities, and all the other reminders that this school is still primarily designed for eighteen-year-old students. Now she is set to start classes, her hopes for her education mixed with fears about skills long unused. Is returning to school a good idea?

Jane Harper, sophomore English major. Jane Harper is a quiet young black woman, the kind of student who doesn't say much in class and can sometimes get lost in terms of the instructor's attention. Her freshman year was hard on her, and it showed in her inconsistent academic performance. At times she felt she didn't really know what was going on in class. Teachers would say things she didn't understand, and other students would talk in class as if they really knew something. Her grades were marginal, a shock after her academic success in a large urban high school. She clearly wants to succeed in college, but she is not sure she is smart enough.

Wesley Singleton, sophomore art history major. Slightly older than the traditional college student, Wes Singleton has a strong sense of his own intellectual gifts and of the significance of his field. For him, art history is the way to appreciate the formation of Western culture, and the history of Western culture is the core of any important study. Along with his strong confidence and convictions, Singleton has a thinly disguised disdain for people of lesser intelligence and for those who work and study in fields of so-called practical importance. Like Deffenbach, Singleton is an elitist enduring in a populist institution. Perhaps too, like Deffenbach, he will soon burn out.

Steven Petrovski, freshman engineering and technology major. Steven Petrovski comes from a rural area near Exemplar, and his college experience has already been both an adventure and a shock to his system. He knows a lot about farming, farm machinery, and animals but doesn't know much about history, dormitory living, or campus life. His placement tests shook him a bit, asking about a lot of things he didn't really recognize. Petrovski is still trying to adjust to all of the different ways people talk and behave. Everyone, including classmates and professors, seems so different.

Scene: Exemplar Campus, Second Day of the Fall Term

As Gretchen Karpoff downs her granola, she finds her mind wandering from breakfast to the classes ahead. Introduction to Psychology is usually not a course teachers anticipate with excitement, but she is excited. This year, for the first time, she is going to try all the interactive techniques she has been hearing about, learning about, and trying in small pieces. She also has some hope that her ideas might inform the direction of the curriculum committee, though that is less clear. The committee, however, is important, and Vice President Kirkwood made it clear that she wants Karpoff on the committee for her ideas.

Sitting in his dormitory room at 8:30 in the morning, Steven Petrovski views the day with anxiety. His roommate has already left, and Steven sits alone wondering what lies ahead. The writing course worries him because he never did much writing in his small-town high school. Psychology should be easier. At least he can sit quietly and listen. There is so much here he is not sure of. He feels a pang of memory for the farm, his animals, and his family and friends back home.

At 8:55, Betty Cordell is walking into her first class, Professor Deffenbach's European History. Betty had planned to arrive extra early to purchase some books and supplies, but things didn't go as planned. The family was no help this morning. Her son, Eric, had to have his favorite clothes and expected to be waited on. Cari, her daughter, suddenly wanted to be held and talked to as she prepared for her own return to school. Betty's husband had to leave early for work and could offer no help. When Betty finally got to campus, parking was terrible. She found a spot several blocks away. This early class was going to be a problem, she realized, especially with getting the kids to school.

Seated in class, Betty is suddenly nervous. The other students look very young and seem unfazed by all of this. They trigger doubts about her own skills and her role as a returning student. A young black woman is sitting next to her. Betty turns and introduces herself. The young student's name is Jane Harper. She seems nice, if a bit reserved. Before Betty can reflect further, Professor Deffenbach enters the room, so she turns, opens her notebook, and prepares to experience her first class.

As Burke Deffenbach enters the room, he feels both the excitement of beginning a new class and the sameness of yet another first day of an academic term. To fight the boredom, he decides to do more than go over the course requirements today. Seeing Jennifer Stephens in the front row reinforces that decision. She will expect a lot from him and will in turn respond to his ideas.

Passing out the course outline and the requirements, Deffenbach starts in on the easy beginning point, "What is history?" As he toys with the idea of chronology and the role of time, Jennifer Stephens adds a question that opens up several themes, including "wholes and parts," "tradition and change," "subject and object," and "objective and subjective perspectives." Deffenbach writes these pairs on the board. He finds himself weaving the ideas in and through each other, letting the contradictions and complexities interact and resonate. His mind roams freely, taking him from history to philosophy, literature, and politics. He notes that the students are industriously taking notes, and he feels his power as a teacher fill the room.

Jane Harper, writing feverishly, struggles to keep up with the flow of words. She writes as much as her pen will capture, knowing that at some future time she may have trouble figuring some of this out. Betty Cordell is unsure of what to write. The ideas are exciting and exhilarating, making her feel that she is now really in college. She remembers the way complex ideas confused her when she was eighteen. "No wonder I dropped out of college when I did!" In the midst of her own thoughts, she suddenly realizes that she has just missed one of the professor's major points. Can she sort all of this out? Can she keep up with these younger students, especially that bright one up front? And can she concentrate on the lecture, rather than wandering off into her past?

For Wes Singleton, all of this is a bit exasperating. Professor Deffenbach is off on a tangent and fails to point out the importance of art and architecture in the history of Europe. Taking history like this is frustrating because it is both close to the truth and yet so incomplete. In addition, this looks like another typical Exemplar class, with a couple of good minds mixed into a large group of students who, in Wes's eyes, should not even be in college.

For Betty Cordell, this is a demanding day, a morning class followed by a couple of quick errands, then home for lunch, back to work during the afternoon, and another class in the evening. Since leaving the morning European history class, Betty has struggled with registration issues at the financial aid and physical education offices. One problem is solved: the financial aid officer was wrong when she told Betty that her parents' signature was required on her loan papers. However, she still cannot convince the assistant director of physical education that she should be able to waive the activity course requirement in PE. As Betty said in arguing her case, she does feel the need to get into better shape. However, it is embarrassing to imagine matching physical skills and body size with all those active, trim young women.

Looking at her watch, Betty is startled by how much time this took. It is now 12:40 P.M. She decides to extend her already delayed trip to work to go to the bookstore. Edgy from the pressures of a second day at Exemplar and tired from waiting in lines at the bookstore (where she found only two of the three books for her history course), Betty returns to her car to find a parking ticket on her windshield. Betty slams the car door, stuffs the ticket in her purse, and begins wondering whether college was such a good idea after all.

At 1:15 P.M., Steven Petrovski has just finished his lunch in the cafeteria. He didn't see anyone he'd met in orientation, so he sat at a table with three guys who didn't seem to mind his presence and who involved him a bit in one of their conversations. Steven didn't know much about pro football, but they didn't seem to mind his ignorance of what was for them an obvious passion. His psychology text under his arm, Steven now heads for his Introduction to Psychology class.

Gretchen Karpoff begins the class by introducing herself and asking the students to do the same and mention one thing that they have heard about the field of psychology that they think might not be true. For Karpoff, this is a chance to get the developmental process going right away, as well as to find out some of the preconceived notions that students are bringing to the subject. She will use these notions later when discussing the basic tenets of the field.

Steven Petrovski is thoroughly confused. He doesn't feel he knows anything yet about psychology—certainly not enough to know what is true or not true. Indeed, he sort of expected the professor to tell him some true things, so this vagueness is troubling. While the other students are introducing themselves, Steven desperately tries to come up with something to say. He remembers that one of the students at lunch had said that pro football players often "psych out" their opponents. When his turn comes, it is the only possibility he can think of, so he states: "Athletes often say that psychology can be used to confuse the people you're competing against." Professor Karpoff asks Steven, "Do you think this is accurate? Do you think that psychology can be used in the competitive situations we find ourselves in every day?" Steven is not at all sure what she means or if that is what he meant, but he says yes so that she will turn her attention to the other students.

At 3:00 in the afternoon, Burke Deffenbach walks away from campus. His head is filled with images of home—the woodwork that awaits him in his garage and the idea of sitting in his favorite chair and reading. He thinks with pleasure of the summer of carpentry that has produced his new den: "The room I built is truly splendid. Sitting there helps me forget about the hassles at Exemplar." He smiles as he steps up to his front door and enters his home.

Gretchen Karpoff leaves campus at 4:00 P.M. Settling into the front seat of her car, she reflects on the seeming passivity and dependence of her students in Intro to Psych: "They seem reluctant to speak up. They don't get involved even when I open the door for them and invite them in. Are they so stuck in their habits of waiting for me to provide answers that I can't get them free? These kids seem so much less mature than the students I worked with at the community college." She also reflects on the general education committee and the other faculty members on the committee. Does she really belong on this committee? Does she really belong in a place like Exemplar, with its entrenched traditions and "old boy" faculty network? Though she has never used the label "populism," Karpoff is puzzled as to why Exemplar seems to have abandoned (or perhaps never fulfilled) its populist mission.

By 6:30 in the evening, Steven Petrovski is in his room, lying on his bed looking up at the ceiling. The day has been long and confusing. He feels vaguely lost and alone. "I don't understand what was happening in either psychology or calculus. I walked through the day alone, even ate dinner all by myself. Roommate Jim has been away all day—though when he's here, he's so involved in meditation that we don't talk much anyway." Steven anticipated having a roommate who would also be a friend, but Jim seems to have already made other friends. Steven looks over at his books and feels the need to get started on his homework. He sits up, looking at his books without enthusiasm.

After a harried afternoon at work and then returning to school for an evening class, Betty Cordell sits down in the nearly empty student lounge and lets her emotions swirl. Her feet hurt, but not as much as her soul. She just isn't up to facing home and family yet. She knows she will get a barrage of excited questions from her husband the moment she walks in—questions she doesn't want to answer yet. She had looked forward to this first week of school for such a long time; her entire family had helped her get ready. Her daughter had even supervised her makeup and choice of clothes. After more than fifteen years, she's a student again. But today didn't go as she had planned. In fact, she is afraid that if she thinks about it much more, she will cry from disappointment. She can't let her kids see her this unhappy; maybe she has made a mistake.

Betty feels like such a fool. Every line she is in seems like the wrong line. She doesn't want to think about how many times she has had to start over in another line or about all the time she has spent standing in lines today. Everyone else seemed to know exactly what to do; registration seemed much more confusing and exhausting than she remembers. Maybe she is too old for school. When she dealt with the parental approval forms, she had wanted to fall through the floor. She doesn't know what to do, and she feels ancient and out-of-place.

She knows that she should go home because it is past her usual bedtime. She would like to come back tomorrow for a meeting of the Women's Network at Exemplar, but she didn't finish registration before lunch today, so she'll probably have to concentrate on that tomorrow. The Network meeting had been the one bright spot for Betty. If only she didn't have to go back into the great hall to finish registering. Her thoughts drift back to an initial luncheon meeting of the Network that she attended last week. A number of returning students had talked about their experiences at Exemplar. One young woman described a general education seminar that she took last year: "I hated to go to class. I didn't bother to read the book. The instructor wouldn't let me participate in class. The class was straight recitation, plugged into a formula. It reminded me of fifth-grade geography. I was so glad when a new teacher took over the class and I could use my brain instead of just memorizing."

Betty wishes she had asked the teacher's name—it sounded like someone she could do without. Yet another woman described an entirely different experience with Exemplar. Betty thinks about the second young woman for a moment. If only she had some of that young woman's brain power, maybe she'd know how to deal with parental permission slips! At the lunch, the second young woman had described how she chose Exemplar:

I had several choices for university. I had excellent training, excellent high school grades, a straight 4.0, a solid SAT combined score of 1375. I short-listed my options to a state school and a private school and visited each campus. The state school was especially bad. In the cafeteria, all the students were gazing off into space. They all looked like robots. Here, at this school, everyone was warm and friendly. Everyone took time away from what he or she was doing to talk to me. I can get the academics anywhere. I wanted something different. I've been treated like a freak all my life; I wanted to belong to a community. I'm not interested in just being the brightest student in the college in special classes; classes just for me. I've never had a chance to learn about me, to be part of a group and learn from other students. Here I have that chance. It's wonderful. I'm finding that I *am* special—special as a person, not some sort of a high-brained freak. I've always run on brain power before; here I'm learning to use person power, and I love it.

"Why did this seem like such a good place for her and not for me?" Betty muses. "Of course: she's a young woman, whereas I'm not young anymore." Betty wonders if she really wants to finish her degree. School had been so much fun before she married, but now it just seems noisy and confusing, with no place for her. Even though the lunch had been interesting, she must have been the oldest person there. No one else seemed to have kids. All the other women were so bright. They were probably smart enough to finish school before getting married. Betty had never thought of herself as dumb, but she hadn't taken a test or written a term paper for years. Maybe she should have listened to her brother. He had told her to stay home and take care of her kids, warned her that she would never be able to compete with the "real" students at Exemplar. The literature from the college that she'd read had mentioned special programs for reentry women, but maybe Exemplar didn't mean someone as old as she.

Her husband and kids will want a full report. Maybe she could make up a story for them so they won't see how scared she is. Maybe first thing next week she could try to get a refund of her tuition. She hopes she won't have to deal with the registrar again to get her money back. But what of her dream? And she'll have to tell her family if she quits. Miserably unhappy, Betty leaves for home. As she goes out the door, she sees a sign describing the cocurricular activities for the week: dorm dances, floor meetings in the dorms, seminars on "living with your roommate," "surviving away from home," and "coping with dorm food." She supposes that that is where the students are, eating in the dorms. Suddenly Betty is angry. "What about me? I don't live in a dorm, have a roommate, or want to go to a dorm dance. I can't even eat on campus if I want to because I don't live in a dorm." Her anger charges her dash to the car through the deserted campus. She knows that before she reaches home, she has to have a story ready about her first day at school. The truth is too terrible to admit—she doesn't belong here.

Historical Background

To understand something of why Betty Cordell and Steven Petrovski seem to be in their current dilemma, why Burke Deffenbach and Gretchen Karpoff face such difficult challenges, and how the populist perspective relates to an institution like Exemplar, a bit more reflection is needed on the history of American education, and some attention must be focused on populist-oriented curricula.

As our modern, postindustrial society moved from a competitive, entrepreneurial capitalism to a more complex corporate capitalism, with applied science and technology and occupational specialization, higher education also changed. No longer was higher education the preserve of a limited, elitist governing class; higher education was for everyone interested in being part of the new capitalism of the corporate state. As Rudolph (1984) notes, "The growth of professionalism changed who went to college, what they sought there, and who taught there" (p. 16).

In the populist curriculum, size was paramount—numbers of courses, majors, enrollments, and growth—a banking model approach to learning. There was a move toward acquisition and imperialism. Department and discipline areas became the centers of power—especially departments that reflected the overall growth patterns in enrollments and courses. With this change of power from an integrated curriculum to individual departments and courses, subjects and courses were offered "because an essentially autonomous group of academic professionals could and would teach nothing else" (Rudolph, 1984, p. 16). This confirmation of authority on the professors, and to some extent on students, robbed the curriculum of its authority and robbed higher education of its concern for community. With unbridled growth, a system of departments and courses, isolated and separated, replaced unity and community.

With a meritocracy in the higher education system came a national upper middle class concerned with equity and fair play, aspiring to neutrality in regard to regions, religions, and ethnic groups. To be fair, equitable, and neutral required separation from the community—individualism (Jencks and Riesman, 1968; Rudolph, 1962, 1984, 1985). The curriculum lost the coherence and authority of the classical tradition; it "quickly became a bazaar and the students tourists looking for cheap bargains" (Rudolph, 1984, p. 16).

The Modern Populist Perspective

Whereas the high-status, elitist-oriented collegiate institution in America was the product of the premodern British college and early modern German research university, the high-access, populist-oriented institution was clearly the product of the modern era—and was often cited as one of its great accomplishments. With modernism came an emphasis on size, quantification, bureaucracy, and the isolated educational experience (within a specific discipline or career track). I will examine each of the dimensions of organizational life studied in Chapters One and Five.

Size and Complexity

From the populist perspective, success is measured largely by growth rates. Rapid growth is typically taken as a sign that the institution is successful and that it is effectively serving its mission of access. Put succinctly, big is better. Big, in turn, means increased differentiation and specialization of functions, the compartmentalization of these specialized functions, and the concomitant need for their effective integration (Lawrence and Lorsch, 1967). This balance between differentiation and integration is one of the major challenges facing any growing organization and reflects the importance of decisions made by any organization about an increase in size (Bergquist, 1993).

Modern postsecondary educational institutions have long operated under the assumption that increased size will inevitably lead to increased efficiency and lower per-student cost in the delivery of educational services. In his seminal work on the "multiversity," Clark Kerr (1963)—then chancellor of the very large Berkeley campus of the University of California—defined the virtues of large, multipurpose postsecondary educational institutions. Ironically, under Kerr the leaders of American higher education (administrators, state system coordinators, state legislators) witnessed not only the success of his multiversity vision but also his ineffective encounter with leaders of the student free-speech movement in Berkeley. Thus, even as the multiversity culminated a quest for the perfect modern educational bureaucracy, it also signaled the start of the postmodern era in which bureaucracy and traditional administrative and faculty-based decision-making modes became obsolete.

Populists are committed to uniformity, for only with uniform systems can one ensure equity of treatment. Hence the systems of a populist-oriented institution may be very large, but they are also relatively simple and replicable—which is to say highly bureaucratic and receptive to such management technologies as were offered by the National Center for Higher Education Management Systems

(NCHEMS) of Boulder, Colorado. This federally funded center flourished during the 1970s, giving American colleges and universities the tools to measure and potentially control complex educational budgets. NCHEMS provided funding formulas and classroom enrollment projection procedures and helped transform educational leaders into institutional managers and isolated educational institutions into complex postsecondary educational systems.

A basic assumption of populism—and the managerial culture that undergirds the populist perspective—is that the organization and its dynamics are essentially nondistinctive and therefore unimportant in terms of defining a unique and specific educational experience for the students attending the institution. Formulas and statistics are at the heart of the populist operation. From the populist perspective, distinctive differences are signs of the failure of the institution to develop and maintain uniform standards, thereby opening the door to the muddled and arbitrary organizational processes of the premodern world (Weber, 1947).

Mission and Boundaries

As in the case of many modern organizations, a populist-oriented postsecondary institution tends to proclaim a mission that is either unclear or inconsistent. Populism in its narrower form is defined much more by its boundaries—or, more precisely, its absence of traditional status-based boundaries—than by its mission. Students are typically brought into a college or university by the thousands, but it is rarely clear what they are going to receive or should receive in terms of education once they have been admitted to the school. The leaders of these institutions tend to be enamored with numbers and efficiency of service. They are often more likely to define themselves as educational managers than as academic leaders.

As a result, discussions about the educational purposes of the institution are often absent, with attention focused instead on the nature and challenges associated with the increasingly diversified student population being served by the institution. With an emphasis on efficiency, the concept of effectiveness takes a back seat: we know that we are delivering an educational service at a specific cost (with the assistance of cost-finding tools such as have been developed and marketed by the NCHEMS), but we don't really know if these services are of value to anyone (student, community, world). An inexpensive education can be very expensive if it yields little of value.

To the extent that populists do tend to assess the quality of the services that they offer, these measures tend to be outcome-oriented. For example, how do graduates of this institution fare in terms of employment, admission to graduate school, earned income after a given number of years, and so forth. Unfortunately, these outcome measures tend to drive the populists' definition of quality rather than being driven by the definition. Because they can be measured, job placements and admissions to graduate school become central ingredients in a populist institution's implicit (if not explicit) mission. But are these outcomes what the college or university really values? Aren't these criteria of quality highly vulnerable to economic forces in the community and shifts in graduate school admission standards and licensing laws that are beyond the institution's control?

From the populist perspective, admissions boundaries are quite clear. Once a collegiate institution has made a commitment to access and has opened its doors to nontraditional students, it must ask two questions. The first is, what is needed for a potential student to be admitted to this institution? Populist-oriented colleges and universities can't be for everyone; otherwise the degree would have no meaning. Since family background, socioeconomic level, and status of other schools attended are no longer acceptable as standards for admission, careful attention must be directed to the formulation and imposition of new standards that very clearly spell out admission requirements. Second, populists must ask the question, access for whom? Access is defined in many ways. Exemplar is representative of the American populist tradition. It strongly emphasizes access in numerous ways—often in ways of which its leaders are only marginally aware. Populism, like elitism, is often so deeply embedded in the institution and its members that there is little overt awareness.

The first form of access, which was common during the early years of emphasis on equity and education for upward mobility in nineteenth-century America, is an appeal to young men and women whose parents did not attend college. These "first-generation students" tend to attend institutions like Exemplar because of geographic access. Whereas the previous generation of Americans often did not attend college for socioeconomic reasons, family deemphasis on education, or a lack of sufficient schooling, the primary barrier for the parents of our current college-age students in many instances has been geography: they simply did not grow up near a college campus.

Second, Exemplar attracts some black, Hispanic, and Asian-American students, as well as a few Native American students. Several of these particular ethnic groups have a long history of nonaccess—a "double whammy" in terms of both ethnic discrimination and geographic remoteness. These two factors tend to reinforce each other. Students such as Catherine Chung and Jane Harper have been pressured to remain in ghettos because of their ethnicity. It will be a major challenge for Exemplar and other populist institutions to break through these boundaries.

As a career-oriented school, Exemplar also tends to appeal to students from lower socioeconomic levels (the original dream of American public education). Furthermore, Exemplar is located in a major urban area and runs evening and weekend programs that specifically attract men and women who are returning to school. Many of its students are middle-aged men and women who are pursuing second careers. Leaders at Exemplar—including President Gravitz—acknowledge the value of career shifts. This is a particularly controversial issue at present: should postsecondary educational institutions support shifts to second careers, or does responsibility end with assisting with the first career? (California public education has come down recently on the side of the one-career option. Students coming back for a second degree at the same level will have to pay considerably more money for their education than students working on their first degree at that level.)

One question lingers at Exemplar, as at many other contemporary colleges and universities: Is Exemplar's commitment to returning students in this urban area just an opportunistic attempt to pull in eligible students, or is there a deeply rooted commitment to access? Mayhew, Ford, and Hubbard (1990) rightly challenge the motives of many struggling colleges and universities regarding the validity and depth of their populist rhetoric. Fortunately, Exemplar is old enough to be well established in its community. In such a setting, there is likely to be a deep-rooted interplay between populism and patriotism. Exemplar is likely to be committed in its actions as well as its rhetoric to serving as a partner (with other schools, businesses, churches, community agencies, and so forth) in building its local community. This seems to be part of the small-town mentality of American populism, reflected in Fourth of July parades, Veterans Day celebrations, war memorials, and the like. As a result of the interplay between populism and patriotism, we often find strange mixtures of conservatism (reflected in the patriotism) and liberalism (reflected in the populism).

Though Exemplar may be dedicated to access, a dominant concern (as in the higher-status colleges and universities) is that the "proper" people get into the school. From the populist perspective, the proper person is someone who has been admitted through absolutely impartial, standardized entrance exams. There is no room for individualized attention or exceptions in the populist school—that smacks too much of the "good old boy" biases of elite colleges or universities. The emergence of the populist institution heralded the era of testing. It is also ironic that another set of boundaries is particularly important in the populist institution—the boundaries set up by faculty that masquerade as "academic freedom."

Leadership

Leadership is defined from the populist perspective primarily by events and systems rather than by the personal characteristics of the men and women who run the institution. Presidents are perceived primarily as managers, not as great leaders or educational visionaries. Attitudes about leadership are also reflected in the populist perceptions concerning faculty and student roles. These perceptions have become particularly important, given the efforts of many populists, under the influence of the managerial culture, to define and measure quality. Faculty members tend to be treated by the management and populist-oriented administration as employees rather than as colleagues or fellow professionals. Students are viewed as profit centers by these same administrators and as knowledge receptacles by the often patronizing faculty. At the heart of the populist perspective we often find a primary concern for jobs and career advancement among students, faculty members, and administrators. Jobs—for everyone—are seen as the primary products of the institution.

By contrast, from the elitist perspective, faculty are viewed as the surrogate parents of the students and the colleagues or revered leaders of the administration, students are looked on as children to be raised by the faculty by means of the curriculum, and maturation is considered the primary product of the school. Faculty and administrators generally neither worry about their job nor consider their current position as a springboard for other jobs. Where would they go? They have already arrived at a high-status institution.

When the central quality-management question is asked—"Who is the customer?"—the populist will initially tend to answer, "The student." This rarely holds up to further scrutiny, however, because populist-oriented institutions do little to hang on to students, considering that so many other people are waiting to come in. In these increasingly hard-pressed colleges and universities, the customer often seems to be the legislature or, in the case of private institutions, the person paying the tuition—which is less frequently the student or parent and more frequently the state or federal government (through student loan programs).

Many populist-oriented colleges and universities rely on student loan programs for their existence and could not survive without generous government support for these programs. Given that most student loan programs are tied to regional accreditation and increasingly to low default rates on the repayment of student loans, the new customer for many populist-oriented institutions thus becomes the regional accrediting association or even graduates who are repaying their student loans.

Faculty leadership in the classroom is often particularly hard to exhibit in the populist-oriented institution because of an overwhelming concern for uniformity and the elimination of personal idiosyncrasies. We saw this in earlier years through the movement away from primary sources (selected by the faculty member) and essay exams (graded by the faculty member) to formally approved textbooks and standardized, objective tests. Although most populist colleges and universities have never had to bend to the pressures of standardized textbooks prescribed by the state (as the elementary and secondary schools have), they have given in to standardized tests to ensure "quality of instruction." Furthermore, in moving from original sources to textbooks, most faculty members have, sadly, eliminated the unique and even idiosyncratic perspectives of a single author in favor of the more homogenized and often overly generalized and simplified perspectives of the college textbook. Unfortunately, old eccentric faculty members like Exemplar's Burke Deffenbach and young, innovation-minded faculty like Gretchen Karpoff often find little support for their unique ideas and teaching styles in populist-oriented educational environments that emphasize uniformity of teaching and learning practices.

Because many faculty members in large, underfunded high-access institutions have many classes to prepare for each term, they tend to rely on the textbook not only for outside reading by the students but also for the content of their own lectures. Thus the oral traditions (tutorials and discussion) of many collegiate institutions (especially those that are elitist in orientation) have become merely surrogates for textbooks used in the course. This reliance on the written word is further reinforced in technologically advanced (modern) populist institutions through the widespread use of various visual aids and technologies, ranging from the old-fashioned blackboard, overhead projectors, closed-circuit TVs, and flip charts to computerized teleconferencing and electronic bulletin boards. All of these technologies tend to take faculty out of the limelight and into the backstage role of instructional manager rather than leader.

Capital and Educational Values

From the populist perspective, capital is defined primarily in tangible terms by the buildings and financial assets of the institution. Many university planning officers dream of large building complexes, of uniform architectural style, and technological interfaces linking all of the facilities to a central office. Along with the massive modern-day corporations that were built during the 1950s and 1960s came high-rise university campuses noteworthy more for their buildings than for their grounds (in contrast to the premodern elitist institutions). The modern populist college or university was also to be a financial empire, given the strong public support for education during the 1960s and 1970s. Managed efficiently, these institutions did not have to scramble for dollars prior to the 1980s. Taxpayers assumed that the leaders of these institutions would be good stewards of their generous yearly appropriations. All of this changed in the 1980s and 1990s, leading these institutions to become either beleaguered or more efficient.

With regard to educational values, the populist institution offered first and foremost a certificate, a degree, a "union card" that was to help the student advance in a career. As Bledstein (1976) has shown, the middle-class structure was patterned around a vertical career path, a path that required a continuous upward climb. "Professionalism," according to Rice (1980), "emerged as a culture—a set of learned values and responses—by which the middle class man shaped his emotional needs, measured the power of his intelligence, and made critical decisions about the patterns and direction of his life" (p. 34).

The hope of upward mobility existed for everyone in the populist institution, not just the students. Unfortunately, it was usually a myth. Individual students obtained better jobs as a result of obtaining an education and receiving a degree; however, more often, the jobs that they acquired were ones that had previously gone to job seekers with lower degrees, as Jencks (1972) noted years ago. Based on a study of work in America, O'Toole (1977) predicted in the 1970s that underemployment (people being employed in jobs for which they are overqualified) may be as great a problem as unemployment in the future. Underemployment is directly related to the myth that additional education will enable one to find a better job.

Given the actual (or potential) diversity of students at a college or university committed to populism, a common measuring stick is needed. The multiplicity of values and aspirations represented by diverse constituencies calls for some mode of uniformity and some shared criteria for quality. The central question that many populists at Exemplar and other contemporary colleges and universities face is, how do we sustain a viable, creditable educational institution that is acknowledged (and, ideally, accredited) by other institutions, the state government, and the federal government while also being responsive to unique student needs and interests?

Facing these conditions, many populist leaders assume that learning at their institution is quantifiable. If it can't be quantified, they fear, the door is open to arbitrary judgments based on the values of one specific constituency or, even worse, to the "soft" assessment of the premodern, elitist institution. For any populist, leaders must always be particularly vigilant about standards in the classroom. It is easy to become obsessed with standards in a populist institution—so bureaucratic and focused on admissions—and to become very punitive. Marchese (1985) notes that the instructor often stands in front of the class and "transmits 'bits' of information that students write down and parrot back on so-called 'objective' tests." The result is "a pronounced 'leveling down' of traditional standards" (p. 6). Furthermore, higher-order intellectual functions that require analysis, synthesis, or original expression tend to be pushed out of the picture.

When the populist curriculum changed to an assortment of bargains that students shopped for, the community life of the college also changed. Professors had become professionals, with a narrow specialization and "complete neglect in their training of any concern with teaching or with any professional responsibility other than to scholarship" (Rudolph, 1984, p. 41). What kinds of changes had been occurring for students, especially in the areas outside the classroom? With the rise of populism, the faculty built its own culture, one that maintains the separation of the classroom and extracurricular activities.

The focus in our Exemplar mini-drama is on teaching and learning at Exemplar because that enterprise is at the heart of American populism. From the elitist perspective, a college or university serves many functions—research, scholarship, culture (through the arts, social analysis, and so forth). Perhaps that is why Mayhew, Ford, and Hubbard (1990), as elitists, are so concerned about narrowing the mission of American higher education. From the populist perspective, an educational institution is essentially in a single business, that of providing an education to men and women who would probably not otherwise be served by a postsecondary institution—certainly not an elitist postsecondary institution. For a populist, the success of an educational institution depends on its ability to serve its students, especially those traditionally underserved.

How is Exemplar doing in this regard? One underserved population in the local community where Exemplar is located is adult learners like Betty Cordell. We observed Betty at Exemplar on the second day of the term. She felt left out and confused, off to a terrible start for a new adult student at an educational institution that needs students like her to survive. Another underserved population consists of young men and women who do not live near a community where a major college or university is located. Yet an Exemplar student from an isolated community, Steven Petrovski, is also not being very effectively served, at least so far. Like Betty Cordell, Steven feels isolated and unappreciated. Betty may have to juggle family responsibilities, but at least she has a family to return to in the evening; Steven feels very much alone, having been pulled out of his supportive local community, where people shared and supported his values and aspirations. He now dwells in a world in which he feels like a stranger, even an alien.

Like many young men and women who come out of geographic or ethnic isolation, Steven wants to learn about the new place but also wants people to appreciate the place from which he comes. He would not be attending college if he didn't want to learn new ways of life and explore new values, but he doesn't want or have to give up his old ways. He wants to integrate the two different worlds, with the help of mentors, teachers, and models from both.

What is Exemplar doing to help him with this integration? When we provide programs, under our populist mission, for young men and women who are Native Americans, Hispanic, African-American, or Asian-American, what are we doing to facilitate effective integration? Are we leaving this demanding task up to the student—as seems to be the case with Betty Cordell and Steven Petrovski? At a more immediate level, what are Burke Deffenbach's and Gretchen Karpoff's attitudes about Exemplar's populist mission, and what are they doing to further it?

Deffenbach loves to interact with his "bright" students, like Jennifer Stephens, who have received excellent training in their previous educational institutions (the kind of teaching and learning that Deffenbach values) and also share many of his own values,

thanks to the similarity of their upbringing and socioeconomic status. Even Wes Singleton largely shares Deffenbach's values and
background and hence will probably be able to have his needs met
in the course. But what about the other students in the class? What
about Jane Harper, who is scrambling to keep up and has already
become a stenographer, a passive learner? And how will Betty
Cordell ever be able to apply her own rich life experiences to this
class? How will Deffenbach come to recognize and acknowledge
their unique perspectives and expertise?

Gretchen Karpoff must also rethink her approach to education.
She is certainly a committed teacher and rightly wishes to increase
student involvement as a way of enhancing the teaching and learning process. Yet some students in her course will be unaccustomed
to and even frightened by active student participation. How will
she make this a safe place for these nontraditional students? Making college exciting for traditional students coming from middle-
class homes straight out of high school is relatively simple; the
challenge is making it an involving experience for students from
other backgrounds.

Involvement is especially difficult to achieve in a diverse student setting because the attitudes of both instructors and traditional
students about the potential of learning from nontraditional students are typically negative: "I have nothing to learn from that old
lady!" "Why would I want to spend time in class with this person,
who comes from such a different world—a world that, frankly, I
wish to know very little about?" The payoff is tremendous, however—for involving students from diverse backgrounds who hold
diverse perspectives and values greatly increases the richness of the
educational mix and accelerates and expands the domain of new
learning for everyone, including instructors.

Historically, students tried to correct gaps in the curriculum by
organizing activities on their own. At the Women's Network lunch
that Betty Cordell attended, the first young woman she spoke with
hated to go to class; little was happening there except aversive

conditioning. The second young woman made her selection of Exemplar based on what was missing at the state school. Students sitting around staring blankly like zombies was not her idea of a learning community. Yet we continue to plan and organize colleges as pieces and then wonder about the loss of the hallowed halls of ivy.

A populist-oriented institution is challenged in yet another manner with regard to its educational values and aspirations. In our colleges and universities, we are slow to change our procedures, policies, and curriculum to include reentry students. Yet many of our students are more than twenty-four years old. Along with this lack of acknowledgment of an entire segment of the student body, colleges and universities have often ignored the learning that occurs outside the classrooms, learning that is not extracurricular and goes beyond cocurricular activities.

Betty Cordell is a mature student returning to school for the first time in more than fifteen years. Betty has learned much during her first two days of school. Unfortunately, most of what she learned would not be discussed with her teacher, Professor Deffenbach, or with any other members of the faculty. Betty's basic assumptions about learning, about Exemplar, and about herself were strongly influenced by what she learned during just these first two days of school. Even the luncheon, designed to help her adjust to Exemplar, did not contradict the strong message that she did not belong, that she was too old to learn. If her feelings persist, she may decide that she has no business attending any institution of higher education.

As noted in the description of the early premodern institutions of America, extracurricular activities were historically to be the "making of the young man" or the "collegiate way" (Rudolph, 1962). Sports, drinking parties, and fraternities were to produce adults who would somehow be better leaders for our country than young men who had not participated in such activities. The supposed benefits for young women were less clear. The social aspects of activities and sororities would help a woman in her future role as social director or wife for the men who would become leaders. Little attention was given to the rest of her time at college.

What about a populist institution like Exemplar? Were people (young men, young women, older men and women, blacks, Hispanics, Asian Americans, disabled citizens) being "made" or shown the "way" in this setting? Given that populist students typically cannot afford to live on campus, the collegiate way must step aside for the commuter way, which requires an entirely different set of assumptions about what a collegiate institution can offer its students and about costs associated with providing a high-quality education. How the time is used during one's stay at a college is important, and the populist institution must do much more inside the classroom than the elitist institution, which typically has the student in residence.

Hattie Bishop, a community college administrator who helped in the preparation of this book, moved in with her students. She found students hungering for attention, in the form of nurturing and acceptance—acceptance of ideas, and hope for a structure on which to arrange ideas, time, and values. They were also hunting— even hurting—for a sense of belonging. Most of the students had never known a traditional family life. For example, one young woman had lived with her mother most of the time. Her mother had progressed through five divorces and six marriages before the young woman had finished high school. Her biological father, with whom she stayed on occasion, seemed like one in the parade of her mother's spouses rather than her father. He had also had an assortment of wives and live-in girlfriends.

This example may seem extreme, but it conveys the family turmoil that many students have experienced. At Bishop's college, more than 60 percent of the students came from families marred by substance abuse (primarily alcoholism and cocaine addiction). One of the effects of family turmoil, especially where substance abuse is involved, is that the young person must often take on the role of the adult in the family from a very early age. A great many of Bishop's students had never had the opportunity to be the dependent child and were therefore coming to college without the skills or insights needed to learn the adult role properly.

During a weekend seminar with thirty-one of these students, Hattie Bishop learned that only two students reported having had a stable childhood in a supportive family free of physical, sexual, and substance abuse. These students were attempting, through cocurricular activities, to replace what they had not had. They knew they wanted something, but too often they did not know what that something was. The programs designed by the college often failed to meet this hungering. Faculty members, absorbed in their own discipline areas and problems, were not addressing the needs of the students for mentoring and nonclassroom contact.

What should a consultant to Exemplar recommend for improving the institution's quality? If Exemplar were a successful populist institution doing an effective job of meeting the needs of its students, what would its primary characteristics be? How might it do an even better job? My premise is that quality and access must be fully integrated as concepts, rather than being considered antagonistic. A new approach that acknowledged this essential unity could mean that what a student at Exemplar learns during the first few days is explicitly discussed and is acknowledged as important. Exemplar faculty and administrators must make it clear that students' assumptions about learning are part of the institution and that Exemplar wants to convert the negative messages of the first few days to a message of acceptance. If Exemplar cannot change its hidden curriculum because change is slow, the hidden curriculum can at least be made explicit.

In addition, the Exemplar faculty and administration can acknowledge the students' fears and struggles. The research of Mary Belenky and her colleagues (Belenky, Clinchy, Goldberger, and Tarule, 1986) indicates that a nonresidential student's initial difficulties may be just the tip of the iceberg. Family support at the start of the return to school often evaporates. One woman reported that "her angry husband had first hidden, then burned her schoolbooks" (p. 79). Men have similar difficulties as reentry students. The entire phenomenon could be studied and used as part of the learning process. For a large percentage of our population, returning to school has become part of adult development. The halls of academe can provide a learning process that is inclusive of all students, non-resident and resident, as well as all other members of the collegiate community, be they faculty, administrators, staff, or board members.

Key Points

1. Populism in the United States arose to meet two challenges: practicality and equity. While high-status institutions in nineteenth-century America served the academic needs of the elite, the emerging state-supported colleges and universities were addressing more practical needs. Ever since, the battle has raged between elitism and populism.

2. With elitism and populism established as conflicting values, most colleges and universities, needing to address both, found themselves with a confused vision and no clear way to set priorities. Individualism became more important than concern for society or community. While the high-status, elitist-oriented institutions focused on preparing leaders for society, the lower-status, populist-oriented institutions focused on helping graduates achieve personal goals and climb the socioeconomic ladder.

3. In many ways, the tension between elitism and populism in pre–World War II American higher education was resolved as the system of community colleges grew. These new institutions took much of the pressure off four-year undergraduate institutions both public and private. In the emerging post-modern era, however, four-year colleges and universities must

themselves confront the issues of access and quality, for the community colleges can no longer cope exclusively with the unmet educational needs of the growing nontraditional population.

4. As a product of the modern era, the populist perspective tends to emphasize large institutional size and uniformity of practices to meet the needs of the general population in an equitable manner. From the populist perspective, institutional boundaries are critical. Primary attention is given to admission standards and evaluation of student performance. The nature and quality of education at populist-oriented colleges and universities is not given as much thought.

5. From the populist perspective, leadership is expressed through carefully constructed and managed systems, rather than by individuals (a more elitist approach). Faculty members become instructional managers of large classrooms that are dominated by standardized textbooks, advanced technologies, and uniform testing procedures. Administrators become cost-conscious managers of large bureaucratic systems who hold together highly specialized and discipline-based subsystems of the institution.

6. From the populist perspective, the capital of collegiate institutions resides in the buildings and financial assets of the school, and educational values focus on career preparation and advancement.

Chapter Seven

The Beleaguered Perspective

For many leaders of contemporary colleges and universities, the interplay between quality and access is a moot issue, for they are fighting for the very existence of their schools. The beleaguered perspective is not a chosen perspective, nor does it typically exist when someone first enters the arena of postsecondary education. No collegiate leader intends to create or manage a beleaguered institution, just as no monarch intends to preside over a beleaguered castle. We must therefore appreciate that the issues of quality and access recede in the deliberations of besieged colleges and universities—not because members don't care but because they are distracted by other matters.

Collegiate institutions have always struggled to survive. Many colleges and universities founded in the nineteenth century are no longer in existence; by contrast, most set up in the twentieth century are still around. Public support for higher education, in terms of tax dollars and number of students enrolled in colleges and universities, is much greater now than at any time in history.

Yet as the century approaches its end, we find that many of our collegiate institutions are in serious trouble, and there is little prospect that this condition will change in the near future. Funding higher education through state lotteries and student loan programs reflects short-term and perhaps ultimately counterproductive strategies for sustaining our institutions. Colleges and universities have become beleaguered due to inadequate support. But they have also become beleaguered by failing to respond to the challenges (and potentials) of the postmodern era into which society is now moving. Thus, as we begin to define strategies for addressing the needs of beleaguered institutions, we must first look at the post-modern conditions these colleges and universities now face.

Exemplar from the Beleaguered Perspective

In setting the stage for describing and discussing the beleaguered per-spective, I return to Exemplar College/University. It is not hard to imagine in this day and age that Exemplar is beleaguered, for it is a school that is hard for students, doesn't have much money, and is viewed negatively by many community leaders. Exemplar's presi-dent, Kevin Gravitz, spends most of his time, like many college and university presidents, struggling with the triple problem of enroll-ment, funding, and public support.

Scene: President Gravitz's Home, Fourth Week of the Fall Term

It is late in the evening. The fall semester is still young, but it is already a source of considerable stress for Kevin Gravitz and other leaders at this beleaguered institution. Kevin settles into bed. This has been a long day, but he has looked forward to reading a bit this evening. In a now-dated ("I never have time to read!") major national report, the following quotation catches his eye: "How an institution's mission statement is written and used may well express the priorities of the academic community, including that of aca-demic advising. On the one hand, mission statements may be used to guide the direction and planning activities of an institution; on the other, they may be rarely reviewed or considered at all. Thoughtful administrators and their advisory boards and staffs take responsibility for assuring that the institution's mission statement is used as an overarching rationale for the educational enterprise they are charged to lead" (Winston and Associates, 1984, p. 67).

Gravitz takes off his glasses and rubs his eyes. This last sentence is a real stinger. "When I was a professor of developmental psychology, I don't think I ever read our mission statement, except perhaps when I came in for the job interview. Yet here I am getting upset because none of my colleagues at Exemplar seems to build on our mission statement when they're doing some planning. They probably haven't even read that document in the past five years! Is all of this mission statement stuff just so much wasted time? Should we really have any kind of a statement to guide our planning, or should we do without? Are we really that chaotic?"

Gravitz goes back to reading: "Just as an institution may state that its mission is undergraduate liberal arts education, it can also state that it endorses and emphasizes academic and personal development of students and that it strives to facilitate educational growth through advising and programming activities designed to be responsive to the needs of students. Mission statements are, after all, usually written by the institutional leaders responsible for their implementation" (Winston and Associates, 1984, p. 67). At that moment, Gravitz begins, somewhat against his own will, to reflect on all the dreams he had for Exemplar as its educational leader. "Educational leader!" He wasn't a leader, he mused. He was a used-idea salesman. "Maybe not even a good one, if enrollment trends are any measure. Does it really feel bad to sell used ideas—not even good used ideas? If I could, what would I want to be selling?"

Gravitz returns to the book: "While it is one thing to prepare a written mission statement to guide an institution's approach, it is another to put that statement into operation. Although mission statements should specify the values of the institution and serve as guides to the development of programs that are consistent with those values, it is sometimes quite difficult to bring such ideal consistency into reality through the operating policies of the organization" (Winston and Associates, 1984, p. 67).

"Difficult! Difficult indeed." Gravitz puts his glasses back on and thinks about tomorrow's meetings. His development officer has been telling him for some time that the Exemplar mission statement wasn't marketable. What makes a collegiate institution marketable? Should we focus on marketing as the major purpose of our school? The dean of admissions was saying much the same thing. To get new students, the curriculum at Exemplar has to be more relevant to today's students. "Well, at least these members of my staff are reading the catalogue. Does our mission statement and curriculum need to be 'relevant' to the faculty, the board, or even the admissions officer? What makes a statement relevant? What would happen if I told development and admissions to market us *as we are*? Do they know what we really do here, and could they make it sell to donors and students?"

Gravitz is suddenly jerked back to reality. What was he going to do about Saunders, the meddlesome board member? How could he sell Saunders's concept of a college? "We could certainly use some of his money, but so far he's given only peanuts to the college." Gravitz continues: "I don't think I can stand one more committee meeting on the college's mission statement. A statement that would please the development office, admissions office, and Saunders would not be acceptable to the faculty—or to me, for that matter. I seem to be making the mission statement into a political arena where all parties are 'satisfied' and the statement is 'acceptable.' *Acceptable*—what a lukewarm word." He sighs. "Maybe I should try selling cars or something," he concludes, with a touch of seriousness. Even if Gravitz could come up with a widely acceptable statement, he knows that Exemplar as a whole would pay little attention to it. Rather than read further, he turns out the light, hoping to erase the feelings of discontent and failure from his mind and heart with sleep.

The Postmodern Beleaguered Perspective

I now analyze the same dimensions of organizational life as in Chapters Five and Six; here, however, I look at them from the perspective of postmodern institutions that are in trouble, unable to cope with the transformations that the era requires.

Size and Complexity

Many beleaguered postsecondary educational institutions—especially those that are state- or community-supported—began with a strong populist mission and a commitment to serving as many people in the local or statewide community as possible. Many state universities and some community colleges are now included on this growing list. For these institutions, rapid expansion in size during the halcyon days of the late 1960s and early 1970s led to several major problems of growth that are shared by many large modern organizations as they enter a postmodern era.

First, large beleaguered colleges and universities need extensive integrative services to hold together the many diverse, specialized, and often warring factions of the institution. Figure 7.1 illustrates the common relationship between institutional size and age, on the one hand, and levels of institutional effectiveness, on the other. As organizations become larger, a greater proportion of the total resources of the institution must typically be devoted to integrative services (coordination, monitoring, personnel services, finances, and so forth) that do not directly relate to the product or service

Figure 7.1. The Dilemma of Growth and Age.

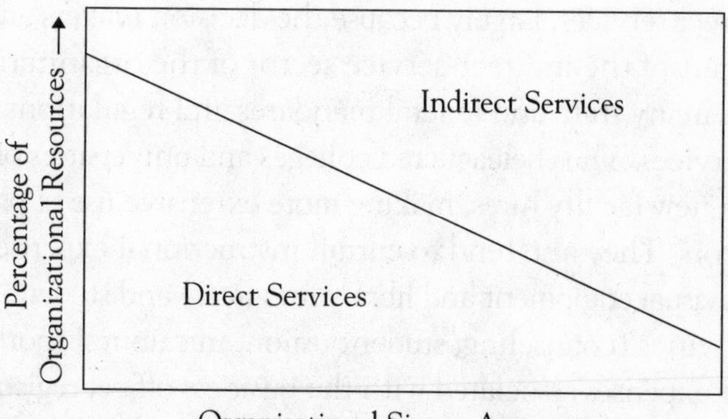

Source: Bergquist (1993), p. 49.

being offered by the organization. A decreasing proportion is devoted to direct services (teaching, supervision, student advising, research and scholarship in the case of elite-oriented institutions). Very large and very old organizations (such as corporations, utilities, and governmental agencies) often devote more than 90 percent of their total resources (people, money, time, energy, technology, space, and so forth) to integrative services or intermediate services (such as sales, marketing, and promotion), with the remaining 10 percent or less of the resources being devoted to direct services.

The large (and aging) educational institution is often caught in this integration-versus-differentiation trap. These institutions often grew precipitously during the 1960s and 1970s, then, in the 1980s, experienced budget cutbacks and the public's demands for greater efficiency. Unfortunately, most of these colleges and universities had already built large bureaucracies to serve the indirect integrative needs of the rapid-growth years. It is not unusual for many contemporary colleges and universities to expend at least 50 percent of their resources on indirect services. Administrative overhead now runs very high, and educational institutions, like most other modern organizations, are often reluctant to cut back on administrative services to reduce costs.

Facing this problem, most large modern organizations tend to cut back on resources devoted to direct services before cutting back on indirect services, largely because the decision makers are themselves part of the indirect-service sector of the organization and because many state and federal mandates and regulations require these services. Thus beleaguered colleges and universities often cut back on new faculty hires, making more extensive use of part-time instructors. They also tend to curtail instructional expenses (such as audiovisual equipment and library resources) and student services and activities (counseling, student union, intramural sports). The indirect expenses associated with the business office, registrar, personnel office, administrative support staff, and other bureaucracies often remain relatively immune to cutbacks, though there are many exceptions—primarily colleges and universities that have been in existence less than thirty years. As a rule, schools add indirect services slowly and later find them impossible to eliminate. Thus, as the school grows older, indirect expenses increase. Much as in the case of biological growth, maturation, and death, institutional integration (indirect services) requires an increasingly large percentage of the school's total resources as it grows older. Death of an organism or institution tends to occur when there are no longer sufficient resources to ward off the inevitable disintegration.

As a result of the inefficiency of beleaguered state-supported institutions, the original populist mission of these schools is now in jeopardy, for often these colleges and universities can survive (in the face of reduced financial support from legislatures and community governments) only by increasing tuition and related student fees. In many instances, out-of-state fees for state-supported colleges and universities are comparable to or higher than tuition fees for so-called independent (private) colleges and universities in the region. Even in-state tuition for some state-supported collegiate institutions has risen to the level of private school fees.

In the case of the Professional School of Psychology, the current tuition level for master's-level students is approximately $6,000 per year. Master's-level students at the nearby California State University campuses are paying almost $4,000 per year. If this is a Cal State student's second master's-level degree, the fee will double to more than $8,000 per year. How can the tuition at a private school like PSP be competitive with or even lower than the tuition at a public institution supported by tax dollars? Part of the answer is that it costs PSP, a much younger and smaller school, about $5,000 per year to educate each master's-level student, whereas the state university, much larger and older, requires about twice that amount. PSP need not charge as high a tuition because its costs are much lower than those for a comparable program in the state university system.

The provision of lower-cost services is a difficult challenge for state universities (and other beleaguered colleges and universities) as they try to improve educational quality through smaller classes, greater faculty access, and more substantial student services. If they fail, small private institutions such as PSP will soon take away their students and their credibility.

Leaders of the California State University system are not to be criticized for the problems they face. They inherited these problems from their predecessors in the state legislature and in the California postsecondary educational system who advocated indiscriminate growth in the size and complexity of their educational institutions. There are perhaps no more important decisions that an organizational leader can make than those associated with growth. It is tempting to ameliorate organizational problems by seeking expansion; yet growth itself can cause some of the institution's most difficult and enduring problems.

Private colleges and universities that are beleaguered often were founded either with an elitist mandate or a populist mission to serve a particular underserved population. The problem of bureaucracy and efficiency is usually not as profound for these independent colleges and universities, given that they have usually been run for many years on a financial shoestring and typically did not overexpand during the halcyon 1960s and 1970s.

A corporate leader recently told me that his organization had offered to provide technical (administrative, financial, and personnel) assistance to small, struggling liberal arts colleges in his region. These private colleges graciously accepted the assistance, and several of the most successful and creative managers from the corporation were sent out to them. When these managers returned to the corporation, they reported that they had been warmly received and that their ideas had been openly embraced. However, they also found that they had very little to offer the leaders of these colleges, who were engaged in much more creative financing than the corporation and could "squeeze more out of a dollar" than any of the corporate managers. The managers found that they learned much more than they taught, and most sat back in amazement, witnessing effective organizational leadership in action (see also Peck, 1985). They helped the colleges by letting their leaders know that they were better managers than even the collegiate leaders realized.

Size problems at beleaguered private colleges and universities are often of the schools' own doing. Like their public counterparts, private colleges and universities, even the small ones, tend to be greatly compartmentalized. Compartmentalization tends to occur primarily in the academic sector and is usually associated with the isolation of the academic disciplines and professions. Each academic department or division establishes its own turf and erects its own protective walls. The result is often an overabundance of mid-level academic administrators (deans, associate deans, department heads and chairs) to provide integration in this highly differentiated environment, leaving little room for institutionwide innovation or creative responsiveness to change or crisis.

With so little coordination between programs, the center cannot hold. Moving beyond distribution requirements in the construction of a general education program is often strongly resisted. The mid-level administrators themselves typically devote most of their energy to protecting the turf of the faculty they represent rather than bridging the gap between departments, divisions, and schools. They are consequently unable to create courses and programs that meet campuswide needs and interests, and they are often hampered in reducing costs associated with instructional redundancy and overlap.

Although all postmodern organizations tend to be fragmented and inconsistent in form and structure, beleaguered colleges and universities are often especially so, making it even harder for these schools to provide adequate integrative services (such as institutional planning, institutional research, personnel services, and financial services). This accelerates the movement to even more integrative services, resulting in lower efficiency and higher costs per student.

Why is the beleaguered institution fragmented? First, it typically faces multiple governance forums, each of which commands the attention of certain campus constituencies and makes a valid claim to legitimacy on campus. On the one hand, we have the formal administrative structures of the college or university, which were dominant at the founding of the institution if it began with a populist mission. The academic and nonacademic administrators rightly expect to govern the institution and work with the appropriate overseeing board (trustees, directors, regents) in creating and implementing school policy, procedures, and goals.

A second governance group also has legitimacy in the beleaguered institution, though its power is on the wane in many schools. This second group is the faculty, especially the faculty senate (or other representative body) and its many subcommittees and forms of representation on other governing bodies. Built on the old collegial model (Bergquist, 1992), faculty governance in the beleaguered college or university is likely to take on a rather protective stance, being concerned primarily with salaries, benefits, tenure, and full-time versus part-time status. The beleaguered faculty governance system is less likely to be concerned with purely academic issues, such as curriculum, academic standards, and student counseling, than faculty governance groups in elitist colleges and universities (where they are particularly strong). Faculty governance concern for educational matters is even likely to be stronger in more managerially oriented institutions that are dominated by either the populist or the expedient perspective.

Because they tend to be protectionist, faculty governance groups in beleaguered institutions are often in direct competition with a third governance group, faculty unions. Based as they are in the negotiating culture, faculty unions tend to be strong and often quite aggressive in the beleaguered institution. Concerns for job security, adequate salaries and benefits, and acceptable working conditions rightly dominate the attention of faculty union leaders in these institutions. In some instances, we even find alliances between faculty government (collegial) and faculty unions (negotiating).

Typically, the faculty union has much credibility, and the beleaguered institution's administration often plays directly into the hands of union leaders by attending primarily to nonacademic, fiscal matters (cost cutting) in attempting to save the institution from further decline, if not demise. Ironically, the beleaguered institution is likely to be helped more by administrators who attend to academic matters, such as recruiting new student populations, better serving existing student populations, and rebuilding institutional reputation (marketing, public relations, lobbying), than by those who attend to issues that alienate faculty and union leaders.

A fourth governance group that contributes to the fragmentation is representative of the developmental culture (Bergquist, 1992). People working in faculty, curriculum, and student and administrative development tend not to be very visible, yet these people are sometimes highly influential and potentially of great value to the beleaguered institution. People in this fourth group are often rather naive and overly optimistic about the ability to transform a beleaguered institution into one that is more expedient (even if it can't return to its elitist or populist roots or move to a more unified stance). Naïveté and optimism may be particularly appropriate for leaders of an institution that is beleaguered, for they are likely to feel powerless under these difficult conditions and must break out of deeply embedded patterns of helplessness and hopelessness.

Even though the existence of these four governance models and the four cultures that underlie them is inevitable and can be highly beneficial in any contemporary collegiate institution, they strike the leaders of a beleaguered institution as disruptive—particularly when they address the central issues of quality and access. These leaders often perceive themselves as ineffective in dealing with the diverse values, change strategies, and needs of these four groups. Given all the other problems their school faces, beleaguered leaders are likely to dismiss dialogues across these cultures regarding quality and access as irrelevant or as a luxury that need not be indulged in at present rather than as essential to the survival of the school.

Beleaguered collegiate leaders are usually unable to articulate a metastrategy that will bring these four groups together to work their way out of the current mess (Schön, 1983, 1987) and to find a new and distinctive mode for uniting quality and access in the institution. They are also unable to articulate a single vision or mission for the institution that is acceptable and inspiring to each of the four groups. Thus, beleaguered leaders like Kevin Gravitz often imagine themselves as stymied by a number of immovable forces. They regard quality and access as incompatible (and dismiss them as unattainable anyway). These men and women often look forward to their own retirement or transfer to a less beleaguered institution.

The fragmentation and inconsistency of beleaguered institutions are further exacerbated by the typical existence of both "regular" daytime programs that serve traditional college students and special "extension" programs that serve nontraditional students, usually in the evening and on weekends. Traditional courses are frequently offered by the full-time core faculty of the college or university, whereas nontraditional courses are taught by part-time contract faculty. Furthermore, there are usually two sets of administrators. Those running the nontraditional program are typically younger and more innovative than those administering the traditional programs. The nontraditional administrators may be employed part-time at the college or university and frequently, like part-time faculty, feel that they are marginal to the institution and its inner workings.

The old and the new, the traditional and nontraditional don't mix very often or very effectively in the typical beleaguered institution. Traditional faculty, administrators, and students usually emphasize quality and view the "other" programs, faculty, administrators, and students as temporary "add-ons" to the "real" programs of the college or university. These unwelcomed and supposedly temporary additions are needed only to raise money or increase public support for the institution and rarely relate directly to or influence the substance of the mission and long-term vision of the school.

Even the faculty, administrators, students, and alumni of a college or university of populist origins tend to become highly elitist when facing the prospect of an innovative new program that effectively meets the needs of an underserved population (such as middle-aged women returning to school, retooling business executives, or retired men and women participating in an "elderhostel" program). The leaders of a beleaguered institution, who should welcome these fresh new ventures and view them as a partial solution to their problems, often instead adopt a defensive and counterproductive posture, and the institution ends up even more fragmented. Policies and procedures regarding old and new programs become ever more inconsistent and more isolated, quality and access are viewed as even more incompatible, and the beleaguered college or university is that much more in need of costly integrative services (a provost, an academic vice president) to hold it together.

Mission and Boundaries

For Kevin Gravitz, as president of a beleaguered institution, the problem of the mission statement is of a different order from that of men and women who preside over elitist or populist institutions. Gravitz must grapple directly with the difficulty of translating or reformulating a mission statement that will enable his institution to survive. The process of redefining boundaries and rethinking mission statements is usually painful—as Gravitz knows all too well. Typically, most beleaguered college and university presidents, vice presidents, deans, department chairs, and faculty members are so deeply embedded in the problems associated with institutional survival that they have little time to think about these broader issues of purpose and mission unless it is to mount a new promotional campaign that will bring in more students.

Unless Gravitz is blessed with extraordinary wisdom and

patience, he is likely to think about the mission of his school not in terms of quality and access but rather in terms of marketability and cost. He is also likely to attribute the discrepancy between word and action at Exemplar to the fact that not everyone there accepts the current mission statement (or perhaps is even aware of it). Frequently, leaders can't even agree on an alternative statement of the institution's distinctive purpose. The statement is intentionally vague where campus constituencies cannot agree—another victim of fragmentation. Gravitz is concerned by that ambiguity. If a mission statement is related directly to action, it is open to inspection. People at the institution can be held accountable for consistent and successful movement toward the goals expressed in the statement. Collegiate presidents like Kevin Gravitz recognize the power and potential threat inherent in a clear statement of mission.

Gravitz and beleaguered faculty, students, and parents (like Joseph Chung) have experienced and identified problems involving the Exemplar mission statement that are shared by virtually all collegiate institutions, beleaguered or not. The situation is just more difficult in the beleaguered institution. With the possible exception of colleges and universities operated by churches, societies, or foundations with a specific, focused mission, all institutions of higher learning find it very difficult to write mission statements that provide both direction for the institution and courage to enable the institution to move in that direction with decisiveness and force. At an even deeper level, these institutions have generally given very little consideration through their mission statement to the basic issues of quality and access or the relationships between these two basic guiding principles.

Boundaries in a beleaguered institution—as in most postmodern organizations—are unclear. There are multiple statuses and entry points for students, faculty, and administrators. Diffuse and ambiguous boundaries allow chaos to reign, which in turn provides the opportunity for profound change. Cohen and Marsh (1974) speak of the artful use of "garbage pails" in collegiate institutions. These pails (what chaos theorists identify as "strange attractors") are provocative, complex proposals or issues that we throw out to a faculty or campus committee to distract them for many months in argument and debate. In that way, we can quietly get on with our own work, implementing a new program unilaterally, without having to worry about interference from members of the distracted committee or college community.

Ironically, beleaguered institutions are potentially open to change in many other ways as well. Michael Rossman (1984), a leader of the free-speech movement at Berkeley during the 1960s, notes that often we can get more done by ignoring the formal governance structures of the school than by trying to get formal approval from beleaguered committees and bureaucrats. If we simply go ahead with what we want to do, the committees and bureaucrats must themselves work slowly and painfully through the massive structures that they have set up in order to get us to stop doing what we are doing. Typically, by the time they work through the structures (which were initially set up to block our unilateral actions), we have already completed our work or project. At this point, we can move on to something else or show the committee members and bureaucrats that our project has worked very effectively, has taken little money, and is loved by the students. Put more simply, in a beleaguered institution, with minimally effective communication, it is often much easier to beg for forgiveness after taking an action than to ask for permission to take the action in the first place.

Also ironically, while beleaguered institutions tend to lower the boundaries of student enrollment and readily shift the institution's mission, the boundaries between units within the institution tend to remain strong. As a result, the beleaguered college or university becomes more fragmented, like many postmodern organizations in our society. Each faculty member and department separates from the whole to do what is best for the individual or department rather than the institution. With each segment of the college or university divided in this way, the institution no longer has leaders or followers, just separate parts. Difficult decisions are avoided. Budget cuts, if necessary, are made across the board rather than selectively in weak areas. Levine (1985) says of fragmentation, "Not only does it deprive colleges and universities of their dreams," but it also "robs them of their reasons for being" (p. 8). The price, according to Levine, is quality. The concepts of purpose, mission, and learning get lost.

Leadership

Leadership in a beleaguered environment is obviously very difficult. In the beleaguered college or university, as in other postmodern organizations, leadership is situational. A leader can't rely on any one style or mode of leadership but must instead shift styles and modes depending on the state of the institution at any point in time and, even more specifically, depending on the constituency with which he or she is interacting. This makes leading very difficult, for the leader cannot behave consistently or predictably. Shifts in style and mode are in turn often interpreted as manipulative, insincere, ambivalent, or simply wishy-washy.

Even as we see this type of leadership becoming more prevalent in large beleaguered federal bureaucracies, and even in the U.S. presidency, the college and university president of our time is often unfairly portrayed as inconsistent or even unprincipled. Dorothy Kirkwood, as administrative vice president of Exemplar, became very frustrated with President Gravitz because of his lack of courage in shifting professional development funds to the general fund of his institution. How many other collegiate leaders are caught in a similar bind and are forced to make similar seemingly unprincipled decisions?

Other members of a beleaguered institution face the same kinds of challenges. Faculty are rarely respected as leaders by their colleagues or their students. Earlier (Bergquist, 1992), I wrote about a

faculty member at a beleaguered university who described his institution as "sociofugal" (borrowing from Robert Sommer's concepts
of social space), meaning that all the dynamics of his university
tend to propel faculty, students, and administrators away from campus. The university itself is practically deserted. Faculty and students spend as little time on campus as possible because there is
nothing there that they particular admire or respect and because
they have more important things to attend to (including tuition-
paying jobs for students and moonlighting jobs for faculty). How
can leadership be nurtured or exerted in such a vacuum? Administrators have no more than a caretaker role to play in a sociofugal
institution, and both faculty and students are likely to find other
venues in which to exert their leadership.

Capital and Educational Values

The nature of capital and educational values in beleaguered collegiate institutions is quite easy to describe. Typically, these institutions have neither capital nor enduring values. Their only guiding
principle is continuing their existence. With regard to capital, the
beleaguered institution usually has neither an abundance of tangible assets (such as land, buildings, or endowment) nor an abundance of less tangible assets (such as reputation or demonstrated
quality of teaching and learning). The assets that are present have
often been mortgaged, literally or figuratively, in order for the institution to survive. Land is traded off. Buildings are sold or sublet.
Endowments are depleted, and, as in the case of Kevin Gravitz,
even dollars that are encumbered get used illegally or at least inappropriately to shore up a crumbling financial edifice.

Psychologically, the beleaguered college or university will often
mortgage whatever reputation and credibility it has left by picking
up programs with low credibility, by substituting new student enrollment for the mission of the institution, or by instituting a massive
tuition increase. I have known several beleaguered college and uni-

versity presidents who have lived out the Faustian drama by selling the soul of their institution to the highest bidder. Unfortunately, these institutions are rarely challenged by regional accrediting agencies, even though these agencies are supposedly in the business of policing just this sort of betrayal (Marchese, 1991). Why do they tend to miss these acts? Usually because the beleaguered college or university is an old and established institution. Regional accrediting officials know that if they call attention to the wrongdoing of these institutions, they could bring about their demise, and no one wants to take responsibility for bringing down a good old (and long-accredited) institution.

Accredited colleges and universities of long standing rarely lose their approval (though they may on rare occasions be placed quietly on probation for several years). Rather, new colleges and universities, which are likely to be expedient or unified, are frequently denied accreditation in the first place. Understandably, there seems to be much less concern about shutting down a college or university that has never achieved accreditation than about killing off an institution that has been accredited for many years.

The real issue for many contemporary collegiate institutions is how to respond to the postmodern conditions in a creative and effective manner. Many collegiate institutions haven't responded effectively to the postmodern world, and that lack of response has left them beleaguered. Others have responded inconsistently, without a clear mission or sense of purpose; they have become expedient and may soon become beleaguered. Chapter Eight looks at institutions that have chosen or been forced to become expedient.

Key Points

1. For many leaders of contemporary colleges and universities, the interplay between quality and access is a moot issue, for they are fighting for the very existence of their school.
2. The beleaguered perspective is not a chosen perspective. Rather, it becomes prominent when a college or university

faces problems of declining enrollment, inadequate funding, and diminishing public support—all common problems in our emerging postmodern world.

3. The beleaguered college or university often experiences problems associated with unbridled growth decades earlier (typically during the 1960s and 1970s). Functions in the school have become differentiated, specialized, and hence fragmented. As a result, considerable attention must be devoted to integrative, coordinating, and bridging functions; these in turn divert the scarce resources of the school away from direct services (teaching, advising, library services, and so forth), further reducing the institution's capacity to address changing student and community needs.

4. From the beleaguered perspective, mission statements often become the battleground for competing internal factions, representing different collegiate cultures. Even when agreement on mission is reached, it can rarely be operationalized in a beleaguered institution. Instead, the mission statement becomes rhetoric that masks the underlying fragmentation and visionless status of the school and its leaders.

Chapter Eight

The Expedient Perspective

The expedient perspective is a recent development in American higher education. Whereas postsecondary education is noted more for its conservative posture than for its visionary stance on most educational matters, some contemporary colleges and universities have become bastions of innovation and experimentation, and their administrators, faculty, and staff have led the way in terms of reform. Unfortunately, in many instances, that is all that one finds at these institutions—a willingness to try out new ideas (in keeping with John Dewey's legacy of learning by doing) but not necessarily a willingness to relate these ideas to the mission of the institution or to the issues of quality and access. Many expedient leaders have never bothered to determine how the new ideas will be assessed in order to select those that will become an integral part of the institution and those that will remain peripheral or short-lived.

Clark Kerr (1991) calls this perspective "survival drift." He observes that many liberal arts colleges without high status and large endowments have begun to resemble comprehensive collegiate institutions with the introduction of vocational programs in an effort to sustain their operations. He notes that the effectiveness of the president (and board of trustees) of such an institution is critical to its success—more so than for more stable and better established colleges and universities, which seem to be more dependent on the quality of their faculty. Kerr also points to the institution's capacity to respond to shifting community needs and its capacity to mount a limited number of successful programs as crucial to its success and reputation. I agree with his assessment and would cite the capacity of the expedient institution to cross traditional boundaries between educational and noneducational institutions as also crucial to its success and viability.

One factor that is often lacking in the expedient perspective is a systematic and sustained concern for quality and access. Whereas expedient administrators or faculty members are likely to advocate both quality and access at various times, they usually bounce around from program to program, rarely building a solid base of support for a particular concept of either quality or access. I have found this pattern of expediency in many colleges and universities that have been very successful in obtaining outside funding for new program initiatives—though there are notable exceptions, such as Alverno College and The Evergreen State College, which have built new programs on existing structures and priorities.

In my own work with several national higher education associations during the 1970s and early 1980s, I think we were guilty of being too expedient in our planning for new program offerings. We were often overly influenced by the fluctuating priorities of foundations and the shifting funding patterns of federal agencies. Gary Quehl, president of the Council of Independent Colleges and the Council for the Advancement and Support of Education, was a notable exception. He consistently built one program on top of another and insisted that each new program initiative link in a coherent and systematic manner with other current and contemplated program initiatives.

As in the discussion of other perspectives, the examination of the expedient perspective will begin with a minidrama at Exemplar College/University. I will then assume the expedient perspective in looking for ways in which Exemplar can effectively address its financial and recruitment problems.

Exemplar from the Expedient Perspective

In setting the stage for this vignette, I will introduce three additional actors—Joan Broadhead, Jacques Rochambeaux, and Joshua Wheat—all faculty members at Exemplar.

Joan Broadhead, assistant professor of business administration. Joan Broadhead was a moderately successful midlevel executive at a large computer manufacturing company. She decided to leave the corporation because she saw little career advancement for herself (glass ceiling and all), especially when the company ran into financial difficulties. On a more personal level, she felt that life in the fast lane of corporate work was not for her. Joan wanted to find a slower pace for herself and her family and had always wanted to teach.

This is Joan's second year at Exemplar. Her background is primarily in marketing and public relations, though she teaches courses in many other fields (personnel, organizational behavior, strategic planning) that are not specifically her areas of specialization. Joan must teach in these many different fields because her department is growing rapidly but is unable to recruit people with both a strong background in business and good teaching skills. Joan feels overworked and underappreciated by her more traditional academic colleagues.

Jacques Rochambeaux, associate professor of art. "Bo," as everyone calls him, is a study in constant motion, both in words and in physical energy. As an artist, Bo is legendary for his productivity and his imagination, which ranges across several styles and modalities. He is currently famous for his massive ceramic abstractions (the kind that fill whole rooms) and huge kinetic sculptures that exhibit wild patterns of movement. Some of his reviewers praise his work as "provocative"; others wish he would be more attentive to the quality of the final result. As a faculty member, Bo exhibits similar inconsistency, making comments that are at times creative and at other times disjointed and irrelevant.

Joshua Wheat, professor of English. Joshua is a nationally known expert in the teaching of writing to traditional college-age students. At this point, he spends much of his time consulting at colleges and universities that wish to upgrade their writing programs and make writing a more developmental experience. On campus, Wheat has become a champion for interdisciplinary education and teaching innovations, working with the assistant to the dean on teaching innovations at Exemplar. Wheat is alternatively encouraged and discouraged by Exemplar's debate on interdisciplinary versus discipline-focused education.

Scene: Faculty Lounge, Sixth Week of Fall Term

At 10:10 in the morning, Burke Deffenbach's class is over, and he goes in search of his morning cup of coffee. In the faculty lounge he bumps into two of his colleagues, Joan Broadhead and Gretchen Karpoff. "Well, Burke," says Joan, "do you think this curriculum committee stuff will be a waste of time?" She launches into a discourse that is familiar to Burke, mixing arguments about efficient decision making with her assertion that an education should ultimately be "marketable, manageable, and mathematical." The three *M*'s replace the three *R*'s for Joan Broadhead. It is an argument that she has trotted out often during her short tenure at Exemplar, and Burke feels slightly irritated at having to listen yet again to the recurrent conflict. It seems to have begun long before Joan was hired—perhaps it began on the day when Exemplar hired its first business professor. Any sense that this will be a better academic year than usual is soon squashed under the burden of Joan Broadhead's shallow rhetoric.

Gretchen listens to this recitation with discomfort. She agrees with part of what Joan is saying; however, other parts have little to do with her view of education. Could someone like Joan Broadhead hear her plea for education that is developmental as well as functional? Can Burke Deffenbach hear some ideas for a new kind of education, or will the committee again be served up his old proposal for the "heritage of ideas"? Will the curriculum committee work together in a process of mutuality and growth, or will committee members repeat the arguments that have been a part of this institution for decades? Gretchen thinks about arguing with Joan, but before she can decide, the one-sided conversation breaks up, and the other professors leave the faculty lounge.

At the far end of the lounge, Bo Rochambeaux is holding forth on creativity and postmodern art as they apply to current Exemplar students, who are (like many of Bo's faculty and administrative colleagues) still stuck in the modern era. As always, Bo's words tumble out in long, emotional bursts, punctuated by his waving arms and bobbing eyebrows. Joshua Wheat listens with half an ear, his attention to Bo competing with thoughts about his own scheduling problems. Joshua has to find a way to balance his Exemplar duties with the requests he receives for speeches and consultation. Right now, Bo's familiar artistic sermon is both a comforting ritual and an irritating distraction. This is, however, the faculty lounge, and Joshua forces himself to relax.

A few minutes later, Joshua is back in his crowded office, setting up his spring travel schedule. His new teaching assistant seems well qualified, so he thinks he will risk letting her teach three full weeks of class in the spring. Joshua feels a twinge of guilt at the thought of letting a TA do what a good teacher should do himself, but he is drawn to the invitations before him. To speak at such a major conference, to organize the writing program at such a prestigious university, to sit on a federal endowment panel—these are opportunities too good to pass up. Joshua knows without asking that the Exemplar community will approve: the publicity value will make the public affairs office very happy.

Historical Background

Because the expedient perspective is much more contemporary than the elitist, populist, and beleaguered perspectives, I will construct the history not around the recitation of events and forces from the past but rather around a more contemporary story. In the early 1980s, I traveled to a moderately well known state university in the southeastern United States to attend a conference. The state and the community in which this university is located are not known for their support of postsecondary education; I was therefore surprised that a major conference on innovation in American higher education was being held at this university.

When I arrived, I was taken on a tour of the university's facilities and given an overview of its programs. I was overwhelmed and came immediately to understand why it had been selected as the site for the conference. The leaders of the university had begun a program or created a facility for practically every major innovation that had been introduced in American higher education over the preceding decade. I was shown the autotutorial lab and the new computer literacy lab and the fully automated student study skills lab and the foreign-language laboratory. Faculty members described their new and comprehensive faculty development program, their writing-across-the-curriculum and critical thinking programs, and their major initiative to bring women back to campus for age- and gender-sensitive orientation programs that build on life planning and experience assessment activities.

I could go on and on listing the new programs and resources being offered at this somewhat obscure institution. One question that came immediately to my mind (and that of my colleagues from elsewhere in North America), however, was this: how did this university acquire all of these resources? The answer came consistently from everyone I talked to: the president was a visionary and a great fundraiser. He would wander the United States, attending conferences and visiting innovative schools, then bring ideas back to campus, where he would invite a design team to come up with an adaptation of the idea for the university. His staff of development officers would then work with the design team to come up with a fundraising strategy—usually involving federal, state, or philanthropic dollars matched by private donations or funds from the president's unencumbered "war chest," the university's foundation.

I was impressed with the president's (and university's) success but also concerned about the future of this institution. The new program ideas seemed to exist in isolation from one another and were never clearly linked to an overall mission statement or sense of purpose for the university. I agree that the president had a vision for his university, but his vision seemed to be primarily one of means (raising funds, starting new programs) rather than of ends. He seemed to hold a Darwinian notion about institutional develop-ment: try out a lot of new ideas and stick with those that survive institutional politics and can be sustained by hard-money support or other donated funds after the initial dollars dry up.

Like many successful fundraising leaders, this president seems to exemplify both the positive and the negative aspects of the expe-dient perspective on collegiate institutional life. I was reminded of the roller-coaster rides taken by men and women working with another fundraising president of a university in the Northwest and, later, of a liberal arts college in the Midwest. A former government official and friend of many wealthy donors to educational institu-tions, this man brought exciting new programs and perspectives to both institutions over which he presided. Both thrived—at least initially—under the inspiring leadership of this remarkable man. But the programs could not be sustained after federal or philan-thropic funds dropped off and state funds or alternative private phil-anthropic support failed to kick in.

This expedient leader raised hopes, and when he moved on (just as matching state or private funds were supposed to increase substantially), he left the sad legacy of foundering programs, hopes, and dreams. This was especially true among "fringe" members of society (women, Third World students, students from disadvantaged backgrounds), who had been the primary beneficiaries of his new programs and consequently the primary casualties of program fail-ure at both institutions.

Similar stories of success and subsequent collapse are to be heard at many colleges and universities that were flourishing during the 1960s and 1970s. Previously, outside funds, in the form of grants, donations, and the like, were being given primarily for research and scholarship, usually only to faculty in privileged, elitist universi-ties. In the 1960s and 1970s, external funds were given for more

populist-oriented demonstration projects and various social engineering efforts to anyone in a collegiate institution with a good idea
and a few connections. Social observers and analysts (like the expedient president) who had worked successfully in both academic and
governmental agencies could thrive in this new setting. One such
man, Bertrand Gross (1980), describes these shifting conditions as
follows: "Alongside the older motto 'Publish or Perish' (which puts
the fate of many younger people in the hands of establishment [elit-
ist] faithfuls on editorial boards) has risen an additional imperative:
'Get a grant or [a] contract and prosper.' This imperative also applies
to department heads, deans, and college presidents who—like professors—are expected to bring in the 'soft money' to supplement the
'hard money' in the regular college and university budgets" (p. 96).

Gross noted that the largest amounts of this "soft money" during the early 1960s came from governmental agencies that contracted for military and aerospace expertise. During this immediate
post-*Sputnik* era, federal funds were going mainly for scientific
research, which was in turn being conducted almost exclusively at
major elitist research universities. However, by the late 1960s, as
Lyndon Johnson's Great Society and War on Poverty programs were
getting under way, funding patterns changed. Federal funding now
favored populist and expedient institutions that had experience in
human service fields, even though they did not have adequate (and
capital-intensive) research facilities. Gross (1980) reports that "with
the civil rights and antiwar movements a minor avalanche of 'soft
money' was let loose for research, field work, and demonstration
projects in the so-called 'anti-poverty' and 'model cities' programs.
The word went around quickly among the new generation of academic hustlers that 'Poverty is where the money is'" (p. 96).

Expedient leaders in the 1990s, like expedient presidents from
the 1970s and 1980s, are often, at least superficially, at the cutting
edge of American higher education. They champion and often help
initiate programs that truly advance the quality of instruction as
well as increase access for underserved populations. The develop-

mental culture in particular is often beholden to expedient presidents or other institutional leaders. Expedient leaders and proponents of developmental programs have entered into a marriage of convenience because the values and desired outcomes of the developmental culture are often espoused and financially supported by philanthropic institutions and governmental agencies.

An examination of the expedient perspective in the United States, therefore, will reveal both positive and negative aspects. Expediency may be an interim answer to many of the problems facing contemporary colleges and universities, but I suggest that it will not do as a long-term solution and that we must look to unified models (described in Part Three of this book) for longer-term answers.

The Postmodern Expedient Perspective

As the beleaguered perspective exemplifies the madness and disorder that can accompany an unsuccessful transition to a postmodern organizational form, the expedient perspective exemplifies a somewhat successful transition in terms of creatively addressing postmodern issues associated with size and complexity, mission and boundaries, leadership, and capital and educational values.

Size and Complexity

Successful expediency-oriented collegiate institutions tend to incorporate mixed organizational models with regard to size. They are simultaneously both small and large. They make extensive use of satellite programs and consortial alliances with other institutions. Through the combinations of small, flexible, and autonomous units with larger, efficient organizational structures, the expedient college or university leader can efficiently address problems associated with differentiation of functions and their simultaneous integration. The use of satellite programs is of value in both small and large institutions, while consortia are particularly valuable in small collegiate institutions and matrix or cluster program models in larger ones. I will briefly consider each of these models.

Satellite programs are typically considered appropriate when a college or university is attempting an outreach to a new geographic location. Satellite programs permit the extension of program services to other locations without having to establish a whole new institution. They allow the creation of new, highly flexible, and responsive program units that are relatively autonomous while not having to replicate basic administrative and instructional support services (such as registration, financial record keeping, and library reference), which the home campus can provide.

This mixed model enables the new program venture to be distinctive and unencumbered by precedent on the home campus. Innovative leaders of the new venture need not initially run after or even worry about financial resources for support of basic administrative services. The services are already available on the home campus, enabling leaders of these satellite programs to devote most of their time and attention to program development and the identification of local community needs. Unfortunately, regional accrediting agencies and state postsecondary educational commissions often take a very critical attitude regarding satellite programs. They should be more supportive, recognizing the "pilot-testing" potential of these new programs. Of course, one must be concerned about quality control and equity in the distribution of resources to satellite programs, but these can be readily resolved and should not blunt visionary initiatives.

Consortia have been of great benefit over the past three decades to the survival of small liberal arts colleges in the United States. Founding consortia has enabled financially pressed small colleges to explore new programs, reduce instructional costs through mutual curricular offerings, and share administrative expertise and even services through joint programs. For example, during the 1970s, liberal arts colleges in the Northeast and the Midwest formed several consortia (College Center of the Finger Lakes, Great Lakes College Association, Associated Colleges of the Midwest) that were at the forefront in offering jointly sponsored faculty and administrative development services. These same consortia enabled member colleges jointly to initiate innovative environmental, cross-cultural, and governmental study programs (domestically and abroad), as well as more conventional cross-registration and interlibrary loan programs. Even more tightly linked consortia, such as the Claremont Colleges in Southern California, share library resources, classroom space, and various student services.

Consortia blend the advantages of small and large size. Each of the participating liberal arts colleges preserves its distinctive mission and its close working relationship with a small student body, loyal alumni, and a committed faculty and administration—characteristics not as commonly found in much larger public and private colleges and universities. Yet consortia also provide for economies of scale and serve as relatively safe places where new ideas can be tried out without any one institution having to risk a large amount of its scarce resources.

A small college can keep its internal resources distinctive and fully integrated with its mission, and the consortia can also remain integrated as an agency that is not meant to compete with the member colleges but rather complement the distinctive mission and character of each. Consortium-based programs make greater long-term financial support possible because funding support is shared by several institutions; also, each institution can focus on one or two special groups, and exchange programs can be offered so that most or all groups in the consortium are served, thereby allaying populist concern about the potential elitism and excessive homogeneity of small liberal arts colleges.

In the case of Exemplar College/University, there are no satellite programs. However, many of the issues being debated by Burke Deffenbach, Joan Broadhead, and Gretchen Karpoff could be at least partly addressed through the use of a consortium. These three faculty members are committed to different versions of a general education program. Could not aspects of each person's proposal be tested out in a consortium-sponsored program? Karpoff could try out her developmental model along with similarly inclined faculty members from other institutions. Couldn't Deffenbach establish a wonderful Heritage of Ideas program along with several senior faculty members from other colleges in the consortium who similarly decry the decline in cultural literacy among their students? This heritage program might even become a relatively permanent addition to the joint curriculum of the consortium, at minimal cost to Exemplar (one course release each year for Deffenbach) and the other schools.

What about Broadhead's interests? Given that she feels a little isolated from her academic colleagues at Exemplar, wouldn't she benefit from a regular consortium-based meeting of all business faculty? Better yet, what about a consortium-based college-corporation alliance that provides for student internships, corporate-college executive exchanges, and college credit courses being taught inside corporations? The untapped potential in satellite programs and consortia is almost unlimited. So much more could be done for the faculty and administration of hard-pressed institutions like Exemplar. Only the stubborn clinging to institutional autonomy and the equally as stubborn resistance of some accrediting agencies to alternative institutional forms prevent this more open exploration.

Collegiate institutions that are oriented toward expediency often tend to blend not only small and large academic structures but also various organizational forms within the institution itself. Specifically, I would point to matrix or cluster models, which are particularly effective in large institutions that want to preserve their traditional program activities but at the same time provide opportunities for new program development.

In the case of a matrix organization, a collegiate institution is structured not only around traditional academic departments but also around interdisciplinary program units. For example, a matrix-structured college or university might offer not only programs in psychology, history, and physics but also interdisciplinary programs in urban studies (involving faculty from sociology, economics, and history), child development (faculty from psychology, education, and biology), and so forth. All or most faculty members in a matrix organization are affiliated not only with an academic discipline but also with one or more interdisciplinary programs. The disciplinary program serves as a permanent "home base" for the faculty member, while the interdisciplinary program in which he or she teaches may change from year to year.

The cluster model differs from the matrix model in that most faculty in cluster organizations spend most of their career within a traditional academic department, affiliating only occasionally with a specific interdisciplinary cluster college. Typically, a college or university offers three or four cluster colleges at a time. Much as in the case of matrix-based universities, the cluster colleges often focus on specific interdisciplinary problems or themes, such as urban studies, women's studies, black studies, or entrepreneurship. In many instances, the cluster colleges are established for specific periods of time or are subject to review every three or four years and may be replaced by other cluster colleges as problems change or specific themes increase or decrease in popularity or relevance.

Whereas satellite programs provide an excuse for new program ideas to be tested off-site, matrix and cluster organizations allow for the testing of new programs on-site—in the backyard, as it were, of the home campus. Matrix models tend to involve a much larger proportion of total campus resources than cluster colleges do and are less frequently sustained over a long period of time by contemporary colleges and universities. The faculty in cluster colleges, by contrast, are more likely to become isolated, and these colleges are less likely than matrix models to have an impact on the core of the institution.

The classic matrix organization in an American collegiate institution was the University of Wisconsin at Green Bay, which was initially set up to provide environmentally oriented education. The matrix at Green Bay enabled traditional disciplines and academic departments to interface with interdisciplinary project or problem-oriented fields (such as pollution or environmental politics). Unfortunately, the Green Bay matrix eventually broke down, the faculty retreating to their traditional disciplines and departments at the expense of the environmental programs.

Cluster colleges also have a somewhat spotty history. Many of the early cluster college models (for example, at the University of the Pacific) have pulled over to the side of the road; however, several cluster models have remained in existence for many years (for example, Concordia University, Montreal) and seem to be firmly established as viable alternative models for the organization of academic programs. Through cluster colleges, special programs can have their own unique culture and identity. The leaders of these cluster colleges can remain relatively autonomous because they are accountable for building and sustaining a viable financial base (often through independent funding).

The cluster college also allows traditional (collegial and managerial culture) and innovative (developmental culture) programs to exist side by side. At Concordia University, a small cluster of semiautonomous colleges exist along with this university's traditional programs. Each of the cluster colleges focuses on a specific topic (for example, feminist studies) or a specific thematic structure (for example, the work of one seminal thinker each year). These cluster colleges shift from year to year, and students may take a small or relatively large proportion of their work in one or more of the colleges. Through their cluster colleges, Concordia University faculty can meet the distinctive needs of their diverse student body; can try out new curricular ideas in a small, manageable setting; and can obtain revitalizing professional development experiences by choosing to participate in one or more of the cluster colleges. As a public university with a strong populist tradition (having resulted from the merger between a Jesuit university and a public one, both with strong populist commitments), Concordia is able, through its cluster colleges, to offer special programs for the general public (such as small humanities seminars) that are often found only at elitist institutions. Similar features are seen at The Evergreen State College, a public institution.

Though Exemplar is probably not ready for a matrix, given its strong traditional roots in discipline-based education, it might be ready for a cluster college. Perhaps the curriculum committee at Exemplar could set up several cluster colleges, rather than supporting a traditional general education program. One of the cluster colleges might support Deffenbach's heritage of ideas theme, another might be developmentally oriented as Karpoff would like, and a third cluster college might be more problem- and business-focused, building on Broadhead's three M's (marketable, manageable, mathematical). Students could meet their general education requirements by participating in one (or perhaps two) of the cluster colleges. Additional cluster colleges might explore some of Bo Rochambeaux's wonderfully eccentric notions about postmodern art as well as serving as a laboratory for Joshua Wheat's continuing exploration of student writing. Perhaps such a laboratory for Wheat would help bring him back to Exemplar. This lab would also more closely link Wheat's national recognition and achievements to the continuing expansion of Exemplar's expediency-driven quest for regional and national recognition and, as a result, attract more funds and higher student enrollments—the dream of most expedient presidents.

Mission and Boundaries

As in the case of the beleaguered collegiate leader, the expedient leader must struggle with the issue of mission, for once an institution begins to stray from its founding mission and venture into the world of fundraising, proposal writing, and new program development—the lifeblood of expediency—it must find a clear and compelling mission to guide these often disparate and even potentially contradictory efforts. An organization that abandons clear boundaries (as is the case in many postmodern organizations) must repeatedly clarify its mission (see Bergquist, 1993).

The struggles of faculty at Exemplar have resulted in part from the decision of its president and board of trustees to become more expedient, to move in new directions, and to find new sources of money and students. By opening up the boundaries and encouraging exploration of new student populations, new funding sources, and new programs, the leaders at Exemplar are adding a new set of problems and tensions that will not necessarily lead to constructive ends, especially if a clear and coherent sense of mission is absent.

To compound the challenge, an institution like Exemplar that is not used to the new postmodern world of opportunism and expediency must also define a mission that is distinctive and responsive to pressing and enduring problems of the society in which it exists. This is a central problem for many collegiate institutions and is potentially a unique advantage held by the expedient ones. A mission statement that is clearly articulated and consistently enacted provides direction for the institution. It defines learning at the college or university, sets standards, provides guidelines and sets priorities (Martin, 1982). A mission statement should tell us what is distinctive about its character and programs.

Many colleges and universities like Exemplar could dust off just about any collegiate mission statement, change a word here and there, and claim it as their own. Exemplar's current statement speaks about heritage (supporting Deffenbach's claim), student growth and development (supporting Karpoff's vision), and responsiveness to changing conditions in society and contemporary careers (supporting Broadhead's claims). You could probably even find support for Rochambeaux's version of the new reality in art as well. This will not do. Exemplar's mission statement was probably constructed many years ago to accommodate a host of faculty, administrative, and trustee interests that were similar in many ways to those held by Deffenbach, Karpoff, Broadhead, and Rochambeaux.

Yet such a broad-based mission statement provides very little direction and is certainly not distinctive. Many studies (for example, Bergquist and Armstrong, 1986) reveal that colleges and universities are more likely to survive and prosper if they are distinctive than if they offer the same educational programs in the same manner as competing collegiate institutions.

Why, then, aren't Exemplar and other expedient colleges and universities more distinctive? These institutions have had sufficient resources to be different from one another. Furthermore, many of these expedient institutions have distinguished themselves from other American colleges and universities that tend to emulate the elites. Several factors come to mind when considering the demise of diversity in expedient institutions. First, as President Gravitz knows, once you bring multiple constituencies into the debate regarding mission, you are likely to end up with a watered-down statement that represents compromise and the lowest common denominator rather than the unique and often controversial vision of a specific individual or constituency. The trade-off between collaborative decision making and creativity is often unacknowledged in many institutional settings, including higher education.

Exemplar has come to a critical point in its life cycle as an organization. Priorities must be set, and a distinguishing mission must be established. Political whims, shifting funding patterns, and pet projects can no longer govern the school. Exemplar can no longer go off in a hundred different directions—especially in light of the cutback in state funds, taxpayer revolts that have hit many neighboring communities, and reductions in state and federal dollars appropriated for new program development in higher education. A set of clear priorities must be established for Exemplar, and a new strategic plan must be created, based on these priorities, to govern the way new and existing programs are reviewed and funded. These priorities and the subsequent plan must be built in a collaborative, participatory manner, with each appropriate constituency at Exemplar and its local community being centrally involved.

At the heart of the matter are the issues of quality and access.

How should Exemplar define quality in setting its priorities? How do the leaders of Exemplar determine the quality of programs and proposals? And what about access? The college is committed to serving community needs; in this sense, it is clearly committed to community access. Should each program at the college necessarily serve specific, local community needs if it is to be of the highest quality? Is quality intrinsically related to access at Exemplar?

An expedient president—like Kevin Gravitz—must negotiate a balance between quality and access. One solution is to bring in one or two special groups (learning-disabled, African Americans, reentry women) and provide them with exceptional, developmentally oriented programs (for which there is funding). This tends to create a major problem, for these programs typically do not have a strong institutional base of support. First of all, they are based on soft rather than hard money support and hence are vulnerable to external funding whims and fads. Second, other students, faculty members, and program administrators often resent the special attention that the program receives. Third, these new programs are frequently incompatible with the deep-seated collegial or managerial culture of the institution and with its elitist or populist origins. Elitists believe that the standards are being lowered for these favored students. Populists believe that there should be broader support for all students, not just a chosen few.

Another reason for the demise of diversity involves risk and flexibility. A distinctive mission statement implies risk taking on the part of institutional leaders. This vision might not "sell." Furthermore, most of our institutions are insufficiently flexible to change in midstream. We can't hedge all of our bets when we move in distinctive new directions. We must identify ways in which we will be indispensable to our community and society and in doing so must risk being wrong (either now or later). However, if we are unwilling to take this risk, we are almost certain of being wrong and expendable. Risk takers and entrepreneurs have been praised in corporate settings (see Bennis and Nanus, 1986; Kanter, 1983) but far less widely in higher education (see Peck, 1985; Riesman and Fuller, 1985).

It is also important, however, that increased risk taking be defined not in terms of opportunism but rather in terms of vision and entrepreneurial spirit. When confronted with problems associated with the formulation and systematic enactment of a mission statement, the leaders of many colleges and universities like Exemplar seem to flounder. Administrators and faculty at Exemplar grasp at what look like opportunities rather than creating their own programs in an entrepreneurial fashion. An important distinction should be drawn here between opportunism and entrepreneurism. In the case of opportunism, collegiate leaders scramble to take advantage of programs that look "hot" rather than addressing the difficult task of setting forth a unique mission statement and using that statement to determine the behavior and activities of the members of the institution at all levels.

Exemplar College/University has been blessed (and cursed) over the past decade with substantial state and philanthropic funding. This has produced an addiction to short-term financial "fixes." Many colleges and universities like Exemplar that have received large external grants (such as Title III–funded colleges and universities) have come to rely on these external funds and are simply unable to exist without them. The leaders of these addicted institutions must now spend much of their time and attention ensuring that outside funds continue to pour in. As a result, they are ready, like all addicts, to sell their soul—their distinctive mission—for these funds.

Exemplar's leaders must be careful about initiating any program that holds the promise of outside funding or the potential for substantial enrollment. School leaders and others who are attracted to the expedient perspective will be inclined to look for the latest federal or state funding initiative or toward an emerging student population with newfound money, such as grants, loans, or personal income, when defining new program directions. Leaders of expedient institutions risk flying from pillar to post in search of new money without reflecting on ways in which these new initiatives relate to the central mission and goals of the institution. Though many of the evangelical colleges that advocate separation of church and state may have lost some financial support by not accepting federal dollars, they have often been more stable than nonevangelical colleges that grew to rely on federal funds. The latter institutions often direct most, if not all, of their planning to the quixotic and changing pattern of federal funding (program grants, student loans, and so on).

Effective entrepreneurial leadership, by contrast, is not reactive, responding to outside priorities and funding initiatives. Rather it is proactive, basing new program development on the mission and goals of the institution. Rather than seek out funding and then try to link it to the priorities of the institution, as seems to have been the strategy at Exemplar, the entrepreneurial academic leader sets priorities, in collaboration with various campus constituencies, and then seeks out funds specifically to support the new initiative. The irony, of course, is that the entrepreneur is more likely to get federal or foundation money because he or she has been able to build on documented institutional priorities and can show how this new program initiative relates directly with other program initiatives at the institution.

Given this seeming confusion between opportunism and entrepreneurism, the curriculum committee at Exemplar should stress clarification of the school's mission. Members of the committee should also encourage school leaders to think in more systemic terms and adopt a longer-term perspective on their institution. They should consider the impact of every new program idea on existing programs at Exemplar and the relationship between the program idea and the stated mission and priorities. The committee should, however, also allow room for the random and risky exploration of new ideas by providing for pilot testing and various short-term cluster colleges. Finally, any educational program that is being started by Exemplar based on external funding should incorporate a plan for eventual movement to hard money support by ensuring solid student enrollment, building an auxiliary enterprise that will yield sustained funds for the program, and similar actions.

A third reason why mission statements tend not to be distinctive and to be of little value to expedient colleges and universities concerns the confusion of means and ends. Exemplar faculty and administrators debate methodology instead of reaching agreement about desired outcomes; furthermore, discussions about methodology are usually quite conservative and self-justifying, leaving the faculty with the same old formula that is being used in countless other colleges and universities in the United States. When speaking of educational quality, considerable attention is typically given to the nature of the means by which information is conveyed to the students ("to lecture or not to lecture") and by which students are assessed with regard to the acquisition of this information. Rarely does the discussion focus on the content of the material being offered or on the manner in which it is being used by students after they graduate.

We often focus on the means: "Did I present the material in an effective manner?" We rarely give sufficient attention to the educational outcomes associated with these means: "Did I present the most important material available on this topic or subject area? Should I be giving this subject area more or less attention?" We avoid consideration of the outcomes because there are no clear statements of mission and goals from which we might generate educational outcome statements. A vicious circle emerges: when attention is directed primarily to means, no clear statement about ends will emerge; when attention is directed from means to ends, we confront the futility of defining these ends in a vacuum without regard to other statements about program ends and goals; hence we are pulled back to the relative security and certainty associated with a discussion of instructional methods and strategies.

The president and other administrative leaders at Exemplar

would therefore be well served if they asked some hard questions about means versus ends:

1. Toward what ends are we raising funds?
2. What would happen if we went away tomorrow or if our outside funding should dry up? Would this really make any difference to the college? To the local community? Would we or this program be missed?
3. How would we know if this program were successful one or two years from now? What difference would it have made in this college? In this community? In the lives of our students?

Finally, the distinctiveness of collegiate missions often seems to be missing because we are not very clear about what students want or need. We look to prestigious universities or to our competitors for guidance about mission and purpose because we are uncertain about what is good and valuable for our students. It is in this domain that student development theory and the accompanying developmental culture have been particularly helpful with regard to the mission statement of expedient college and university leaders.

Advocates of student development perspectives often provide unambiguous statements about what a student should gain from a collegiate education and how a college or university might determine whether or not it has been successful in helping its students arrive at these desired developmental goals (usually based in a value-added approach to the definition of quality). Over the long run, this feature of student development theory may be its most important contribution to the field of higher education. Even in this area, however, student development theory cannot claim a major victory, for much of this work has remain confined to a few devotees and members of the student affairs offices in many colleges and universities. These concepts must receive much more attention if our colleges and universities are to develop and enact distinguishing mission statements.

In his study of new organizational configurations, Kenneth Boulding (1973) identified the "intersect organization." This type of organization is typified by unclear boundaries and unclear status with regard to such traditional organizational categories as public and private, regulatory and service-providing. Many expedient institutions have become classic intersects. As private, independent institutions, they have become increasingly reliant on public funds (student loans, federal grants, state appropriations). Highly entrepreneurial presidents have turned public universities and private liberal arts colleges into major centers for experimentation in the provision of new public services (such as Head Start). Public and state-supported colleges and universities that are expedient have frequently become reliant, conversely, on private funds and philanthropy. Whereas thirty years ago most public universities relied exclusively on state dollars (supplemented by research or instructional innovation grants received by their faculty), now they frequently have a university foundation that enables the presidents of these institutions to compete for philanthropic dollars with the private colleges and universities.

We also see the movement toward intersect status in attempts being made by many colleges and universities (both private and public) to generate additional unencumbered funds from various "auxiliary enterprises" ranging from student bookstores, student unions, and continuing education programs to profitable athletic programs, on-campus movie theaters, and bowling alleys. Some expedient colleges and universities lease some of their campus facilities (including unused dormitories, summertime classrooms, and athletic facilities) to outside agencies or establish long-term leases on unused land at the edge of campus. As in the case of many human service agencies, college and university presidents can no longer depend on stable public funding or stable student enrollment patterns. They have turned instead to the for-profit business sector and often spend much of their time acting like corporate executives, shepherding profits from far-flung auxiliary operations. They need these funds to offset at least part of their institution's budget.

Boundaries are unclear in yet another way in many expedient collegiate institutions. In creating many new programs for a variety of different traditional and nontraditional students, these institutions often offer students (and faculty and administrators) multiple statuses and a variety of modes, points, and times of entry. Students can attend part-time, take individual courses as nonmatriculated students, audit courses, and take courses offered through an extension program that count under certain circumstances as courses in the regular programs of the school. Students taking courses on a nonmatriculated basis may be able to credit the courses and the money they pay for the courses toward a degree program if they apply for one later. Many universities that are expedient in orientation offer enrollment opportunities throughout the year for "busy, working professionals" who don't want to wait for more traditional enrollment periods in the fall or spring.

Multiple entry points may facilitate the recruitment of new students and permit students to tailor their education to their work and family demands, but these multiple points also create problems. The nontraditional commuter student, even more than the traditional student, needs solid social support. These students often do not receive much support from home (their further education often threatens other members of the family) and find that balancing work, family, and education is particularly stressful. When nontraditional students are admitted at different times during the year, they never have a solid support base constituted of other students who began the program with them. At first, the "new kid on the block" will know far less about the program and personal roles in it than virtually all of the other students, traditional or nontraditional. This can be an advantage in terms of the earlier students serving as "big brothers" and "big sisters" to the new students, but more often the expedient institution simply leaves the new students to sink or swim.

The experiences of Betty Cordell, a mature returning student at Exemplar, are not uncommon. She felt bewildered and alone during her first days at the school. It is not even clear that she will continue. Betty couldn't care less whether Exemplar comes from an elitist or a populist tradition; all she knows is that up to this point, she is experiencing neither quality nor access. Betty may join other returning students who drop out of the hostile or indifferent environment typical of many contemporary schools. Multiple-entry programs must be coupled with thoughtful and extensive student support services if they are to be successful. Programs with only one or two entry points during the year still need support services, but the more natural acquaintance processes undertaken by a group of students all beginning the program together make these support services easier to plan and maintain.

Leadership

Successful expedient leaders are situational leaders—as are most leaders of postmodern colleges and universities that are either beleaguered or attempting to integrate quality and access. A situational leader shifts between a task orientation and a people orientation as need be (Hershey and Blanchard, 1977). College and university presidents who are expedient must vary their roles, depending on the situation. Not only must they serve as taskmaster and people person, they must also serve as visionary, mayor, servant, learner, and community builder. Each of these roles requires different and often contradictory skills.

The leader of the southern state university that I described at the start of this chapter was clearly a visionary. He wandered around the country listening, reading, and visiting other institutions. Whereas Johnny Appleseed spread his seeds all over the country, the president of this university collected seeds from elsewhere and planted them in his own backyard. Unfortunately, the orchard that he cultivated back home was soon overgrown, and some pruning was needed. But no one was certain what to prune, for the president hadn't gotten around to determining which of the trees were most valuable; furthermore, none of the faculty or administrators at his university had much personal investment in either his trees or the fruits they bore—primarily because he had found and planted the seeds on his own.

Nearly two decades ago, Jack Lindquist (1978) discovered in an extensive examination of change in American colleges and universities that new ideas will be successfully incorporated into an institution when they are brought in not by the president but by midlevel academic administrators or faculty members. The southern president could have benefited greatly from Lindquist's findings. He would have spent less time being a visionary and more time in one of the other roles that need to be played by an expedient leader. For instance, he might have served more as a mayor, building coalitions in support of new ideas brought in by faculty members and administrators. In this quasi-political role (Birnbaum, 1988), the expedient leader becomes more a champion of other people's ideas and less an advocate for his own (Bergquist and Armstrong, 1986).

The southern president—or the president of Exemplar, for that matter—might also be more effective if he were to serve more as a servant than as a master. We are likely to find the concept of leader as servant (first described by Robert Greenleaf in 1970) particularly appropriate for leaders of postmodern organizations. Given the enormous stress associated with any postmodern conditions, particularly with demands for change in expedient institutions, the leader of such an institution must attend extensively to the care and feeding of his or her colleagues.

Increasingly, the leadership of contemporary organizations is being differentiated from management. Managers are appropriately in the business of producing results and achieving objectives over a specific, usually short term. Leaders, by contrast, must be concerned with longer-term issues such as size, complexity, mission, boundaries, and capital and educational values (the dimensions I highlight in this book). One of these long-term issues is the growth and development of employees. The leader's primary responsibility is to ensure that excellent people are hired, that they are placed in settings where they can be effective, that they are supported and acknowledged for their work, and that their own personal growth and professional development are enhanced within the context of their job.

To perform these functions effectively, a leader must step down from his or her hierarchical position and work more as a colleague, in partnership. Greenleaf (1970) describes this role as one of servanthood, through which we define our first obligation as meeting the needs of our employees so that they can do their job effectively and gain from this experience. Often in playing this role, the leader serves as a buffer between his or her employees and the turbulent postmodern world outside (and inside) the organization. He or she also serves as an expediter, a network broker, and a resource procurer (Schön, 1971). In these new roles, the leader is working on behalf of the employees' job performance as well as their personal and professional development. The role of servant is particularly important for expedient leaders given the challenge they have posed to members of their collegiate institution with regard to new perspectives and programs.

Capital and Educational Values

From the expedient perspective, capital is defined primarily in terms of money: money generated by student enrollment, money obtained from successful grantsmanship, money gained from various auxiliary enterprises, money raised from philanthropic endeavors. Whereas the leaders of beleaguered institutions try to balance their budgets through cutbacks in staff and facilities, the more entrepreneurial expedient leader attempts to balance the budget primarily by raising more funds. Given this emphasis on money, the expedient leader always stands on rather shaky ground with regard to both capital and educational values, for his or her credibility and the viability of the institution often depend on the rather fickle flow of funds into the organization from both tuition revenues and nontuition sources.

Although the reputation, land, and solid endowment of elitist institutions and the commitment, track record, and facilities of populist institutions build up slowly, they also decline slowly. The premodern, elitist institution is built on the personal word-of-mouth testimonials of graduates, beneficiaries, and observers of the institution. Similarly, populist institutions have an accumulated history of service to underserved populations and, at least until recently, a backlog of deserving student applicants. Neither the elitist nor the populist institution is going to go out of business overnight.

Expedient institutions do have reputations, like the elitist institutions; however, their reputations are often short-lived, being dependent on "smoke and mirrors" (press releases, newspaper and magazine articles, radio and television spots, and so forth). Large federal grants or private donations and flashy demonstration projects are very appealing to the public, as are the appointment of an exciting, highly visible faculty member, guest lecturer, or consultant. When a struggling institution like Exemplar tries to be expedient in its new program development, it moves onto shaky ground. Exemplar's leaders may find that when the school no longer has its federal grant or its inspiring community project, the school's reputation will fade rapidly, and it will either shut down or return to its former invisible status. Such was the case with many expedient institutions that relied for many years on Title III grants. These large federal grants, given to struggling colleges and universities that served minority student populations, yielded many exciting and highly visible short-term improvements but often had little enduring impact on the institutions receiving the grants.

Given the emphasis on money from the expedient perspective, it should come as no surprise that the educational values of expediency-oriented institutions tend to be market-driven. Specific educational programs and approaches are considered to be of value (and of quality) if they respond to the identified needs of a specific student population—that is, a specific source of revenues. Though the populist institution, with its dominant managerial culture, would seem on the surface to be most amenable to total quality management (TQM) and other market-oriented strategies for institutional improvement, the expedient institution is in fact likely to be particularly responsive over the short term to TQM and related tools. However, without a clear mission other than fundraising, the expedient institution will readily identify students as customers (the centerpiece of most TQM programs in American higher education) but will not be able to sustain the long-term discipline of a TQM initiative (this will be described in Chapter Ten).

From the expedient perspective, students may readily be defined as customers either because they pay tuition or because they are voters who must pay taxes for the education they receive. Traditionally, the independent (private) college or university was primarily concerned about tuition, while the state-supported (public) institution was mostly concerned with the support of taxpayers. This distinction has now broken down as more and more educational institutions—expedient institutions in particular—have become intersects, with both private and public elements. The leaders of expedient independent colleges and universities must increasingly be concerned about students as both tuition payers and voters, for public dollars are still needed to support student loan programs and various state and federal grants.

Furthermore, in light of the potential creation of vouchers that can be used to pay for either private or public education, many independent college and university leaders are particularly concerned with public relations. In addition, the independent college or university, as noted earlier, must often become involved in auxiliary enterprises to compensate for the inability of students to pay for their entire education. These auxiliary programs may soon become of dominant concern to the leaders of expedient institutions, leading to a neglect of students as customers and a shift to a much broader definition of the customer. The customer becomes anyone who is purchasing services or products from the college or university.

Similarly, state-supported colleges and universities dominated by the expedient perspective are experiencing a shift in their definition of the customer. They must be concerned not only about voters and taxpayers (who may or may not be students at the school) but also about students as tuition payers, given that educational costs can rarely be covered anymore by tax dollars. In addition, the state-supported institution must be particularly concerned in the 1990s with the student as a taxpaying customer, for increasingly the students in many of these institutions are not only old enough to vote but also old enough and sufficiently established in the community to make an immediate and direct impact on community support for the institution.

I am reminded of a consultation with a relatively small state-supported college whose future funding by the state legislature was assured by the firsthand experience of one of the most influential legislators in the state. This legislator decided to take several courses himself at this college and found that he not only received an excellent education but also observed many other mature learners taking courses at the college. As a result of his own experiences as an adult learner and his conversations with other mature students, this legislator became a particularly knowledgeable and persuasive advocate for this college and for adult education in his state.

If students are the customers of expedient institutions, money (generated by enrollment and outside funds that support the students) is the product. Whereas the maturation of the student is the central, defining product of the elitist or collegial institution and career advancement (through degrees and certification) is the product of the populist or managerial institution, financial well-being for the school is the central desired outcome of the expedient institution. Such a shift in emphasis from the student's to the institution's welfare, though regrettable in many regards, is understandable in light of the reduced support for postsecondary education in our society. Such an emphasis, however, might not be necessary, given the option of a unified perspective, to which I turn in Part Three.

Key Points

1. Although the expedient perspective includes a willingness to try out new ideas and take risks, it does not necessarily extend to relating these ideas or risks to the mission of the school or to the issues of quality and access. Expedient leaders often never bother to determine how new ideas will be assessed in order to select which will become an integral part of the institution and which will remain peripheral or short-lived.

2. Visionary expedient leaders are likely to bring hope and inspiration to a struggling college or university, thereby attracting outside funds that can be used to initiate new program ideas and temporarily bolster student enrollment and school revenues. However, when these leaders leave or when funding ends, the legacy is often dismantled programs and shattered dreams. This is particularly problematic in the case of programs that serve "fringe" members of society, who become the primary casualties of program terminations and accompanying disenchantment.

3. From the expedient, postmodern perspective, colleges and universities should construct complex, multiform structures (satellite programs, matrix organizations, cluster colleges) to accommodate the need for efficiencies of scale (usually found in large organizations) as well as flexibility and responsiveness (usually associated with smaller colleges and universities).

4. Expedient leaders tend to be clear about their short-term goals and objectives but unclear about the overall mission of their school, especially as it relates to new program initiatives. This lack of clarity and consistency can be problematic, given

that the expedient leader and institution may abandon their
boundaries in an effort to reach out to new student populations, funding sources, and cooperative agreements with other
schools and noneducational institutions.

5. Expedient leaders are situational in orientation. They shift
   roles in response to shifting needs and conditions. Unfortunately, in shifting roles, they may lose their sense of the
   underlying values and aspirations of the institution and its
   members. The primary product of the school becomes its own
   financial achievements—a shift from the concern of both
   elitists and populists to something above and beyond the
   institution itself.

Part Three

Achieving and Integrating Quality and Access

Chapter Nine

Strategies Based on Creativity, Commitment, and Cooperation

With their unclear boundaries, diverse educational values, and situational models of leadership, postmodern collegiate institutions are by their very nature hard to manage or define. Often the critical decisions to be made by leaders of these institutions concern issues of size and complexity. The critical role played by these decisions in terms of the elitist, populist, beleaguered, and expedient perspectives has already been noted. Can we retain quality if we become a much larger institution? If we limit size, aren't we cutting off access? As we become larger and older, our organizational structures seem to proliferate, and our institution seems to become increasingly difficult to manage. How do we hold back these shifts toward greater organizational complexity, and how do we learn to work in an effective manner in such a setting?

Even when clear decisions regarding size can be made, definitional problems remain, for these institutions have typically become quite complex as well as diffuse with regard to boundaries. In some ways they are very large institutions, for they typically involve effective outreach into the local community or even into the state, nation, or world. In other ways they are very small. In fact, in the future we are likely to find postmodern institutions that are nothing more than "holding companies" (like many "hollow" postmodern corporations) that remain small, supple, and efficient, serving primarily as vehicles for the identification and linkage of student needs and community resources. Increasingly, we are likely to find that postmodern colleges and universities are working in consortial relationships as well as in other even more innovative collaborative relationships with other institutions.

Given these shifting postmodern conditions, three basic strategies are crucial for any college or university that wishes to achieve and integrate quality and access: creativity and sensitivity in the search for quality in a setting of diversity, an ongoing and sustained commitment to the achievement of quality and access, and the development of cooperative arrangements that enable quality and access to be sustained and effectively integrated.

Creative Integration of Quality and Access

In the successful postmodern college or university, access is increased through the enhancement of quality, and quality is in turn improved by increasing access. Improved quality makes an institution more reputable, which in turn makes access that much more valuable to underserved populations. Credibility is a central figure for many underserved students, either because they won't get much of a job without a highly credible degree or because their own self-esteem is tied up with the credibility of the institution from which they graduate.

The interviews conducted at the three case study institutions revealed a prevailing concern with credibility. Students who were interviewed often acknowledged that they either worry about the effect of their school's credibility or accreditation status with regard to future job placements and job security or wonder if they could have been accepted by and successful in a "real" (that is, prestigious and elitist) institution. Alternatively, students were often defiant in their declaration of indifference or antipathy toward traditional standards, and we are left wondering if they "protest too much."

In highly creative postmodern institutions, greater access improves quality by encouraging a diversity of resources and perspectives. Our postmodern era requires the capacity for complex and relativistic thought, which in turn requires exposure to diverse perspectives and experiences not only among faculty and administrators but also among students. Whereas attention has often focused on the value of postsecondary education for students from underrepresented populations, it should shift to the value that these underrepresented students bring to other students attending the school. Jacobs (1989) suggests that this can be a real challenge for classroom instructors. She notes (specifically with regard to older students) that traditional students are likely to be threatened by the rich, alternative perspectives that the nontraditional student brings into the classroom. Jacobs maintains, however, that with effective faculty development and the use of collaborative learning techniques, the nontraditional students can become valued resources for everyone in the classroom.

In the interviews with students from Evergreen, JFK, and PSP, students repeatedly stated that the diverse student body in all three schools is itself one of the most valuable resources that any of these institutions possesses. A sophomore at Evergreen, for instance, speaks of a love-hate relationship between the college and its nontraditional students. She feels that some of the seminars in which she has participated have been disappointing; however, others have gotten to "the second level of understanding, beyond just the ordinary grasp of the material." She notes that with the diversity of students at Evergreen, she benefits from a wide range of experiences that other students bring to these seminars: "You can't prejudge anyone. Your first tendency might be to put people in a box; they would say something, and their ideas would blow away everything you'd expected." Because of this exposure to new people and ideas, she has learned to depend on the strength and validity of her own opinions: "How I judge myself is just as important as how others view me. I have my own strengths and weaknesses, and Evergreen forces me to acknowledge them both."

A much older woman, attending PSP, made a similar observation: "There is predominantly an older population [at PSP]. You become more your own person as you get older. Each of us came to this school with a story—family, children, profession, tragedy, special skills, and so forth. In a school that is geared for students right out of undergraduate school, there isn't any way the student population can be as rich. My classmates are teachers, ministers, parole officers, lawyers, podiatrists, nurses, chiropractors, administrators, theater critics, social workers, counselors in private practice. . . . Doesn't that sound appealing?" She went on to talk about the sense of personal integrity that comes with an exposure to diverse ideas and perspectives. At all three schools, an interactive environment and valuing of student input in classes maximizes the use of diverse student resources. In light of the financial pressures experienced by all three schools—and by many other schools seeking integration of quality and access—the rich student resources of the school are particularly valuable.

Given the intimate relationship between access and quality, two questions become central in sustaining this union. First, we must determine in which dimensions our institution is going to be accessible and the ways in which this accessibility will increase diversity and ultimately quality by asking which of the many underserved populations will be the focus of our commitment and our initiatives. The focus is typically on one or more of six different target populations in American higher education: mature working adults, people without substantial incomes, women, people of non-European origin, people with disabilities, and people who deserve a "second chance."

The second question is even more important; without a satisfactory answer to it, the first question becomes irrelevant: in what ways will we respond distinctively and appropriately to the unique needs of the target populations being served by our college or university? Typically, one or more of six different dimensions of the collegiate institution are altered, in a creative manner, to respond to the distinctive needs of these populations: time (course scheduling), location (where services are offered), cost (tuition levels and payment plans), physical facilities (the setting in which services are offered), content (what is being taught), and style (the way services, including instruction, are being delivered).

More profoundly, the institution must be responsive to these populations by changing its basic character or culture (Skinner and Richardson, 1988) and by fully acknowledging the unique contributions to be made by each of the diverse populations in the institution (Jacobs, 1989). This demands even more thoughtfulness and creativity, for the high-quality and highly accessible college or university must acknowledge and act on the knowledge that quality is enhanced and can in fact exist in our postmodern world only when there is full access to the institution. I will explore each of the six dimensions in some detail, making use of the three case study institutions.

Time

The issue of time is particularly complex and difficult in the postmodern institution. First, with regard to the scheduling of courses, schools like PSP and JFK must offer courses at times when their working students can attend. PSP and JFK offer most of their courses in the evening and on weekends. Mature adults are particularly time-sensitive, and both institutions must respond to this particular need. While students greatly appreciate the availability of courses at times of the day when they can attend, they also often recognize that evening and weekend classes are a source of frustration and may block the learning that takes place because both instructors and students are tired after long days or weeks of work.

A PSP student observes that she doesn't have time to recover from work before having to leap into class at PSP. She knows that she's not alone in this regard:

> Most students and instructors have such full days, other commitments. Teachers sometimes come to class tired and hassled, and so do students. Learning and teaching are not optimal under those

conditions. Since having both a working faculty and a working student body is one of the strengths of the school, I'm not saying that I think anything can be done about it, but it certainly has a negative as well as positive impact on what goes on here. Maybe if we weren't all in such a hurry to get through the program. . . . I feel like there is such pressure to keep on moving. If students would take fewer classes at a time, maybe some of the panic I see in the classes wouldn't happen so often. Sometimes I want to say, "Will you zip it up? We are all tired and have unexpected crises. What's so special about you?" I wish there were some way to handle the pressure better.

Another PSP student similarly describes how she comes to class hassled and distracted, yet she sees this as somehow beneficial and as something that bonds her with her fellow students and instructors:

I arrive in an exhausted state. I sit down, and the class begins. I focus on the class and the other students. Before I know it, it is time for the first break, and I eat my dinner. I look forward to seeing everyone. I feel a strong connection [with classmates]. It's different from my other school experiences. Here most other students are just like me. . . . We are all pretty rushed, we connect, and then we go our separate ways. I mean, the other students all work in related fields; they're working adults with busy lives. . . . In other schools I have gone to, I was the only one who had to work for a living. I feel more like the others here. . . . We're in it all together.

Both PSP and JFK have also explored the option of offering courses in the early morning (before work), at noon, and in intensive sessions held over three-day weekends. The early-morning and noon courses have typically met with little success; they make sense only in a noncredit continuing education situation. But the three-day format has been very successful at both PSP and JFK. Not only has attendance been relatively easy for students to arrange, but they also greatly appreciate the focusing and community-building dimensions of the intensive three-day experience. In many ways, the three-day module replicates in condensed form the residency experiences of younger students who need not work and can live on campus while attending school.

In the near future, we are likely to find that postmodern colleges and universities take even more radical steps regarding the scheduling of courses. They may begin to restructure temporal boundaries and may even go so far as to establish lifelong learning contracts with their students. Such an agreement would enable a college or university to commit itself not to two or four years of education for its students but to the lifelong educational needs of people participating in its collegiate community. A student may attend classes for several years, then leave the college or university to pursue a career, raise a family, and so forth. The student or graduate will then return to school for a short time to reassess life plans, determine which educational resources are needed in conjunction with these plans, get help in identifying the nature and location of these resources, and receive assistance in obtaining these resources (from the college, off-campus, on the job, in the family setting, or in a field or internship experience).

A lifelong learning contract would call into question the traditional notion about graduation and in turn increase alumni interest in the financial welfare of the school, as well as in its educational goals and mission (given that alumni are actually continuing students). In this type of institution, we are likely to find much broader participation in the governance of the school, as well as larger donation of funds and expertise (guest lecturing, field supervision, and so forth). Organizational resources, such as office space, jobs, and conference facilities, would be forthcoming, and the skills of continuing students in marketing and public relations would probably be available. If nothing else, these continuing students could enthusiastically tell other people at all stages of life and in all social roles about the lifelong program in which they continue to participate and from which they derive benefits.

Location

Most nontraditional learners are not only time-sensitive but also location-sensitive. Location is often a mixed blessing for nontraditional students. They end up attending a school not because of its curriculum or degree programs or even because it is in a location that they find particularly attractive or conducive to learning; rather, they chose a location that is convenient to work or home. JFK and PSP have responded in different ways to the issue of location. The leaders of PSP chose to situate their campuses in major urban areas (San Francisco and Sacramento). Though the cost of doing business in these cities is often high in terms of rent, parking, public transportation, and crime, students greatly appreciate the convenience of going to school near their place of business or residence.

PSP maintains a campus in the heart of San Francisco, despite the high cost, because many PSP students either live or work downtown and find the location convenient. Similarly, PSP retains a Sacramento campus despite pressures from the state and regional accrediting bodies to consolidate it with the San Francisco campus. Considering that it is the only doctoral program in its region, PSP remains firm in its commitment to stay, recognizing that the students at the Sacramento campus could not move or commute each day to San Francisco, eighty-eight miles away, due to work and family commitments. Many other colleges and universities in California have abandoned or severely cut their programs in the Sacramento region because of these outside pressures, despite the fact that it is one of the largest and fastest-growing metropolitan areas in the United States.

Early leaders at JFK chose a different strategy. They located in a rapidly growing suburban area where prospective students live and new businesses, it was hoped, would soon locate. Their prediction was accurate, and JFK is now at the heart of a rapidly growing area, though students commuting from jobs in San Francisco, fourteen miles to the west, often find it difficult to get to school on time through evening traffic.

Cost

Increasingly, with the cost of postsecondary education in the United States spiraling ever upward, the issue of access centers on the question of cost. Hansen and Stampen (1989) note that student financial aid has decreased since the early 1980s and that a commitment to financial access in American higher education has generally been replaced by an emphasis on improving educational quality. Others (Lewis, 1989; "Shifting Responsibilities," 1994) similarly document a major reduction in student aid since the early 1980s. In the 1990s, how does a student from a lower-middle-class background pay for an education? What about minority parents who have faced years of discrimination in employment and pay and as a result are unable to afford college for their children? What about potential adult students who face the cost of not only their own education but also that of their children?

Typically, these issues have been addressed since World War II by pleas to increase federal or state financial aid or to increase private donation of funds to financially pressed educational institutions. The National Commission on Responsibilities for Financing Postsecondary Education (1993), for instance, offered several recommendations ensuring that all students receive an appropriate amount of aid (as well as work and tax incentives) to support them in their educational efforts. Yet student aid has not been a reliable source of support for higher education over the years. Hansen and Stampen (1989) have pointed out a cyclical pattern of public support for student aid and, more generally, for programs that address the issues of equity and student access. At times—for example, in 1947 and 1948 (GI Bill) and 1972 through 1981 (federal need-based aid programs)—emphasis has been placed on financial access to higher education. At other times, however, the focus has shifted to private solutions to the financial problems of schools and the students who want to attend them and an accompanying emphasis on quality rather than access. This cyclical pattern is not confined to the United States; similar shifts away from public support toward greater privatization are occurring throughout the world (Altbach, 1991, p. 310).

Even more important, increasing financial aid does not get to the heart of the issue of access. First, if colleges and universities are not prepared for students from lower socioeconomic levels, it is not clear that the investment of public money in their education is justified. If education is not of quality (as defined by its appropriateness for the student population being served), does access really exist? How can we say that we are providing access if the nontraditional student must be shoehorned into an alien world? How can we say that there is access if the alienated student is much more likely than the traditional student to drop out of an ill-prepared school, having gained an even lower sense of self-esteem and lost the wages that could have been earned in some other pursuit?

Second, enrollment trends in American higher education strongly suggest that most lower-income students are restricted from attending traditional liberal arts colleges and universities; they tend to go to community colleges and vocational schools. Rose and Sorensen (1991) found that student aid is more likely to be found in "lower-quality" institutions (as defined by student selectivity categories in Barron's *Profiles of American Colleges and Universities*) than in "higher-quality" institutions. This is true whether the institution is private or public. While community colleges and vocational schools are often best equipped to address the distinctive needs of lower-income students, they are not necessarily appropriate for all such students: "Although the issue of 'choice' is often expressed in terms of public versus private alternatives, opportunity to attend a flagship public university or indeed *any* four-year public institution is importantly constrained by income in many states" (McPherson and Schapiro, 1991, p. 19). Our reliance on these specific institutions to educate our lower-income students means that we restrict these students' educational options and ultimately prevent them from making certain choices with regard to their lives and careers.

Rarely has the other dimension of the financial access problem been addressed—the spiraling cost of collegiate education. The problem of high tuition and financially pressed institutions could be solved in part by changing the way in which our colleges and universities do business. We could concentrate on making them more efficient and more effective. If we could make our colleges and universities less expensive to run, we could reduce or at least cap the tuition they charge. Is such a proposal a pipe dream, the knee-jerk reaction of a misinformed outsider? Perhaps it is; however, all three of the case study institutions have tried to implement cost reduction plans. They have all established cooperative programs with other schools; have challenged traditional assumptions about expenditure for library, full-time faculty, and facilities; and at times have taken painful steps to eliminate unnecessary staff and administrative positions.

The central issue in this regard is not what can be done to reduce costs but where to find the willpower to make these cuts, given the often flimsy commitment of the school to financial access. In the case of Evergreen, PSP, and JFK, sensitivity to cost is indispensable, for all three schools serve nontraditional students who often cannot afford more expensive schools. Both Evergreen and PSP offer education at low cost for people who work or come from middle-class families that may not be eligible for the grants and loans available primarily to lower-middle-class students.

The issue of cost relates not just to student accessibility but also to the roles that alumni can play in society after they graduate. As I mentioned in Chapter Three, students who graduate with large outstanding student loans are restricted in terms of the kinds of work they can do. They need to find jobs that pay enough for them to pay off their debt. The capacity of graduates to serve underserved populations or contribute to the betterment of society is determined in large part by the cost of education and more specifically by the nature and extent of loans that a student acquires before graduation from the institution. Graduates who owe large amounts of money are unable to serve underserved populations, given that they most devote their energy and creativity to the repayment of these loans. Guaranteed student loan programs perpetuate this problem by encouraging students to defer payments on their tuition until after they graduate; this in turn enables colleges and universities who participate in these loan programs to increase tuition without regard for the ability of students to pay these fees, as payment is deferred. So even though guaranteed student loan programs are intended to increase access, they do so at the expense of the subsequent access of other members of our society to the services being provided by these students when they graduate.

The Professional School of Psychology is committed to both access and quality, and the school's board of trustees has consequently had to make difficult decisions. How does one retain the traditional values of graduate education while keeping tuition low, thereby making the school affordable for men and women in the human service professions who do not command large salaries? As the tuition levels of the master's and doctoral programs at PSP continue to fall farther behind the tuition levels of other graduate schools of psychology in Northern California, it is tempting for the board to approve a major tuition hike, knowing that PSP will still be less expensive than other schools in the region.

As is the case with the leaders of many graduate schools, the leaders of PSP know that many of the school's needs could be met with a substantial tuition increase. Such an increase would enable the school to hire more full-time faculty, build a larger library, establish a larger financial reserve, and start to look like schools that are accredited. But PSP is committed to affordable education and does not want to perpetuate the strategy of encouraging students to obtain loans to cover their tuition. Many doctoral graduates of other schools of professional psychology in Northern California owe

$50,000 to $100,000 on student loans, obliging them to seek out wealthy clients who are already being amply served by psychologists. PSP graduates usually owe nothing when they graduate.

Graduate schools are also able to charge high tuition rates by asking some students to help fund the education of other students through scholarship programs. It is not uncommon for graduate schools (and undergraduate institutions as well) to charge a high tuition and then offer scholarships to some students funded not by outside philanthropic sources but rather by a portion of the full tuition the other students pay. This stratagem of "robbing the rich to pay the poor" may be appropriate in some settings, but it certainly is not the only way or even the best way for an educational institution to address issues of financial access.

PSP has also confronted the financial aspect of access by creating a unique guaranteed tuition payment plan. When they enter the school under this plan, PSP students either pay for their entire program up front or participate in a loan program offered by the school that permits them to make monthly payments. In either case, mature PSP students know exactly what the cost of their education will be when entering the school and can control and reduce this cost by accelerating their payments. Because the school, rather than a bank, holds the student's note, PSP can be much more flexible if circumstances favor reducing student payments for several months, accepting additional payments or balloon payments, or restructuring the loan. Furthermore, interest from these loans is funneled back into the school's educational program, rather than being paid by the student to a bank. This helps reduce the cost of education at PSP further without reducing quality.

Physical Facilities

Like many other schools, all three case study institutions have become more sensitive with regard to facilities. All three have built or remodeled facilities that are fully accessible to physically disabled students and provide supplemental audiovisual equipment for students with impaired vision or hearing. When PSP moved into new facilities in both San Francisco and Sacramento, school leaders insisted that all areas of the school be fully wheelchair accessible. Furthermore, PSP has obtained equipment to enlarge printed materials for visually impaired students and has made special arrangements to have available textbook materials, audiovisual aids, and examination procedures for blind and learning-disabled students. These are not particularly noteworthy accomplishments for a large university; such actions in a small, tuition-driven graduate school, however, are remarkable and make all students aware that the school is committed to fair and equal access in all areas (including finances, course scheduling, and location).

All three case study schools (like many other collegiate institutions) have gone beyond the requirements of state and federal law in responding to the physical needs of their student populations. If the accessible college or university is to be successful in providing education for disabled students, it must move far beyond government requirements. An accessible college or university should create equitable admission and testing procedures that encourage high but thoughtful standards and consider such issues as special instructional support services for students with learning disabilities.

Content and Style

The added complexities of a postmodern collegiate institution, in terms of schedule, location, tuition structures, physical facilities, and resources, all help increase access to underserved populations. Yet by themselves, these components of a postmodern collegiate institution are insufficient. Finally able to attend an accessible college or university, the underserved student must be given an appropriate and rich educational experience. Opening the doors is just the first step. These men and women bring unique perspectives and resources that should be honored not only for the sake of their own learning but also for the learning of other students (and faculty) in the classroom.

The unique needs of nontraditional students should also be acknowledged. For instance, Orfield (1990) observes that not only do African-American students rarely have access to the same institutions that white students attend, but also very few institutional changes have been made in response to the introduction of this new student population into the colleges and universities that are accessible. Orfield suggests that changes in institutional policy and procedures have been confined primarily to what he describes as marginal areas of the school: admission policies, remedial training, student support services, and financial aid. The core of the school (curriculum, modes of teaching and learning, faculty counseling, program requirements and structures) have remained essentially untouched. Orfield notes that even in the marginal areas, there has been considerable backsliding in recent years.

Mature adult students, from minority or majority cultures, also want to be heard, and they want their school to be responsive to their distinctive needs. Adult students are often particularly insistent that their past experiences be integrated into their education. When education is really working at JFK and PSP, these adult educational needs are being addressed. Many of the classes at the two schools are interactive, enabling class members to exhibit the skills, knowledge, and experience they have acquired in living their lives. Whereas younger learners (such as those found at Evergreen) often value experiential education because it gives them a taste of the real world, mature adults at JFK and PSP tend to value the opportunity to talk about their own past experiences because the discussion and subsequent analysis confirm the value of these experiences. Furthermore, faculty members can readily make linkages for mature learners between these experiences and the concepts and theories being taught in the course.

Alternative forms of learning are also employed at all three institutions, resulting in a rich variety of experiences for students.

While Evergreen, JFK, and PSP continue to work with certain classic forms of learning, there is a great respect at all three schools for the fact that each student learns in a different way and should be offered diverse means of education. Many of the courses, and especially the field project at all three schools (wherein students are asked to donate time to perform community service or receive internship credit toward licensing), offer students an opportunity to use (or reconfirm) in a new outside environment what they have learned in the classroom or in life.

The issue of designing new programs to meet the distinctive needs of a more diverse student population is certainly not being ignored, despite the disappointing record over the past fifteen years of bringing new populations into our colleges and universities. In recent years, both the American Council on Education (Hall, 1991) and the Western Interstate Commission for Higher Education (Odell and Mock, 1989) have addressed issues related to the need for new programs and structures to serve the new students (especially minority students). They identify curricular changes, multicultural education (for all students), continuing adult education, external degree programs, experiential degrees, and broader-based shifts in public policy and community attitudes. In focusing specifically on community colleges, Nielsen (1991) offers a complementary list: new and more accurate assessment programs, faculty development programs, model student support services, better use of technology, and the formation of partnerships with business, labor, school districts, and other collegiate institutions.

Obviously, these initiatives must go hand in glove with the other four access-related initiatives: time, location, cost, and facilities. Even more important, they must be accompanied by a spirit of cooperation and a commitment to learning on the part of all members of the collegiate community. The leaders of institutions that are committed to access must focus in particular on the creation of settings in which there are ample opportunities for all members of the institution to learn from mistakes and benefit from the support of other people. A commitment to diversity requires an accompanying commitment to learning, for we all will make mistakes and have much to learn from the diverse perspectives, values, and experiences of our students, faculty, administrative colleagues, and other constituencies involved in accessible schools.

Commitment to the Integration of Quality and Access

How does a collegiate institution commit itself to quality while also making itself fully accessible so that quality can be further enhanced? First of all, it is essential that the mission of the school be reviewed regularly in terms of these issues. Frequently, growth in size and complexity is automatically accepted as a goal of the institution when in fact growth has little or nothing to do with the institution's mission. Is it better to serve a large number of students badly or to serve fewer students effectively?

The issue of growth and its impact on both quality and access is particularly vexing for schools like Evergreen, JFK, and PSP, which are relatively young and still establishing their reputations. The three schools exemplify nontraditional institutions established during the late 1960s and the 1970s, a time of great innovation in American higher education. Clark Kerr (1990) characterized the 1960s and 1970s as decades of fundamental transformation. Enrollment in higher education increased 140 percent during this period. The nation's faculty went from 235,000 in 1960 to 685,000 in 1980, and the number of colleges expanded from 2,000 to 3,200. The 1970s and 1980s were also decades in which new hierarchies were established and a sorting out of roles and relationships occurred in higher education. Differential funding made investment in less costly two-year institutions an economical way to increase access. The community college system, which was largely created in this period, was crucial in opening up access to higher education. Community college enrollment went from fewer than half a million students in 1960 to four million by 1980 (Kerr, 1990).

In the state of Washington, as elsewhere, the fates of the two-

and four-year colleges would become increasingly intertwined. By the 1990s, fully half of the students in Washington (and increasingly in the nation as a whole) would enter college through a two-year institution. In many ways, nontraditional colleges and new public liberal arts colleges were caught in crosswinds between different missions for existing traditional four-year institutions and new teaching and community-centered two-year colleges. However, the full implications of this didn't become apparent until the 1980s, when the public liberal arts colleges would argue for a distinctive role and mission. Evergreen occupies an unusual place in the history of American higher education (see Riesman and Grant, 1978; Mayhew, 1978; Dressel, 1971; Levine, 1980; MacDonald, 1973). Not only is it one of the few surviving nontraditional colleges established in the late 1960s, but it also became part of a rising sector in higher education sometimes referred to as the public liberal arts colleges or the "public ivys" (Moll, 1986), uniting the elitist and populist traditions.

This emerging sector came to some prominence in the late 1980s when a group of public liberal arts colleges organized to argue for the value of their distinctive contribution to higher education. Other schools in this sector include the University of North Carolina, Asheville, and Ramapo College (New Jersey), which with Evergreen formed the Council of the Public Liberal Arts Colleges. What these public liberal arts colleges have in common is small size (compared to four-year public institutions), organizational simplicity, and a student-centered identity that attempts to combine access and quality. They strive to provide students at public institutions with the quality liberal arts education previously available only at elite private colleges. Evergreen's dual identity as a nontraditional institution and a public liberal arts college created both stresses and opportunities for the college as it developed.

Evergreen faced many challenges as a nontraditional college, but it was also aided by three critical early factors. First, it had the luxury of a fully funded planning year in which a core of eighteen planning faculty and administrators designed the campus and the program. Neither JFK nor PSP (both private schools) had this luxury, and in many ways the two have been scrambling to catch up ever since. Second, although the temper of the time was profoundly ahistorical, Evergreen learned from the mistakes of the earlier alternatives. It was founded toward the end of the era of expansion in nontraditional higher education and hired a number of faculty members who had participated in those experiments. JFK and PSP were also beneficiaries of earlier experiments, and many of the founding administrators and faculty of these two schools came from other (often unsuccessful) innovative programs. Finally, Evergreen was a more holistic alternative than many similar institutions, less riddled by the dualisms that would eventually drive them back to traditional forms. This was also an advantage of both JFK and PSP as new rather than reformed institutions.

In 1971, The Evergreen State College opened its doors to an entering class of eleven hundred students, becoming the first new public four-year college in Washington in seventy-five years. In its first dozen years, Evergreen was touted in the popular press as a "little-known but high-quality liberal arts college," one of the "ten best-kept secrets among American colleges," "a college with an ivy twist," and "an exceptional value." At the same time, closer to home, bills were being introduced in the state legislature to close the school. Fortunately, the college and leaders in the Washington state legislature were successful in fending off these initiatives.

The issue of how large Evergreen could and should be is a recurrent theme in its history. For many people, the question is intertwined with concerns about the college's mission, cost, and responsiveness. The original forecasts assumed that Evergreen would grow rapidly to more than twelve thousand students by the early 1980s, and the physical plant and administrative structure were planned accordingly. The college did grow rapidly in its first two years, adding a thousand students each year. But then the economy slipped, fueled by recession and huge layoffs at Boeing, which dominated the Washington economy. As a result, enrollments in higher education throughout the state were cut back.

The local newspaper in Olympia, long unfriendly to Evergreen, was filled with stories of layoffs. This negative coverage led to a feeling of failure early on and contributed directly to later problems the college had justifying its cost per student in the face of large diseconomies of scale.

By 1983, it had become clear that the original demographic projections for the college were far off base, and the decision was made to rescale the college to 4,200 students. Most members of the Evergreen community were relieved at the decision to downsize the institution. The campus had been designed largely around small teaching spaces organized to support a seminar-based form of instruction. Most faculty saw the small residential college as the ideal campus environment. But the debate about size and mission continued well into the late 1980s, when the school's mission was officially changed.

Similar demographic miscalculations occurred at a number of other new nontraditional schools, including Ramapo College; the University of California, Santa Cruz; and Southwestern State University (Minnesota). In many instances, these nontraditional schools were forced to revert to traditional curricular and organizational structures. Pressure continues unabated in the 1990s and strongly affects schools such as JFK and PSP that have fewer resources than Evergreen (in terms of money and reputation) to fend it off.

What about the survival of independent colleges, such as JFK and PSP, which have no state funds to support their innovative practices? The critical point seems to be, as in the case of Evergreen, that one must remain committed to the mission of the institution, especially if it concerns both quality and access. An important lesson in this regard can be learned from another independent college that had a distinctive mission involving both quality and access: St. Andrew's Presbyterian College (North Carolina). As an independent, tuition-driven liberal arts college, St. Andrew's retains a strong commitment to serving a particular population of underserved people: severely disabled students. The issues of growth and admissions relate directly to the accompanying issue of financial viability in the case of St. Andrew's. During the late 1970s and early 1980s, St. Andrew's, like many liberal arts colleges, faced financial hardships because of declining student enrollments. The college had a long-standing commitment to mainstreaming its severely disabled students and had set a limit (20 percent) on the number of disabled students that would be admitted each year so that these students would always be interacting with many students who were not disabled.

The 20 percent limit on the severely disabled student population ensured that St. Andrew's would not be perceived as an institution specifically for disabled students. This commitment to diversity was one of its most attractive features. Yet the college was short of students in the late 1970s and could have readily increased its enrollment and at least temporarily solved its financial problems by letting in a larger number of disabled students. The leaders at St. Andrew's chose not to make this move but instead held firm to the mission of the school. This decision not only made sense in terms of long-term benefits but also enabled the school to retain its mutual commitment to quality (defined in this instance as mainstreaming disabled students) and access (attracting severely disabled students and providing exceptional resources for them).

John F. Kennedy University and the Professional School of Psychology, as tuition-driven, independent schools, must also constantly struggle with the issues of growth and financial viability. To be efficient in terms of administrative services, both institutions must attain a certain level of student enrollment, yet the leaders of both must also avoid the typical size-efficiency paradox whereby at a certain point in the growth of an organization, indirect administrative services begin to eat up the largest share of total resources.

As both institutions have grown in size, their organizational structure has become more complex, and their administrative staffs have also increased—at an even greater pace. PSP employed the equivalent of four full-time administrative staffers to serve about 260 students in 1986 (on one main campus and in two small satellite programs); by 1994, with only eighty additional students, the staff had increased to more than ten full-time equivalents (on two independent campuses). Thus, not only has the student population at PSP increased, but the ratio of administrators to students has also increased (from one for every sixty-five students to one for every thirty-four). How can a school like PSP keep tuition low when this ratio continues to shift upward?

Size and complexity also affect the quality of education in a collegiate institution. Both PSP and JFK are favored by some students because of close interactions among faculty, administrators, and students, thanks in large part to the small size of the school. As classes have grown larger (due to cost reduction initiatives or unanticipated growth) and as institutional policies and procedures have proliferated (as a result of pressures toward credibility), students have voiced objections to violation of the basic commitment to small classes and responsive administrative structures.

Critics are inclined to argue that Evergreen, JFK, and PSP are too small, too expensive, or too specialized to survive, particularly in times of economic downturn. All three schools are unaffordable for some prospective students, and the Washington and California economies have suffered substantial swings over the past twenty-five years. No one should start a school in either state if economic stability is a primary concern. But cost hasn't been the only cause for criticism at these three schools. Critics have accused all three of arrogance in choosing to emphasize only one part of their mission—to serve as an alternative college and, in the case of PSP and JFK, to serve nontraditional student populations. However, a nontraditional mission undergirds each of these three schools.

Many critics simply don't like the political, educational, or cultural milieu of these schools. Mayhew, Ford, and Hubbard's (1990) dismissal of such institutions is typical. Evergreen, PSP, and JFK have been tarred with the brush reserved for all nontraditional colleges: they are too soft, too radical, too impractical, and too different from the way "the rest of us" were educated. Under such assault, it is particularly important for schools such as Evergreen, PSP, and JFK to retain their commitment to both quality and access; otherwise, the battle will be lost, and the critics will have been proved right that nontraditional schools are doomed to merely a temporary role in the American higher education community.

Integrating Quality and Access Through Cooperation

In successful postmodern institutions we are likely to find not only a concern for size and uncontrolled growth in administrative structures but also a growing interest in alternative ways by which to expand institutional capacities other than through internal growth. Several of these alternatives (consortia, cluster colleges, matrix models) already have been reviewed in the discussion of the expedient perspective. In the future, we are likely to see many unusual collaborative arrangements between postmodern educational institutions and other agencies in connection with various institutional operations. One such agency, the California Management Institute (CMI), assists colleges and universities in the recruitment of mature, accomplished students from Asia (primarily Taiwan and other Chinese-heritage countries). Enrollment decisions are appropriately left to the educational institution. Once students have been enrolled but before they leave the home country, CMI helps them improve their English skills, get up-to-date in the field they are studying, and even start courses in that field at a university near home.

The staff members at CMI then assist with travel to the United States and make room and board arrangements, obtain and orient translators, and provide tutorial and other assistance to these foreign students. After the students return home, CMI staffers coordinate correspondence between the school and the students. Finally, CMI has been very successful in identifying faculty members for the program (subject to institutional approval) who are particularly sensitive to and effective in addressing the unique educational needs of this student population. The CMI program has been adopted by four California universities and one in the Pacific Northwest. As postmodern colleges and universities begin to define their catchment area very broadly—even internationally—they are likely to establish relationships with organizations such as CMI.

Unfortunately, agencies such as CMI are often dismissed or misunderstood by leaders of collegiate institutions and accrediting agencies. Legitimate concern is expressed about the extent to which agencies such as CMI take over control of the curriculum and student and faculty recruitment from the college or university they are serving. Such concerns have led several schools to terminate contracts with CMI after indirect pressure from the regional accrediting agency and university leaders. It is essential that these decision-making processes remain firmly in the hands of the faculty and academic administrators at the host college or university. Yet these safeguards are in place at CMI. Agencies such as this must be better understood by the higher education community, for they can be of great value in building bridges between various educational institutions and potential student populations.

In the future, postmodern colleges and universities will lower their boundaries and start extending themselves to their local communities and other colleges and universities to form alliances, cooperative agreements, and partnerships. Partnerships have become a key element in Evergreen's attempts to extend the reach of its innovations. A variety of creative efforts have already been undertaken to diversify its student body and broaden curricular options. These new relationships, which evolve and change over time, demonstrate the willingness of the institution to reach out and make long-term commitments and at the same time maximize compatibility with institutional values.

The fit between a postmodern collegiate institution and its partner organizations is crucial. Levine (1980) argues that compatibility and profitability are the key variables in explaining why innovations flourish or fail. Nontraditional institutions like Evergreen, JFK, and PSP probably have some natural advantages in that they aren't constantly facing compatibility challenges from the rest of the institution. Citing Burton Clark's (1970) study of Swarthmore, Antioch, and Reed, Levine argues that distinctive institutions often need to maintain relatively rigid boundaries (especially in their early years) to maintain their uniqueness: "In the case of Clark's three colleges, this meant a small, little-changing core clientele and financial support groups; a student subculture for socializing entering students to appropriate norms, values, and goals; and a true ideology. In combination, these elements preserved the three experiments. At the same time, they ruled out other types of innovations" (p. 170). Several of the projects now being initiated at Evergreen are notable with regard to this dimension of compatibility with institutional norms and values.

One in particular stands out. Evergreen has started serving multicultural communities through its Tacoma campus. This campus started in 1972 with two students in the founding director's kitchen. It grew to 120 upper-division students and was formally recognized as a branch campus by the state Higher Education Coordinating Board in 1983. Increasingly assertive about its sense of obligation to the local community, the campus moved into the heart of the economically troubled Hilltop area of Tacoma to help rebuild the multicultural community. In 1985, an innovative lower-division bridge program was added in collaboration with Tacoma Community College to serve an additional fifty students who needed the lower-division program to enter Evergreen's upper-division curriculum. The bridge program is taught by a team of faculty from the two colleges and located on the site of Evergreen's upper-division program. This partnership represents a radical vision of intercollege articulation, the type that may be increasingly required to boost the baccalaureate completion rate as more and more students—

especially students of color—begin their college career in a two-year institution.

The teacher education program at Evergreen further exemplifies the college's outreach orientation and its accompanying concern for compatibility with its commitment to quality and access. The program slowly evolved from a contractual, traditional program to a distinctively Evergreen program of team-taught coordinated study programs. In 1985, Evergreen switched its traditional teacher education program from a six-year contracted partnership with the University of Puget Sound to a more integrated collaborative program with Western Washington University. In 1990, Evergreen decided to establish its own independent master's program within the teaching program.

Postmodern colleges and universities are likely to expand radically and even to shatter traditional spatial and temporal boundaries regarding what is and is not the campus and when the institution's commitment to the education of its students comes to an end (that is, when graduation actually occurs). At an even more basic level, the very notion of the student will be challenged and expanded. With regard to spatial boundaries, we will see the successful postmodern college or university become more fully involved in its community and in the life of its alumni and others that have been or are now being served by the institution. These institutions will increasingly become intersect organizations (Boulding, 1973)—a mix of various institutional forms (public and private, big and small). We may in the future find much more extensive use of partnerships, alliances, and compacts between postsecondary educational institutions and various other types of organizations (corporations, human service agencies, governmental agencies, and the like).

We are also likely to find not only interrelationships between postmodern collegiate institutions and other educational and human service agencies but also collaborative programs between colleges, universities, corporations, and governmental agencies that all help increase access by cutting costs; expanding the resources available to students, faculty, and administrators; and breaking down traditional boundaries between school and community.

For instance, the Professional School of Psychology recently engaged in a three-year project with a major newspaper publishing company, Lesher Communications, to help it establish self-managed work teams and a sociotechnical redesign of its production process in its new high-tech printing factory. Though many colleges and universities over the years have signed contracts with corporations—the electronics industry has been built around such agreements for years—the PSP-Lesher contract was unusual in that the project became both a source of revenues for the school and an ongoing internship and research venue for PSP faculty and students. Much as there are facilities associated with medical schools that become teaching hospitals, the Lesher project became a teaching organization for PSP faculty and students who were interested in organizational psychology and consultation.

In the future, we are likely to find many more alliances and partnerships formed by postmodern institutions such as Evergreen, JFK, and PSP. New government-supported joint-powers agreements will allow for new collaborative efforts between governmental agencies, private enterprises, and human service agencies (including colleges and universities) that enable a cluster of institutions to provide a variety of quasi-governmental services (limited only in their inability to levy taxes). What might we find when postmodern colleges and universities—be they public or private, nonprofit or for profit—begin to engage in these joint-powers agreements?

Working at the Intersect: Blending Creativity, Commitment, and Cooperation

Chapter Eight described the intersect organization and looked at ways in which expedient institutions have used auxiliary enterprises to raise funds—in most instances having little to do with either quality or access. In other cases, however, the intersect relationships and accompanying auxiliary enterprises have exhibited both a commitment to quality and access and the creative use of cooperation to achieve both quality and access.

Berea College (Kentucky), for instance, was one of the first schools to make effective use of auxiliary enterprises. All of the students at Berea work at the college to pay for their education. Many years ago, the leaders of this college decided to manufacture craft products, with student labor, that could be sold in stores throughout the United States to raise funds for the college (thereby preserving the college's populist commitment to financial accessibility). Many other colleges and universities could benefit from Berea's example. If churches can sell cakes and run flea markets to raise funds and if states and churches can run lotteries to generate revenues for educational programs, college and university presidents are certainly justified in running football games, baton-twirling clinics, and miniature golf courses to support their institutions.

Creative intersects are also being formed in the blending of residential and commuter-based student activities on expedient campuses. In serving nontraditional student populations, the academic and student service leaders of contemporary institutions often confront the reality of these students' having to live off campus because of marital status, low socioeconomic level, or full-time work, by creating new hybrid models of on-campus and off-campus programming. In some instances, weekend residential programs are offered, whereby nontraditional students can live on campus one weekend each month to participate in an intensive program. In other instances, nonresidential nontraditional students are paired up with residential traditional students, providing the former with a colleague to meet with at night or during the day. The traditional student can in turn make use of the nontraditional student's contacts in the community to overcome the isolation typical of many residential students.

In a more extreme case, the unified perspective begins to break down the traditional boundaries between campus and community by defining the whole community as the campus. Lone Mountain College, a visionary liberal arts college for women that was absorbed by the University of San Francisco during the 1970s, used a picture of the city on its promotional materials, indicating that all of San Francisco was its campus. The college provided extensive field placements in the city and offered many activities in collaboration with other city organizations, truly making the entire city its campus.

Flathead Valley Community College in Montana incorporated itself in its community in the 1970s by offering most of its courses during the evening in stores located along the main street of the town of Kalispell. Flathead Valley was a true intersect organization that completely shattered the boundaries between campus and community, in the process reducing overhead costs and increasing community visibility and cooperation. Faculty members, like Exemplar's Joan Broadhead, who come out of corporate settings, can often provide valuable linkages to the community if given some credibility by their academic colleagues and if given a chance to exert some initiative.

The intersect can also be formed in creative ways between the institution and faculty members. Rather than conceiving of faculty as employees, they can be considered partners in a flexible, cooperative commitment to quality and access. Faculty members may be hired part-time to teach one or two specific courses each term. They might be hired full-time, bringing their own personal accounts (as clinical psychologist, financial planner, accountant, engineer, nurse, or physician) into the institution. In exchange, they obtain a stable cash flow, benefit programs, free office, free secretarial services, and colleagueship.

Faculty in elitist research universities are often supported in part or in full by governmental or corporate research grants, and faculty in populist institutions are sometimes supported by state and federal program grants. By contrast, faculty in successful postmodern schools may be supported in part or in full by service contracts that the schools obtain from corporations, governmental offices, or human service agencies. Liberal arts colleges, such as Northland College (Wisconsin), and vocational-technical institutes, such as Fox Valley Technical College (Wisconsin), have supported many of their innovative programs in environmental studies, Native American studies, American history, business ethics, and total quality management through the establishment of self-sustaining or even profit-generating institutes run by faculty, administrators, and students.

What about Joshua Wheat at Exemplar? How might a cooperative, campus-community intersect help him? Perhaps Exemplar should be much more flexible with regard to his boundaries. Wheat is always having to struggle with his own speaking and consulting assignments as they relate to his teaching responsibilities at Exemplar. Couldn't his outside work be more closely linked to the school? I have already mentioned establishing a cluster college that provides a laboratory for him to explore student writing. What about setting up an institute through which Wheat does his speaking and consulting, that would be tied directly to the new cluster college? Couldn't this help make Exemplar a national center for student writing, much as Sonoma State University in California has become a national center for critical thinking (as a result of several entrepreneurial faculty members' being given a chance to pursue their interests)? Expedient colleges and universities like Exemplar could benefit greatly from the loosening of boundaries when this loosening is coupled with a clear sense of the institution's mission and future directions.

Key Points

1. Given the intimate relationship between access and quality, we must first determine in which dimensions our institution is going to be accessible. Which of the many underserved popu-

lations will be the focus of our commitment and our initiatives? Typically, focus is directed toward one or more of six target populations in American higher education: the working adult, people without substantial income, women, people of non-Northern European origin, people with disabilities, and people who deserve a second chance.

2. Typically, one or more of six dimensions of the collegiate institution are altered to respond to the distinctive needs of new student populations being served by our colleges and universities: time (course scheduling), location (where services are offered), cost (tuition levels and payment plans), facilities (setting in which services are being delivered), content (what is being taught), and style (the way services, including instruction, are being delivered).

3. Any college or university in our postmodern era that wishes to achieve and integrate quality and access must repeatedly review its mission in terms of these commitments. Frequently, growth in size and complexity is automatically accepted as a goal of the institution, obscuring the deeper commitment to quality and access. Is it better to serve a large number of students badly or to serve fewer students in an effective, high-quality manner? A commitment to access does not necessarily mean a commitment to serving all populations or to serving a large number of people.

4. Successful postmodern colleges and universities are likely to explore alternative ways in which to expand institutional capacities other than through internal growth, thereby keeping down unnecessary costs and enabling the institution to sustain quality while increasing access.

Chapter Ten

Institutional Approaches to Managing Quality and Access

Quality—clarity about it and a commitment to it—has long been recognized as critical to any effectively running organization. There is nothing new in my emphasis on this concept. In fact, increased attention has being given to the achievement and maintenance of quality in recent years in all sectors of our society. Total quality management (TQM) (and its many variant forms, such as continuous quality improvement) has been enthusiastically embraced in many corporations, human service agencies, and governmental agencies over the past decade, to the point that these programs now seem almost outmoded.

Yet, in higher education, TQM is still a new concept, received with mixed reactions in the postsecondary education community (for example, Carothers, 1992; Sherr and Teeter, 1991; Cross, 1993; Marchese, 1992a, 1992b; Seymour, 1991; Spanbauer, 1992; Whittington, 1992). In part, I would suggest, this concept has been resisted in some sectors because it often flies in the face of three of the organizational cultures (collegial, developmental, and negotiating) that exist in American higher education, being identified with and emerging primarily from the fourth culture (managerial). Despite these problems, I suggest that TQM strategies can be effective in American higher education and that these strategies are crucial to the achievement of not only quality but also access in our postmodern colleges and universities. I propose that any total quality initiative will be successful in our postmodern world only if it informs the ways in which our institutions achieve and maintain quality, and if it also informs the ways in which they achieve and maintain broad-based access and the integration of quality and access. This is the essence of the unified perspective on quality and access.

The key lessons to be learned from the application of TQM principles in higher education institutions are these:

1. TQM is an ongoing organizational process rather than a specific product that can readily be transplanted from one campus or corporation to another.
2. Quality-oriented processes, as described by most TQM-related strategies, concern primarily communication between the consumer (student) and the organization, among the members of the organization, and among the various constituencies that are stakeholders in the organization.
3. The quality of the processes being used in an educational institution is ultimately more important than the quality of the product of the institution.
4. Process-oriented TQM strategies are particularly relevant in higher education (and other educational institutions) because higher education produces no tangible physical product that is subject to direct inspection; rather, higher education is concerned primarily with the quality of extended conversations that are defined as processes of teaching and learning.
5. Proponents and managers of TQM strategies must be particularly sensitive to cultural differences among the various groups that must approve and implement the TQM imperative; these cultural differences relate directly to the four cultures (collegial, managerial, developmental, negotiating) I have described here and elsewhere (Bergquist, 1992).

In this chapter, I relate the issues of quality and access to the emerging interest in total quality management and related quality-oriented initiatives for institutional reform in higher education. I will illustrate the use of these strategies through the three case study institutions I introduced in Part One and offer a general framework for the exploration of institutionwide initiatives for achieving and maintaining quality and access in institutions of higher education.

Three components are central to any institutionwide initiative to achieve quality and access: assessment of institutional functions; clarification of institutional values, mission, and goals; and empowerment of various constituencies. Three communication strategies link these components: benchmarking of institutional strengths and weaknesses, development of professional competencies, and feedback on personal and institutional performance.

I will discuss the achievement of quality and access with specific regard to all six of these elements (see Figure 10.1).

Assessment of Internal and External Environment

An institution seeking quality and access must continuously gather in a systematic manner both quantitative and qualitative information on its own internal operations as well as on the changing environment in which it operates. Whereas a premodern, elitist college or university president could rely on personal contact with students, faculty, and alumni to assess the quality of education in his or her institution, the modern-day more populist-oriented president requires formal institutional research and formal assessment tools and procedures to determine the quality of education being offered. In the postmodern era, notions about assessment are likely to be much more sophisticated and complex, moving beyond the simple collection of information about basic institutional functions and outcomes. The new modes of assessment are much more likely to invite inquiry and dialogue rather than just passive reception of descriptive statistics on student enrollment, financial health, and postgraduate success. In more complex assessments, at least three data sources ("triangulation") are likely to be used

Figure 10.1. The Quality-Access Triangle.

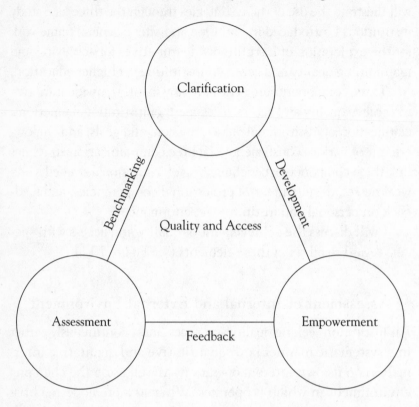

in the assessment of any critical factor inside or outside the institution. All constituencies of the institution will be involved in these ongoing assessment operations to ensure the accuracy, acceptance, and use of collected information.

The managerial culture at most collegiate institutions is likely to promote this strategy and the systematic collection of information about daily operations. The development culture is likely to embrace the linkage of these assessment processes to the institution's mission. Whereas leaders of the managerial culture will ensure that assessment is taking place, leaders of the developmental culture will ensure that this assessment focuses on the educational purposes of the institution rather than on administrative means to these educational ends.

As with many other institutions, assessment came to The Evergreen State College primarily as a result of crisis and external pressures. Institutionally, we often don't wish to look at ourselves too closely and will look carefully and critically only when forced to do so. A crucial turning point in Evergreen's history came in June 1977 when the popular three-term Republican governor of Washington, Daniel Evans, assumed the presidency of Evergreen. His appointment raised a great many eyebrows. Some observers criticized the appointment, arguing that he had set up the college as a "retirement spot"; others experienced greater cognitive dissonance. But Evans brought a new level of respect to the college, and it is difficult to imagine what might have happened had he not assumed Evergreen's presidency when he did. In close collaboration with a much respected provost and founding faculty member, Byron Youtz, Evans played a key role in stabilizing the college and improving its image in the state.

During the first two years of Evans's term, the college experienced absolute enrollment declines, nearly dipping below the critical two thousand mark in 1978. Student retention also reached a low of 55 percent. In 1977, the state legislature asked the Postsecondary Education Council (CPE) to conduct a study of Evergreen to identify actions that should be taken to increase enrollment and reduce the average cost of educating an Evergreen student. The CPE responded with a detailed study of the college's programs, enrollment patterns, and processes; its cost; and its image among current students, area high school students, alumni, and employers. There was particular concern that the college was not attracting a proportionate number of local high school and community college students. Surveys were conducted to ascertain why.

Surprisingly, the surveys indicated that Evergreen provided many of the features that the high school students said they valued, but the students did not associate these features with Evergreen. The areas in which the college was perceived to fall short were areas in which the college actually excelled, such as the ability of graduates to get jobs, teaching as the most important mission, faculty expecting students to work hard, students committed to learning, small classes, accessible faculty, and low tuition. Clearly, Evergreen was not communicating well. The CPE survey questioned whether Evergreen's problem was one of being unattractively different and not offering the right campus environment or curricular options, or merely one of perception. The authors of the CPE report suggested that it was probably some of each but urged the college to improve its communications and to institute new activities and programs to broaden its appeal. The study concluded with twenty recommendations, the most important one being that the college be given a four-year "breathing period" to implement changes and reverse declining enrollment. The CPE report recommended that enrollment be increased to 4,250 full-time equivalents to achieve cost parity with similar institutions. Earlier studies had indicated that the direct costs of instruction at Evergreen were only slightly higher than at other regional public colleges ($1,325 versus $1,219), but the gap was much larger in terms of the overall support costs. Most of the differences were attributable to size.

With very specific directions from the state, Evans and Youtz had considerable leverage to engage the college community in serious self-analysis and corrective actions. Over the next several years, Evergreen assessed many of its processes and implemented most of the CPE recommendations. Though the fundamental approach and values of the institution did not change as a result of the CPE recommendations, the college created a variety of ways of explaining what it did to make it more intelligible to outsiders. These included developing recruiting brochures to translate Evergreen programs into disciplinary equivalencies and transcript fact sheets summarizing traditional course equivalencies. The college also embarked on an intensive and professionalized program of student recruitment and aggressive research and assessment of its efforts. Pressures from outside the college and a successful assessment of the college by the CPE had demonstrated the value of this strategy. Evergreen could not keep its head in the sand. Evaluative information had to be collected systematically and regularly to keep the college viable.

In the case of John F. Kennedy University, assessment is neither a high priority nor a source of particular innovation. Charles Glasser, the president at JFK, speaks of his own intuitive sense of how the university is doing at any point in time. Although his administrators and deans systematically collect information about the functioning of the university, these assessments are being done partly for external consumption (regional accrediting association, federal and state agencies, and so forth). Recent federal regulations on guaranteed student loans suggest that in the future external sources will be even more interested in the assessment of various institutional functions, especially student learning outcomes. But is this information being used by internal sources? Are the administrators at JFK (or any other college or university, for that matter) making effective use of this information? I would suggest that quality and access can be effectively integrated only if assessment is intimately linked to the ongoing operations of the college or university.

Without a substantial flow of information into the decision-making processes, it is easy for administrators to fall comfortably back into their own informal impressions of the dimensions of quality and access. Unfortunately, these informal impressions are often distorted or clouded by traditional standards of quality (primarily input measures, such as number of faculty with doctorates, number of square feet of classroom space, and student-faculty ratio) or by traditional quantitative measures of access (number of minority students enrolled, mean taxable income of all entering students, and so forth). Institutional assessment can challenge this complacency, as it did at Evergreen, and bring the leaders to new levels of awareness about the subtle, even ephemeral nature of both true quality and true access.

What, then, about the Professional School of Psychology? The answer is disappointing. PSP is not doing a very good job, though the key administrator on one of the two campuses strongly encourages the collection of more institutional information. Is there any excuse? Not really. However, PSP's failure to make effective use of institutional assessment points to several important issues related to this administrative function. First, intuition is very seductive. Leaders at both PSP and JFK are convinced that they understand their own institution when in fact they may be quite mistaken.

I know that presidents are often the least knowledgeable members of the administrative staff when it comes to understanding and appreciating the daily operations of the institution. We are much more frequently in the business of envisioning and articulating a vision or a goal for the school than we are in the business of assessing the school's current functioning. We know about and celebrate the construction of a new classroom yet don't really know what goes on there once it has been built. We raise funds for a new library but don't really know how our students and faculty make use of the improved facilities. Years ago, Richard Beckhard (1969) wrote about the importance of moving decision making to the level where the maximum amount of information exists about the decision to be made. This level is usually not in the president's office.

Second, institutional research often takes a backseat to the more immediate critical needs of a low-status, struggling college or university. PSP confronts the need for more full-time faculty and for a substantial increase in administrative staff and library resources in preparation for accreditation while retaining its commitment to low-cost education. It is relatively easy for leaders at PSP to set aside various institutional research operations (such as studies of student attrition, postgraduate performance on the job, or the achievement of specific student learning outcomes). This may make sense over the short term; however, over the longer term, institutional assessment is critical if an institution such as PSP is to retain its commitment to both quality and access. One or the other is likely to drop off if the leaders don't keep a close watch on institutional functions, and this close watch is not possible unless the leaders of the school encourage and make extensive use of institutional research.

Clarification of Mission

The mission of an institution is nothing more or less than an answer to the question, "Why does this entity exist?" (a variant might be, "What difference does it make that this institution exists?"). An institution seeking quality and access must be clear about its mission, for in achieving and sustaining quality and access, the faculty, administrators, staff, and board must know why it exists and what its priorities will be over a specific period of time. There is very little room in hard-pressed postmodern colleges and universities for the misdirected or unguided expenditure of resources on activities that have little to do with either quality or access, especially if they are unrelated to or incompatible with the institutional mission.

In establishing and sustaining the mission of a collegiate institution, a leader, committee, or board must first clarify the deeply embedded values and the personal and organizationally based aspirations of the members and then determine the implications of these values and aspirations for the activating and sustaining vision of the institution. Institutional goals and objectives should be built on these enduring values, aspirations, and vision. In essence, the values of an institution concern the founding and emerging principles and the understandings of the ways in which the institution will operate. New or altered values can rarely be introduced by individual members, no matter how important their leadership roles. Rather, values are born and cultivated in the daily activities of the college or university; they are deeply embedded in the culture of the school and are highly resistant to willful change. Typically, the crucial role played by a leader is not to change the values of an institution but rather to identify and clarify the existing values so that the institution operates with consistency and awareness.

Similarly, the personal aspirations of members of the community are not easily manipulated or modified; rather, they are the givens of the institution. For whatever reason, people are attracted to the college or university as students, faculty members, administrators, staff, or board members. They bring their own assumptions about what the school could do for them in terms of fulfilling personal aspirations regarding career advancement, social acceptance, status enhancement, intellectual stimulation, altruistic gratification, and so forth. These men and women also bring aspirations about the college or university—what they would like the institution to be. These organizational aspirations often relate to their own history in one of the four academic cultures (collegial, managerial, developmental, negotiating) and their own perspectives on quality and access.

Edgar Schein (1978, 1980) speaks of the "psychological contract" that forms (usually unconsciously) between members of the organization and the organization itself. People make certain assumptions (often self-fulfilling) about what they will give the organization (service, competency, loyalty, subservience) and what the organization will give them in return (wages, job security, self-respect, social acceptance, status). The psychological contract may be violated either because the individual's aspirations and expectations are unexpressed or because the organization fails to meet them. It is therefore essential that personal and organizational aspirations among the members of a collegiate community be identified and clarified in conjunction with the identification and clarification of institutional values.

The institutional vision makes explicit where the college or university wishes to be in the future. Typically, this vision is never fully achievable; it serves more as an inspiration than as a goal. Nevertheless, it is tangible—it can be seen, felt, and touched. We know what it would feel like to achieve this vision (see Bergquist and Armstrong, 1986).

This emphasis on the clarification of values, aspirations, and vision is decidedly postmodern. It arises from the diffusion of boundaries in postmodern organizations, including colleges and universities. Collegiate institutions can remain intact only if they are clear about the reason for their existence. Without clear boundaries, organizations must find other ways in which to hold themselves together. The center will not hold in postmodern organizations, unless central purposes and mission are clear. This process of clarification in turn requires what Peter Senge (1990) has called a sustained dialogue (a mutual pursuit of truth) rather than discussion (an adversarial process by which the holder of truth is determined). Values, aspirations, and vision are conservative forces in institutions, but they do change over time (particularly in the turbulent postmodern era); that is why the dialogue must be ongoing and collaborative.

In our postmodern era, it is tempting for a collegiate institution to be expedient in terms of its mission. However, as noted in Chapter Eight, expedient institutions often pay a price for their flexibility in regard to the central mission, values, and aspirations of the school. They run the risk of losing the ability to sustain program initiatives (because of the incompatibility of these initiatives with the culture, values, and aspirations of the school) and to integrate these initiatives with the school's more traditional components. Contemporary colleges and universities will benefit very little from the expedient or opportunistic identification of new values or visions. Typically, contemporary colleges and universities are better advised to build on the existing distinctive culture (especially its values, aspirations, and vision) in response to changing needs and demands among potential customers. In academic circles, the developmental culture is likely to further ongoing substantive dialogue about the purposes of the institution, whereas the negotiating culture is likely to serve as a watchdog of the processes by and through which this dialogue takes place.

Though PSP can take little pride in its institutional assessment initiatives, its leaders can point admiringly to their efforts at clarifying and continually asserting the importance of PSP's vision, values, and mission. The PSP catalogue spells out not only the school's mission but also three underlying commitments and values. At a yearly daylong retreat, members of the board reflect on the mission

and values of the school and whether they are being met. Responding to the complex requirements of regulatory, funding, and accrediting groups can cause leaders to lose sight of the institution's
fundamental commitments.

While I served as president, I frequently reminded myself of
PSP's mission in my dealings with colleagues inside and outside the
school. Even small compromises can lead to abandonment of the
mission. The mission statement in the catalogue might no longer
reflect the work done in the administrative offices and classrooms.
Guarding against this outcome was perhaps my most important
responsibility as president of PSP. In his study of large-scale changes
in American higher education during the late 1960s, Mayhew
(1978) found that many of these changes came precisely at the time
when higher education started to encounter serious financial difficulties. As a result, many of the original nontraditional institutions
were underfunded and forced to become conventional or to lower
standards to survive. These schools often lost their sense of purpose
and values while fighting for their existence.

More than a decade later, Mayhew and coauthors Ford and
Hubbard (1990) contended that many of the nontraditional efforts
of the 1960s eventually produced low-quality education and were
motivated more by survival than by genuine educational objectives. They gave the nontraditional college a bad name and questioned whether nontraditional education is affordable when done
right. Evergreen, JFK, and PSP should be in the business of prov-
ing Mayhew and colleagues wrong by demonstrating that both
quality and access can be preserved in a contemporary college or
university.

Empowerment of Constituencies

All relevant constituencies in an institution must be engaged in its
decision-making, problem-solving, and planning activities if quality
and access are to be achieved. This respect for broad-based participation in academic institutions is of premodern origins. Ironically,

many TQM advocates move into collegiate institutions touting the benefits of high-involvement management. If they come out of corporate settings, they often fail to note that most colleges and universities already have substantial worker involvement, known as faculty governance. Many of the problems faced by colleges and universities in fact result not from a lack of broad-based involvement but rather from too much (ineffective or unpredictable) involvement by too many constituencies. Put simply, a college or university president often plays a role more closely resembling that of an urban mayor than that of the chief executive officer in a corporation (Cohen and Marsh, 1974). The harried postmodern college or university president (as personified by Exemplar's Kevin Gravitz) must typically set some decision-making and problem-solving boundaries if his or her institution is to function with a modicum of order and purpose.

The norms and values underlying this emphasis on faculty involvement originate in the collegial culture, most frequently in elitist colleges and universities. Ironically, strong faculty governance is also present in collegiate institutions that are least elitist, most beleaguered, and pervaded by the negotiating culture. Whereas the collegial culture and elitist institution emphasize the involvement of faculty in the educational governance of the school, the negotiating culture and beleaguered institution emphasize (or are forced to acknowledge) the role of faculty in budgetary and personnel decision-making processes.

In our emerging postmodern era, the tools of involvement that have traditionally been advocated by the collegial and negotiating cultures and dominate elitist and beleaguered institutions will no longer be adequate. Much as postmodern assessment must shift from passive data collection to interactive inquiry and as value clarification must shift from contentious discussion to interactive dialogue, so must empowerment shift from adversarial confrontation to interactive deliberation. The most successful postmodern institutions respect diversity of perspectives and assumptions among the constituencies involved in such deliberation.

This spirit of deliberation and dialogue must be sustained by all participants. The individual rights given to various constituencies must be balanced against collective responsibility assumed by all constituencies for the overall welfare of the institution (Gilligan, 1982). Collegiate leaders must define their role primarily in terms of facilitating these empowering processes. The leader must serve as a synthesizer. He or she must also provide support to these various constituencies in the movement toward and maintenance of highest quality and access. In this capacity, the collegiate leader serves not as master of but rather as servant to the institution.

Benchmarking Against Other Institutions

An institution seeking quality and access must place its assessment and clarification processes against those of other institutions that are comparable, competitive, or potential role models. These other institutions can serve as measuring sticks or benchmarks against which to assess the potential and actual achievement of one's own institution. Such comparisons permit distinctions to be drawn so that the unique quality of one's own institution can be more readily identified and nurtured. Interinstitutional learning is at the heart of this continuous monitoring effort.

Given the growing emphasis on benchmarking in TQM initiatives, we are likely to see increased attention given to consortial arrangements among collegiate institutions. Whereas in the past consortia were established primarily to share resources, they will soon be used more extensively to set standards and provide monitoring of performance based on mutually accepted standards. Many corporate consortia that are oriented toward TQM—such as the Council for Continuous Improvement (San Jose, California)—are built primarily around the process of benchmarking (see Bergquist, Betwee, and Meuel, 1995). Institutions of higher learning are soon to follow in the footsteps of their corporate colleagues, especially if collegiate leaders continue to grow increasingly disenchanted with the standards set and comparisons made by governmental agencies, regional accrediting associations, and national disciplinary associations.

For all three of the case study institutions, the issue of benchmarking is important but troublesome. Existing governmental and accrediting institutions that provide benchmarks (set standards) and form judgments about the quality of education in these three institutions are likely to be inadequate or even unfair, for each of these institutions offers a distinctive educational program and serves nontraditional students. Questions come immediately to the fore when considering benchmarking in distinctive institutions: Are there any other colleges or universities that should be used as benchmarks in assessing the effectiveness of these institutions? What is to be learned from colleges and universities that offer very different programs and serve very different students? How does one know if a good job is being done if there is no one else in the same "business"?

During my many years of consulting with nontraditional schools, I have found that they quickly become isolated and self-delusional. It is too easy to rely on the advantage of being different and to ignore the more difficult issue of being successful at being distinctively different. For instance, how can the leaders of PSP know if the school is truly successful in serving adult learners, given that most of the outside bodies that review the school (such as the state postsecondary education commission and regional accrediting agency) have relatively little experience in assessing schools exclusively devoted to adult learners?

I have found that PSP's reviewers over the past ten years have often failed to notice what I consider major flaws in our delivery of educational services to working adults. For instance, PSP does not provide technical mechanisms (videotapes, audiotapes) for the recording of class sessions. Knowing that our students are called away on business or family emergencies much more frequently than typical twenty-five-year-old graduate students, we should make arrangements for them to review any sessions that they miss. We have responded to this situation by setting limits (no more than three missed sessions per course) and encouraging students to help each other by sharing notes and recording classes. No one reviewing the school has even brought up this issue.

What about The Evergreen State College? How did this institution, as a leader in innovative education during the early 1970s, deal with the issue of benchmarking? By 1974, questions about the way the college operated had been raised internally, and students began to demand more predictability in the curriculum. This led to greater reliance on outside opinions and the first use of benchmarking at the school. Three critical inquiries focused attention on the future direction of the college: a 1974 accreditation report, a 1975 long-range curriculum review, and the report from a 1976 review panel established by the Evergreen board of trustees. All three reports made essentially the same recommendations, some of which would be repeated in the 1978 report by the Council on Postsecondary Education.

Evergreen's first accreditation visit took place in 1974. The visiting team was strongly supportive of the new college but also suggested ways in which it could improve. The accreditation team recognized the power of the coordinated-studies programs and saw this as Evergreen's strongest plus. But the team also found considerable variation in quality among programs and felt a need for better overall balance in the curriculum. The committee suggested that the college face up to some basic questions about boundaries in light of the wide variations in modes of study, in student counseling, in the integration of the program themes, and in the level of challenge in the curriculum.

Many of the issues raised by the accreditation report were addressed by the 1975 long-range curriculum DTF (disappearing task force, Evergreen's name for an ad hoc committee). It recommended that a portion of the curriculum be repeated and that the overall curriculum be organized around interdisciplinary specialty areas to provide more sequence, coherence, and predictability. Also, some additional career-oriented areas were established, such as a specialty in management and the public interest. At the same time, an upper-division program was established in Vancouver, Washington, a community that many people considered a logical alternative site for the original campus. Limited part-time studies were also established in Olympia. All of these moves had the consequence of diversifying the student body and the faculty, but within the framework of coordinated-studies programs and the essential values with which the college had begun.

In 1976, a review panel was appointed by the board of trustees to provide additional benchmarks. Acting like an accreditation team, the panel sought to augment the accreditation evaluation committee's view, particularly emphasizing the extent to which the college was benefiting citizens of the state. This phenomenon of outside reviews assisting internal change processes would be repeated throughout the college's history. At the same time, the academic administration of the college was reorganized in 1976 by the board trustees in the interests of greater continuity. A system of selecting two long-term deans (appointed to four-year terms, renewable twice) and two rotating deans (serving nonrenewable terms) from the faculty was established. This approach was designed to give continuity to long-term functions while still providing the faculty perspective and vitality that comes from having administrators with recent experience in the classroom. This system was later changed in the mid 1980s in the interests of attracting internal deans who rotated more frequently, a decision that again eventually created problems of continuity and curricular instability.

Development of Human and Organizational Resources

Institutions will find that the implementation of a program for quality and access will inevitably follow a developmental path in which the human and organizational resources of the institution are fully enhanced and more effectively used. Although Mayhew, Ford, and Hubbard (1990), using outdated information from the 1970s, suggest that developmental efforts have received little support and are probably not needed in high-quality (elitist) colleges and universities, it is clear that efforts at professional, faculty, and administrative development are a fixture in American higher education, as witnessed by the proliferation of professional development programs throughout North America.

Professional development includes not only the refinement of existing knowledge and skills but also acquisition of new knowledge, skills, and attitudes. Development concerns the creation and modification of institutional structures that support and reward ongoing development. Career ladders must be built for all employees, including faculty members. It is particularly challenging to build career ladders for faculty who have already attained full-professor status in their early forties (not unusual in American higher education). What future challenges can be posed for these faculty members with regard to institutional leadership, continuing intellectual and pedagogical growth, and the mentoring of younger faculty?

Reward systems in a responsive postmodern college or university should be integrally tied to improvement of both current and anticipated knowledge, skills, and attitudes. Ongoing reflection on one's own practices (Schön, 1983, 1987) is at the heart of any continuous improvement effort. This process requires an accompanying clarification of organizational values, personal aspirations, and institutional vision; a sense of personal empowerment; and rich, diverse sources of feedback on personal and institutional performance. Perhaps more than any of the other components and strategies identified in this chapter, development must be integrally linked with the other five.

A second ingredient at the heart of development and continuous improvement is collegiality. In all my years of working in and writing about professional development in higher education, the one fact that has repeatedly struck me about the enduring benefit of professional development relates to the isolation of faculty members (and most administrators and staff members, for that matter). If nothing else, ongoing and effective professional development breaks down barriers between people and encourages them to discuss their teaching, departmental problems, decision making and problem solving, and even life outside the academy.

I am always amazed that faculty, administrative, and staff development workshops are considered a success by everyone concerned if they do nothing more than provide an opportunity for open and thoughtful communication among participants. Members of the higher education community aren't asking for much, but they should be granted their request for a few moments of dialogue and the breaking of barriers between disciplines, departments, and people working at various levels and in various functional areas of the college and university. TQM will be effective in higher education if this simple need for communication is kept at the forefront.

I offer an example from PSP to illustrate this point. During my eight years as president of PSP and during the previous decade as a faculty member at several other graduate schools in Northern California, I consistently advocated the establishment of professional development programs for myself as well as my colleagues. Such a stance would certainly be expected of me, given my work promoting professional development: I would be a hypocrite if I were not an advocate in my own hometown. Yet I have been singularly unsuccessful in these efforts. In one instance, I wasn't even voted onto the professional development committee of a graduate school in which I taught, even though (or perhaps because) everyone knew of my experience in the field. By 1991, I came to the conclusion that my own role as a hometown advocate was doomed. I should stick to my consulting work and leave professional development in my own school to other people.

Ironically, I have been very successful in promoting professional development since then, but indirectly, through a program

I initiated in another part of the world, the former Soviet republic of Estonia. As a result of my sponsorship of an Estonian graduate student at PSP, I began working with several colleagues at PSP and at a university and mental hospital in Estonia to establish a yearly mental health institute in the newly independent country. Since 1991, I have traveled with two of my PSP colleagues several times to Estonia to establish and run this institute. We from PSP and our colleagues from Estonia have benefited immeasurably from this exchange, and my work there has already led to a book on the experience of newfound freedom in Eastern Europe (Bergquist and Weiss, 1994).

My PSP colleagues, too, have been deeply moved by this cross-cultural experience. I vividly remember one, Katherine Czesak, discussing the graduate curriculum at PSP with three Estonian psychologists late one evening at an apartment in Tallinn, the nation's capital. Our Estonian colleagues had been taking many notes during the evening, and as we left, they told us that the PSP curriculum was going to be used as a model for graduate education in their country and would serve as the basis for their new national licensing laws. Katherine was especially delighted to hear this, having played a central role in revising the PSP curriculum.

International experience is not unique to PSP. Many colleges and universities encourage faculty trips to foreign countries and faculty exchanges with institutions in other countries. Unfortunately, this type of experience is often less common in tuition-driven schools such as PSP or JFK or in access-oriented institutions, which consider such activities diversions from pressing financial needs or the school's populist mission. Populism has often been linked to the proclivity toward isolationism in American life. We sometimes seem to believe that Americans are best served if we remain at home and concentrate on meeting the needs of our local neighbors. This has certainly been the assumption at PSP.

Even though virtually all of the funds needed for my two PSP colleagues and me to fly to Estonia came out of our own pockets, students at PSP (and some faculty and administrators) were upset at our paying such attention to foreign matters. We were not very successful in convincing PSP customers (students) and stakeholders (board members, faculty) that our professional development is of great benefit to the school and to our own personal lives.

Despite the objections, work in Estonia has continued to be a rich source of professional development for my PSP faculty colleagues and myself. One of the key lessons to be learned from this experience is that professional development often occurs indirectly, when one is focusing on another set of goals and aspirations. Postmodern colleges and universities should consider that the diversity of perspectives and experiences being offered by the institution (as a result of its commitment to access) is itself a rich source of professional development for faculty, administrators, and staff. This is likely to be particularly true if the boundaries of the institution are expanded or blurred so that its employees and students can freely explore, serve, and learn from many different communities and nations in the world. PSP must begin slowly to expand its boundaries so that an institute in Estonia is not considered a distraction. Other postmodern colleges and universities may find that they must take similar initiatives if they are to avoid the backlash that my colleagues and I experienced at PSP.

A second important lesson for me concerns the fine art of practicing what we preach. Many years ago, Richard Gross, then academic dean at Gordon College in Wenham, Massachusetts, taught me that professional development programs are best promoted by institutional leaders if they take the first step by attending to their own personal development. Gross was the first person in his own institution to participate in the professional growth contracting process he had initiated at the college. I had forgotten this important lesson with regard to promoting professional development at my own institution. In pursuing my own professional growth through the Estonian project, I had not only modeled this process in PSP but also shown my tangible support for this strategy through participation in a project that yielded professional development for myself.

The Estonian project also illustrates the potential for development to break down barriers not only between employees at a single institution but also, in this instance, between men and women from different parts of the world and even from nations that were recently on opposite sides of the political fence. A somewhat less dramatic but even more important example of professional development programs that shatter interinstitutional barriers is to be found at one of the other case study institutions, The Evergreen State College. Evergreen has initiated a statewide professional development program that focuses on innovations in Washington and builds on the values and experiences of the college. In 1985, with support from the Exxon and Ford foundations, Evergreen established the Washington Center for Improving the Quality of Undergraduate Education, a unique statewide public service initiative. With the establishment of the Washington Center, Evergreen assumed an explicit leadership role in reforming undergraduate education in the state. A primary focus has been supporting adaptations of Evergreen's curriculum, commonly referred to as structural reform, through "learning communities" (Gabelnick, MacGregor, Matthews, and Smith, 1990; MacGregor, 1987, 1991; Smith, 1991, 1994a). The effort has been remarkably successful (Smith, 1988, 1994b). More than thirty-four Washington colleges now offer learning community curricula, and forty-four Washington colleges are affiliated with the Washington Center. The center has also attracted major funding for statewide projects in such areas as calculus reform, cultural pluralism, and interdisciplinary approaches to the sciences. It acts as a statewide support system for educational reform and sponsors a variety of activities including faculty exchanges, conferences and retreats, assessment initiatives, and technical resources.

The success of the Washington Center—a winner of the Hesbergh Award for excellence—suggests that a third-party organization can expand institutional boundaries to create and nurture a larger community committed to professional development and educational reform. Diffuse boundaries, complex styles and sources of leadership, and continual review of the mission seem to be key elements in the center's success. The work of the Washington Center has demonstrated that many aspects of the Evergreen experience are transferable. Perhaps the same can be said of other postmodern institutions that have been successful in sustaining both quality and access. Given the need for these hard-won successes to be replicated somehow in other colleges and universities, the Washington Center model should be considered by other state higher educational systems. The very positive response of traditional educators to the Washington Center also suggests that learning communities and collaborative learning can be used successfully with diverse learners and in diverse institutional settings.

Feedback on Program Performance

Institutions that wish to achieve and sustain both quality and access must provide communication channels that allow for and encourage the rapid diffusion of valid and useful information (Argyris, 1970) on the performance of all program units, new and old. Decisions about program units should be made at the point of maximum information. In our complex postmodern era, mistakes cannot be avoided (especially if risk-taking behavior is encouraged); however, failure to learn from these mistakes is unacceptable. Learning from mistakes as well as from successes should be considered an essential competency. Organizational learning is at the heart of this continuous improvement effort (Argyris and Schön, 1978; Senge, 1990).

In an institution that seeks to integrate quality and access and in doing so recruits a diversified student body, faculty, administration, and staff, it is particularly important that all constituencies receive frequent and timely feedback on their performance from a variety of sources and through a variety of modalities. For instance, faculty members should regularly reflect with their students on their own teaching practices, and administrators should likewise engage in the kind of reflection articulated by both Schön (1983, 1987) and Senge (1990). In essence, the emphasis on feedback in a TQM program helps break down the isolation that is typical in academic institutions. While benchmarking helps break down the isolation between institutions and development tends to break down the isolation between colleagues, feedback helps break down the isolation between consumer (student) and provider (faculty) or between two internal constituencies (for example, faculty and administrators).

Charles Glasser, president of John F. Kennedy University, believes that the most important feedback mechanisms at JFK concern teaching and learning, given the centrality of this dimension of organizational life at his university. During our interview, he identified the traditional modes of feedback to faculty—student evaluations and peer reviews—but also spoke of the importance of administrators at JFK keeping their doors open to informal feedback from students about their classroom experiences. Much as in the case of PSP, the students at JFK are not naive consumers of education. They have received instruction for many years in a variety of settings, ranging from formal classroom and corporate training to television and involvement in their own children's learning. Furthermore, mature adults (like younger commuting students at many colleges and universities) have nothing else by which to judge the quality of JFK or PSP than what occurs in the classroom, for they do not live on campus and have few nonclass interactions with the staff.

As a result, the formal and informal feedback of mature students about teaching and learning at JFK and PSP must be taken seriously, for they know what they are talking about and are likely, as Glasser noted, to leave the school if their feedback is ignored and if the education they receive remains inadequate. Glasser also noted that unlike other students, those enrolled at JFK tend to choose not between JFK and other schools in the area but rather between JFK and no formal education at all. As is the case with mature students at many other schools (including PSP), JFK students are often severely restricted in regard to location and scheduling of courses. They are simply unable to travel very far to school or take classes during the daytime. Furthermore, students at JFK (and PSP) often cannot afford to attend any other undergraduate or graduate schools, especially with the declining access of mature, second-career students to the state universities in California.

Thus, if students at JFK or PSP have a bad experience in the classroom, they are unlikely to transfer to another school; they are instead likely to conclude that they made a wrong decision in returning to school and that JFK (or PSP) failed to deliver on its promise of providing a relevant and responsive education for mature adults. Feedback under these circumstances must occur not just at the end of the term but throughout the term. This ongoing feedback is typically not available in most classes, though many rich instructional feedback and improvement processes are now available. Frequently, we must, like President Glasser, rely on the informal comments and complaints of students throughout the term. Is that sufficient? I would suggest that it is inadequate and that we must obtain more extensive and more frequent feedback if we wish to achieve quality in teaching nontraditional and increasingly diversified student populations. The challenge for our postmodern colleges and universities will be to discover or invent these alternative modes of feedback.

Key Points

1. Efforts to achieve and integrate quality and access are ongoing organizational processes, not specific products or ends. These efforts primarily concern communication between the consumer (student) and the organization, among members of the organization, and among various constituencies that are stakeholders in the organization.

2. The quality of the processes being used in an educational institution is more important than the quality of the product of the institution. Process-oriented strategies are particularly relevant in higher education because it produces no tangible physical product that is subject to direct inspection.

3. Any efforts to achieve and integrate quality and access must be particularly sensitive to cultural differences among the various groups that must approve and implement these initiatives; cultural differences relate directly to the four cultures of the academy (collegial, managerial, developmental, negotiating).

4. An institution seeking quality and access must systematically and continuously gather both quantitative and qualitative information about its own internal operations, as well as about the changing environment in which it is located.

5. In order to determine the mission of an institution, organizational values, personal aspirations, and institutional vision must be identified and clarified on an ongoing basis, and these values, aspirations, and vision must be used to determine the institution's goals and objectives for a specific period.

6. All relevant constituencies within an institution that is seeking both quality and access must be engaged in its ongoing decision-making, problem-solving, and planning processes (a process-oriented approach to quality). There must be a broad-based respect for diversity of perspective and for assumptions among those who are involved in the ongoing deliberations and dialogues of the institution. The individual rights given to various constituencies must be balanced with the collective responsibility assumed by all constituencies for the overall welfare of the college or university.

7. An institution seeking quality and access must place its assessment and clarification processes within the context of other institutions that are comparable, competitive, or potential role models. These other institutions can be used as measuring sticks for assessing an institution's distinctive potential for achievement as well as its actual achievement.

8. Institutions will find that the implementation of a program for the integration of quality and access inevitably follows and

is enhanced by a developmental path that improves the quality of personal and organizational resources within the institution (a value-added approach to quality). A developmental program introduces new knowledge, skills, and attitudes, as well as expanding existing knowledge and skills; it must relate to the reward systems and career paths of the institution, as well as reflecting norms of collegiality and broad-based participation (by the leaders as well as the led).

9. Institutions that wish to not only achieve but also to sustain quality and access must provide communication channels that allow for and encourage rapid diffusion of valid and useful information about institutional performance. In our complex, postmodern world, mistakes cannot be avoided (especially if risk taking is encouraged); however, failure to learn from these mistakes is unacceptable. Learning from mistakes as well as from successes should be considered an essential competency in the learning-oriented colleges and universities of our postmodern era.

Chapter Eleven

Critical Roles
for Campus Leaders

The integration of quality and access is achieved by individuals collaborating with one another. In postsecondary education, only people can produce quality—it is not now and probably never will be a machine-intensive business. Similarly, the decision to make a college or university accessible to a particular group of potential students is always a decision that people must make. It involves much more commitment, courage, and creativity than it does either statistics or technology. Behind all of these people is leadership, which animates, directs, or at least encourages the commitment to and integration of quality and access.

As we look at the dimension of leadership in the integration of quality and access, two primary characteristics come immediately to mind. First, an institution that achieves both quality and access must be led either by people who are themselves flexible in the style of leadership they exhibit or by a succession of leaders each of whom exhibits a style of leadership that is appropriate to the developmental stage of the organization. Whether in the hands of a single, flexible leader or of several leaders, a successful postmodern institution must commit, through its leadership, to a balance between quality and elitism, on the one hand, and access and populism, on the other. Second, leaders must work effectively with complex issues of authority both inside and outside the organization. They must learn to be comfortable with ambiguity of authority and with rapid changes in the nature and source of the authority they must confront and accommodate.

Successful postmodern institutions require diverse forms and sources of leadership, for they usually operate in complex settings and must struggle against powerful and resistant forces and sources of authority. As has already been noted with regard to the beleaguered and expedient perspectives on contemporary higher education, leadership in the postmodern institution is inherently situational. Even more than in the expedient institution, the president of an institution that wishes to achieve and integrate quality and access serves as mayor, learner, servant, visionary, and community builder. Leadership is interaction-oriented, with knowledge of the institution being built on the lessons learned from various attempts to integrate quality and access.

Much will be learned about the institution and the type of leadership needed to ensure its continuation from encounters between its leaders and the leaders of governmental and quasi-governmental agencies that oversee and ultimately determine the future of nontraditional, unified colleges and universities. This concluding chapter will focus on the attitudes of leadership that are inherent in efforts to integrate quality and access and returns once more to the three case study institutions. Four interrelated attitudes will be explored: willingness to take risks, willingness to shift styles, tolerance of ambiguity, and willingness to work with arbitrary or ambiguous authority. These attitudes are required not only of the administrators of successful postmodern institutions but also of their colleagues and subordinates.

Willingness to Take Risks

What immediately strikes any close observer of a new alternative college is the long arm of the founders and the self-absorption of the community in these beginning moments. For many of the early participants, the founding of an institution represents a singular turning point, the rare and pure opportunity to innovate, to create, to pursue a vision. Later leaders are guided, inspired, and at times encumbered by tales of these visionaries.

Evergreen's founders apparently had unusual latitude to experiment. The college was chartered with a threefold mission: to serve as a nontraditional institution, to maintain a special relationship with the state government, and to serve southwestern Washington. Senator Gordon Sandison, then chair of the Senate Higher Education Committee, is credited with establishing the mandate to be experimental in a comment he made at an August 1967 meeting with the newly appointed board of trustees. He advised the board to study innovations around the country and called for "a college that . . . can be as modern fifty years from now as at the present" (*Daily Olympian*, Aug. 31, 1967).

As Peter Tommerup (1993) noted in his ethnographic study of Evergreen:

> Working to create a new kind of college within this flexible though ambiguous environment had a discernible impact on the founders. On the one hand, . . . they enjoyed the freedom afforded them by this flexibility and the opportunity to create a new world. The flip side of this inspirational high, however, was frustration due to the large amount of ambiguity involved in the project. It was difficult at times for the group to determine whether they were still on track due to the lack of a preexisting model for this sort of school. Additional burdens included pressure from interested outsiders as well as the participants' internal desire to create something truly special, something that reflected their ideal image of what teaching and learning should be about [pp. 46–47].

Two figures loom large in Evergreen's early history: the founding president, Charles McCann, and one of the founding deans, Mervyn Cadwallader. McCann came to Evergreen from a deanship at Central Washington University. An unassuming humanist devoted to the liberal arts, McCann would seem to be a more likely candidate for an academic position in a traditional, elitist institution than in a brand-new nontraditional institution with populist goals. McCann didn't think he had a chance of winning the presidency of the new college against a national pool of candidates, but the opportunity was unprecedented, so he applied for the position anyway. He was candid with the board of trustees about his views that the new college should be different. He saw no reason to replicate traditional colleges, especially when they were so obviously flawed and ill-suited to the needs of the late twentieth century.

McCann's earliest comments indicate a special interest in decentralizing education by placing responsibility in the hands of faculty and students rather than committees, departments, or faculty senates. Narrative evaluations and integrating the world of work into the curriculum were also two of his passions. Although McCann had certain notions about the new college, he did not have a detailed curricular design or an organizational structure in mind when he assumed office. He came, however, firmly convinced that he had been given a mandate to design a distinctive institution that was not a carbon copy of the other colleges in the state. McCann's job description actually included a charge to ensure that Evergreen would not be "just another four-year college." As in the case of many unified institutions, the emphasis was on process rather than specific outcomes.

One of the most influential founding deans, Mervyn Cadwallader, recounts the early discussion at Evergreen:

> We met for the first time in a trailer. The conversation was absolutely formless. Nothing happened. We were talking about lectures and courses. We looked at floor plans. . . . Lecture halls, . . . big lecture halls, little lecture halls. . . . Finally, to get things moving, I described my previous coordinated-studies program at San Jose, and I said I'd like to have an opportunity to do that with a hundred of the thousand students we admitted. And then, as I recall, Don said if it's good for a hundred, it's good for a thousand—and that's how Evergreen got committed to coordinated studies.

Cadwallader also recalls being astonished at this turn of events:

> The moment Don said if it's good for a hundred, it's good for a thousand, I was really appalled and shocked and scared. I started to backpedal and emphasize the difficulty of finding faculty who could teach cooperatively and across disciplinary lines in coordinated studies. When I came to Evergreen, the most I was hoping for was two coordinated-studies programs, one starting each year and a hundred to two hundred students, counting for the work of ten to twelve faculty. I was completely bowled over when in a matter of hours, we found ourselves committed not to one coordinated-studies [program] but to twelve on opening day!

The planning faculty were a diverse group with many different and sometimes contradictory views about education, but they were all taken by the notion of establishing a team-taught, theme-based curriculum in which students and faculty would work together in yearlong programs rather than discrete three- or four-credit courses. After hearing Joseph Tussman's (1969, 1988) account of the Experimental College at the University of Wisconsin and its replication at Berkeley, it was agreed that the college would resurrect the structural and pedagogical features of the Experimental College established briefly at the University of Wisconsin from 1927 to 1932 by Alexander Meiklejohn—though they did not as a group choose to emulate the basic content of the Meiklejohn curriculum, the so-called moral curriculum organized around the history of Western and American civilization topics. Like many other successful innovative leaders, these educators were not afraid to borrow good ideas from other schools (Lindquist, 1978). This means first of all that they identify themselves as educators and not just as representatives of a specific field of study or discipline. Second, it means that they read about and visit other people and institutions rather than remain parochial.

278 Quality Through Access

Cadwallader doubted whether the entire institution should be organized around full-time coordinated-studies programs. He argued instead for a more hybrid type of institution in which the lower division was organized around thematic interdisciplinary programs but the upper-division curriculum was more conventionally structured. Debates among the faculty about the desirable curricular structure continued to revisit this point of view, which was dubbed the "two-college approach," especially in times of enrollment shortfall, but there was never a serious attempt to alter the basic structure established in the early years. Although full-time programs created certain rigidities in the college's curriculum, the wholesale commitment to coordinated studies at this early date was probably critical in preserving the college's distinctiveness in the tough times that followed.

Many of the founding faculty had previous experience that proved valuable in designing a new institution. They came from diverse institutions—from elite private colleges such as Reed, Harvard, and Oberlin, or from new "alternative colleges" such as New College in Florida; the State University of New York, Old Westbury; and the University of California, Santa Cruz. Still others came from innovative cluster colleges within traditional institutions, such as San Jose State. A half dozen of the founding faculty were familiar with other Meiklejohn-like programs. They brought a variety of progressive education ideas with them—narrative evaluations, interdisciplinary study, internships, self-paced learning, individualized study, community-based education, and hands-on experience in the sciences.

The founding faculty also brought a litany of lessons from their mistakes. Many came with concerns about the nonacademic turn that many alternative colleges had taken and the endless haggling about governance. The founding faculty may have been wiser for their hindsight, but their enthusiasm for educational reform was undiminished. Much to their surprise, the more experienced veterans found themselves in the awkward position of being the conservatives—the "Cassandras," as one put it—as they cautioned their more inexperienced colleagues about the perils of interdisciplinary studies and team teaching.

Evergreen's main features emerged in the first year and changed little over the next twenty-five: a stress on collaboration and avoidance of hierarchy (no faculty rank or tenure, a uniform salary scale based on years of experience, rotating academic administrators, use of narrative evaluations rather than grades), interdisciplinary study in the context of structural innovation through yearlong programs, and a strong commitment to a diverse faculty. Organizationally, the college was decentralized and firmly based on the assumption that faculty teams could be trusted to develop strong academic programs. Dozens of new practices—such as student portfolios, teaching team covenants, narrative evaluations, and required weekly faculty seminars and a reappointment policy based on faculty portfolios—gave life and structure to these new values, resulting in a largely holistic environment devoted to interdisciplinary and collaborative teaching and learning. In the process, Evergreen developed new forms and languages that would become part of its identity and also part of its problem in relating to the outside world.

Willingness to Shift Styles

In all three case study schools, the situational form of leadership derives not from a single leader but rather from the mix of leadership styles and transitions between them as the schools have grown and matured. This shift occurred at Evergreen as the deans and faculty of the new school began to assume greater responsibility. JFK's first president, Harry Morrison, was a builder and a dreamer in the populist tradition. A businessman, Morrison brought in many of his friends to provide initial administrative services for the school, and it remained a relatively small but distinctive institution from its founding in 1964 until his death ten years later.

Though enrollment had increased from sixty students in its first year of classes to four hundred students in 1974, it was still a small "mom, pop, and friends" shop when Bob Fisher came in as president from a faculty position at the University of California. As Elinor Fisher (1982) notes about Morrison's presidency, "The tribulations of the University and the fluctuation in its fortunes in the Morrison years made the small number of staff and the large number of volunteer people around them highly interdependent. The President's style was collaborative as he communicated quite openly those things which were happening in the University and those things which were on his mind. He was a 'dream weaver.' He enjoyed regaling others [with] his latest ideas. Everyone thrived on the joy of the challenge, and he nurtured them in this way" (p. 336).

True to the populist mission of JFK, Morrison encouraged the contribution of time and talent to the university. Whereas elitist colleges and universities tend to encourage the contribution of money, populist institutions tend to emulate the barn-raising tradition in the United States—they want your labor, not your dollars. Morrison also exemplified the egalitarian and visionary tenor of the populist tradition. Like Charles McCann at Evergreen, Morrison encouraged participation and spoke like populists before him (ranging from Abraham Lincoln to William Jennings Bryan or even Huey Long) of an alternative vision for his institution and society.

When Robert Fisher was appointed JFK's second president, he brought a more elitist perspective to the institution, having graduated from or taught in several of the most elite universities in the United States and England. Fisher believed that there was no reason why working adults shouldn't receive the same excellent education as younger traditional students. He effectively brought elitism into the cultural mix at JFK. To enhance this more elitist tradition and encourage the growth and maturation of the university, Fisher hired more full-time administrators and relied less on volunteers and the goodwill of friends and family.

Like the presidents of many elitist institutions, Fisher served in a public, charismatic role, bringing greater visibility to the campus by recruiting high-profile speakers and recipients of honorary doctorates. Whereas Morrison had been charismatic in his building of internal commitment to the university, Fisher brought an external orientation. This helped place JFK on the map in the San Francisco Bay Area. He also brought in a more collegial culture by emphasizing the relative autonomy of each academic division at the university and moving the school to a setting that was somewhat more "collegiate" in appearance, a former elementary school.

Fisher recalled recently that the JFK registrar during his presidency served wine and cheese to students while they waited in line to enroll in courses and that the JFK librarian served fresh-baked cookies to the students using the library. These often-told stories about the Fisher era at JFK are in keeping with the collegial culture that Fisher brought to the university. These stories differ very little from comparable "collegial way" stories about sherry hours and the baking proficiencies of dorm mothers that have been told in traditional American liberal arts colleges for the past three centuries.

As in many institutions that are infused with a collegial culture, authority was somewhat confusing and contradictory under Fisher's leadership. On the one hand, he played a powerful role at the university and continued Morrison's tradition of taking an active role in the internal matters of the school. On the other hand, Fisher empowered members of his executive staff to make more decisions and gave considerable authority to his academic deans. Throughout the history of American higher education, we find elitist presidents in collegially oriented colleges and universities who draw substantial attention to themselves and assume enormous power in the institution while simultaneously moving the institution to a more collaborative mode of governance and management.

The picture gets even more complicated, however, when a university such as JFK tries to blend elitism and populism. Fisher was loved by many colleagues but also distrusted or disliked by others, who felt that he was moving the university away from its populist roots. They missed the vision and camaraderie of Morrison and felt that they were no longer "friends" of the university as they had been under the first president. A successful institution must somehow blend the voluntary and visionary spirit of American populism with the more dignified and stratified spirit of American elitism. This is not an easy blend.

Two men followed Fisher at the helm of JFK; though both were competent academic administrators, neither was a good match with the school. The fifth president, Charles Glasser, comes from a very different mold. First, he is himself a graduate of JFK, having obtained a law degree as a mature and successful adult. He later returned to JFK as dean of the law school and now serves as the university president. Glasser represents the populist tradition and an accompanying emphasis on management and the managerial culture. Unlike Fisher, who valued elitist credentials, Glasser looks to men and women who are good managers and who know how to run their own shops without extensive interference from either himself or other administrators.

Glasser speaks of JFK as being much more complex and sophisticated than it was when Fisher was president. The school hires many more full-time faculty than it did just a few years ago. Many of these faculty members expect to play an active role in campus governance, and the head of the faculty senate is now a member of the university's executive staff and board of regents. Glasser notes that the university can no longer be run by one charismatic leader. In his role as president, Glasser believes that he always runs the risk of inhibiting and distracting the university from its primary mission, which is teaching and learning. According to Glasser, a bad president blocks progress while trying to be progressive. Conversely, as president of a university that is now large and complex, Glasser believes that his primary role is one of facilitating and promoting the work of other people toward the university's primary mission.

Thus, in an effort to integrate elitism and populism at JFK, there is also a need to blend different styles of leadership and different organizational cultures. Elitism usually requires charisma, for the leader personifies quality in the institution. It is particularly important that the president of an elite college or university be accomplished and publicly acknowledged as successful because the criteria of quality in such an institution are more easily demonstrated than measured. Among populist presidents, conversely, there is great value in being "one of the common people." As mentioned, Glasser is a graduate of the university, and he speaks of broadening the base of participation in the governance of JFK. Although President Morrison was also a populist, his style of leadership could not be sustained, for a populist institution can serve its underserved population for only a limited time through volunteerism and the sacrifice of committed and visionary men and women like Morrison and his friends and family.

Tolerance of Ambiguity

The Professional School of Psychology faces a challenge similar to that of JFK, though PSP is a much younger institution. Like JFK, PSP survived and even thrived during its first ten years on the basis of the vision and sacrifices of its original leaders. Many stories about the three founders and, later, the San Francisco campus dean, Nancy Barber, and myself as president make the rounds. These stories—like those at JFK—tell of low salaries, bailing out the school with short-term loans, and extra hours of work to make the school successful in terms of its commitment to both quality and access.

Yet in the case of PSP, an additional factor gives this vision and this sacrifice a different meaning. The school is privately owned—initially by the three founders and later by myself and two other people. Thus several questions seem always to linger: Are the owners' and leaders' sacrifices a sign of personal commitment to the mission of the school or merely actions taken to protect a long-term business investment? Are the owners making sacrifices to benefit underserved populations (in this case hardworking, low-paid human service professionals), or do they really simply hope to make a profit? Can a humanistic vision and an entrepreneurial vision be combined?

Answers to these questions may have changed over time, for ownership and leadership at PSP have changed over the years, much as they did at JFK. The three men who founded PSP tended to be more business-oriented, while I tended to be more idealistic and education-oriented. All four of us blended elitism and populism in our perspectives on PSP. The campus deans and deans of students and faculty seem to have a comparable perspective. Two of the three leaders of the school during the past three years came from elite undergraduate or graduate programs. Yet two of the three also received their doctorates from freestanding graduate schools of psychology (one from PSP). The other leader has a distinguished record of serving underserved populations as the director of a major urban mental health system and as a long-term advocate for the homeless in San Francisco.

One of the most important organizational challenges facing PSP at present concerns the shift from a more personal and charismatic style of leadership to a more formal, systematic style. Much as in the case of JFK, PSP must move away from leadership and management based on friendships and family ownership, sacrifice and vision, to one based on administrative competencies and role clarification. This shift is critical if the school is to mature and ultimately become independent of any one person or small group of owners. In the near future, PSP must either become a nonprofit institution or remain private with broad-based, financially secure ownership. Though all young organizations must go through such a transition (see Adizes, 1988), a collegiate institution that is trying to retain a commitment to both quality and access will find this transition particularly challenging. The leaders of such an institution must simultaneously hold the vision of populism and access, and the standards of elitism and quality. They must broaden the base of participation in the governance of the institution while ensuring that students are receiving an excellent education.

As a leader of PSP, I often found myself torn between these various purposes and roles. I wanted to broaden the level of participation in part through serving (in elitist fashion) as a role model and person to emulate. Yet most of the people with whom I worked—administrators, faculty, students—had neither the time nor the inclination to model or emulate me (or anyone else, for that matter). They were leading their own lives and trying to build an educational program at PSP for themselves or their students that somehow fit with the complex, demanding lives they were leading.

Wine and cheese at registration and cookies in the library are wonderful elitist touches and suggest, as Bob Fisher noted in our recent interview, that students are "welcomed" at the school. These niceties, however, do not address the central populist needs of PSP students, which relate directly to tough issues of access (such as cost of the program, scheduling of courses, and location of the school) and credentialing (accreditation, preparation for the state licensing exam, and postgraduate eligibility for third-party payments for psychological services rendered). The current leaders of PSP must find ways of addressing these difficult issues in a forceful and timely manner, yet they must also build a climate of collaboration and camaraderie—which is more in keeping with the elitist tradition—and ensure that the quality of education is not hindered but is instead enhanced by successfully addressing these access issues.

Willingness to Work with Arbitrary or Ambiguous Authority

The exertion of external authority (by state, regional, and disciplinary accrediting groups, as well as community boards, regents, and other external agencies) is a very complex problem that has significant bearing on the issues of quality and access. Conflicts regarding the authority exerted by external bodies begin at the administrative level in most colleges and universities. It has been observed that successful executives are usually effective at working downward in their organization and are thereby able to exert authority in a sensible manner. They find it much more difficult, however, to relate laterally with colleagues, vertically with their own board, or upward to outside regulatory and accrediting groups. They are likely to experience conflict about authority exerted from above because this authority is usually ambiguous in terms of its form, its message to the executive, and its capacity to reward or punish, and it conflicts with the executive's own motivation to achieve higher positions out of a desire to transcend or avoid authority issues (David Bradford, personal communication).

In the three case study institutions, this dynamic is particularly salient. My own interaction with state and regional authorization groups as the president of PSP, an unaccredited institution, were troublesome, much as these interactions have been for the presidents of many nontraditional colleges and universities. I remember a conversation I had with the president of a nontraditional university that is now accredited. After he left the presidency of this school, he indicated that he had rarely in his long career been as nervous or upset as he was when facing his "peers" at regional accreditation commission meetings. This highly capable and accomplished leader indicated that he not only became nauseated when attending these meetings but still, many years after leaving the presidency, felt queasy whenever he drove past the hotel where the commission meetings were held. What kind of process brings about such distress? Would he have felt this way if he had been the president of a traditional, established college or university?

At the heart of the matter is a college or university president's preparation for and capacity to sustain personal identity and integrity in a world that demands radical shifts in roles and in emotions from moment to moment. Collegiate leaders are likely to experience the dilemma of ambiguous authority repeatedly in their postmodern roles (Bergquist, 1993; Vaill, 1989; Quehl, 1991). Leaders of postmodern colleges and universities must spend an increasing amount of time looking outward to the unpredictable and volatile environment that surrounds their institutions. They must somehow manage outward in a world that is turbulent and essentially out of personal control—what Vaill describes as the "white-water world" of contemporary leaders. Both Vaill and Quehl speak of the spiritual dimension of leadership that becomes central in this type of turbulent world. Perhaps those of us who serve in these leadership roles should work a bit more in this dimension in preparation for our continuing encounter with ambiguous authority.

Given the complex interplay between accreditation, authority, and the integration of quality and access, there are three sets of questions about the role that accrediting agencies might play in promoting and sustaining the process of achieving and integrating quality and access: first, how does an accrediting agency foster and protect institutional diversity, thereby ensuring or increasing overall quality and access in higher education? How does it ensure diversity while also preserving the standards that are essential to community and to the equitable use of authority?

The issue of authority and accreditation with regard to this tension is clarified by a longer, more historical view on how authority has changed in modern America (Sennett, 1981). The Western world has moved from paternalism to a more autonomous form of authority, a shift from authority being exerted through personal power and influence to authority being exerted through rules, procedures, and standards derived by consensus. This conclusion has numerous implications in terms of the shift from external to internal modes of authority. Sennett writes of contemporary authority being exerted through psychological "shame" and informal power residing in knowledge and skills. He contrasts this with older, paternally based and position-based authority that is exerted through formal power, coercion, rewards, and punishment.

Accreditation agencies, like many corporations and human service agencies, assert authority not by mandating certain changes in an educational institution but rather by suggesting (often rather ambiguously) that the institution is simply not of sufficient quality and must examine its internal operations to determine the nature and extent of its flaws. Much as in the case of a knowledge worker who has been told that she should be able to discover her own flaws and failings if she is to be an effective employee, so must a college or university up for review find its own answers—provided that the answers ultimately match the expectations of the accreditors. Thus authority is exerted subtly in forms that force institutions to look inward for faults and never look outward for blame. This shift from external constraint and punishment to internal control and shame provokes internal ambiguity, anxiety, and fragmentation (Sennett, 1981).

On the opposite side of authority we find a renewed emphasis on the building of community. Once again, the role of accreditation with regard to the building and maintenance of community affects the issues of access and diversity in American higher education. As noted by Robert Bellah and his colleagues (1985), there is a dilemma in the United States about the nature and extent of community that is desired. We find ourselves in a struggle between individualism and individual rights on the one hand and community and collective responsibility on the other (Gilligan, 1982; Eisler, 1987).

Accreditation is a balancing act between these rights and responsibilities. Accrediting agencies and the processes they manage must ensure that the integrity and distinctiveness of individual institutions are not violated (a matter of rights), yet they must also ensure that these institutions continue to serve the public interest (a matter of responsibility). Comparably, an institution that is seeking accreditation or reaccreditation must ensure that it acts in a responsible manner with regard to this process and that all information presented to the accrediting body is accurate and not misleading. Each institution, however, also has a right (and a responsibility to its board, students, and community) to pursue its mission and not sacrifice it for the sake of accreditation.

A second question about accreditation and the unification of quality and access is, how does an accrediting agency build and maintain appropriate levels of authority within the context of collegial community when given the responsibility by governmental and quasi-governmental agencies to provide a critical assessment of an institution's overall quality? Obviously, the challenge for enlightened accrediting groups—and for our society in general—is to establish community in the context of distinctiveness. We must, as several observers have noted, conceive of American society not as a melting pot, in which the distinctive features are lost to general cultural uniformity, but as a stew, in which each of the diverse elements preserves its distinctiveness.

Many years ago, Martin (1969) and Jencks and Riesman (1968) offered very thoughtful critiques of American higher education with regard to conformity and the lack of diversity among colleges and universities. The situation has not improved greatly since. If accreditation is to help reestablish the American higher educational stew, it must find a way to balance its legitimate concern for uniformity of standards and equity of treatment against an equally important concern for preserving and nourishing diversity and the application of distinctive and varying modes of assessment in any institution that is being reviewed.

A third question concerns the criteria of quality: how does accreditation encourage and help sustain multiple criteria of quality—particularly criteria that encourage the integration of quality and access? PSP's candidacy review brought forward several problems related to the issue of quality. How do we measure quality? We could rely on input measures: size of library, number of full-time faculty, financial resources, physical plant, and so forth. Alternatively, we could look at output measures: success of graduates, number of publications, number of grants, number of graduates, and so forth. What about value? Can quality be defined by "value-added" measures? How would we go about determining what difference we

290 Quality Through Access

make in the lives of the students (and faculty, administrators, and alumni) who participate in PSP in terms of skills, attitudes, knowledge, character, and so forth? Finally, in what ways are the processes of PSP themselves being studied as indices of quality? Each of these four definitions of quality seems important, yet only the first (and occasionally the second) is to be found in the current standards used by most accrediting agencies.

Do we avoid the second, third, and fourth criteria because those aspects of quality are hard to measure? Or do we really believe that the definition of quality is contained in the measurement of input? If the latter is the case, higher education is unusual, for no corporation would measure its success primarily on the basis of input measures (size of plant, number of workers, level of professional preparation of workers, or quality of materials brought into the company). Rather, success is measured in terms of output measures (sales of product, net revenues, quality of product), value-added measures (increased value or quality of the product after processing by the company), and process measures (how well work is performed and how people feel about it).

In light of the outside pressures toward conformity and entrenchment, a nontraditional institution like PSP (or JFK and Evergreen) must discover and encourage creativity and collaboration with other institutions in the acquisition and use of new resources. Substantial creativity and collaboration are needed if the institution is to confront the standards of licensing and accrediting agencies while also encouraging both quality and access. It is essential that these institutions increase their own efficiency while providing opportunities for greater access without sacrificing quality.

Unfortunately, the tendency for accrediting bodies, at least implicitly, to define quality primarily in terms of traditional input measures requires the extensive expenditure of funds for often unneeded resources (such as independent libraries) and discourages the collaborative interinstitutional sharing of resources that boosts institutional efficiency. Traditional input-oriented standards also tend to discourage increased institutional access, for the quality of the institution is being defined in part by the extent to which its student body meets outmoded standards of excellence (high school average, College Board scores, and so forth). Risk taking in admissions is discouraged, and there is little incentive to produce new admission standards or ways of assessing student potential.

Even when output measures (such as the competencies and career success of graduates) are encouraged by accrediting groups, these output measures are often confounded with input measures (in this case, the level of competency of these graduates when they first entered the institution). Institutions that measure only output, either by choice or in compliance with accreditation procedures, are forced to reduce access in order to enroll students who would be successful after graduation regardless of the school they attend. Similarly, input and output standards are often confounded in the measurement of such variables as library use and student performance on the Graduate Record Exam and other graduate exams. Governmental agencies, accrediting and licensing agencies, and college and university administrators and faculty must rethink their policies and procedures in terms of how they help or hinder the essential union between quality and access.

Clearly, there is much to be learned by all members of the postsecondary education community about the pursuit of quality and access. Men and women who have assumed the responsibility of reviewing the status of colleges and universities with regard to accreditation face issues that are as difficult as those faced by the people who lead and work inside these institutions. Accrediting authorities must themselves struggle with issues of quality and access. They must themselves discover ways in which quality and access can be integrated and ways in which the accrediting associations can promote rather than ignore or discourage this integration. Each party can learn from the other in what Senge (1990) calls a dialogue rather than a discussion. Given the critical role played by both quality and access in the contemporary and future lives of postmodern colleges and universities, it behooves us all to remain open to the often surprising and illuminating insights of our colleagues in all domains of the postsecondary education community. Our colleges and universities deserve this careful dialogue.

Key Points

1. Four attitudes are critical with regard to effective leadership in facilitating the achievement and integration of quality and access: willingness to take risks, willingness to shift styles, tolerance of ambiguity, and willingness to work with arbitrary or ambiguous authority.

2. Governmental agencies, accrediting and licensing agencies, and college and university administrators and faculty must rethink their policies and procedures with regard to ways in which they help or hinder the essential union between quality and access.

References

Adizes, I. *Corporate Lifecycles*. Englewood Cliffs, N.J.: Prentice Hall, 1988.

"Affordability Concerns Reemerge Among American College Freshman in 1992." *Postsecondary Education Opportunity*, July 1993, pp. 1–6.

Altbach, P. "Patterns in Higher Education Development: Toward the Year 2000," *Review of Higher Education*, 1991, *14*, 293–316.

Anderson, C. "Enrollment by Age: Distinguishing the Numbers from the Rates." *Research Briefs*, 1990, *1*(7), 1–8.

Anderson, W. *Reality Isn't What It Used to Be*. San Francisco: HarperCollins, 1990.

Argyris, C. *Intervention Theory and Method*. Reading, Mass.: Addison-Wesley, 1970.

Argyris, C., and Schön, D. A. *Organizational Learning: A Theory of Action Perspective*. Reading, Mass: Addison-Wesley, 1978.

Aronson, E. *The Social Animal*. (4th ed.) New York: Freeman, 1984.

Astin, A. W. *Achieving Educational Excellence: A Critical Assessment of Priorities and Practices in Higher Education*. San Francisco: Jossey-Bass, 1985.

Astin, A. W. "Educational Assessment and Educational Equity." *American Journal of Education*, 1990, *98*, 458–478.

Ballesteros, E. "Whatever Happened to Access?" *College and University*, 1988, *64*, 91–121.

Barber, N. "The Organization as Curriculum: An Exploration of the Learning Implications of Organizational Culture and Administrative Practices in Colleges." Unpublished doctoral dissertation, Wright Institute, Berkeley, Calif., 1984.

Bateson, G. *Mind and Nature: A Necessary Unity*. New York: Dutton, 1979.

Beckhard, R. *Organization Development: Strategies and Models*. Reading, Mass.: Addison-Wesley, 1969.

Belenky, M., Clinchy, B. M., Goldberger, N. R., and Tarule, J. *Women's Ways of Knowing*. New York: Basic Books, 1986.

Bell, D. *Coming of Postindustrial Society: A Venture in Social Forecasting*. New York: Basic Books, 1976.

Bellah, R., and others. *Habits of the Heart.* Berkeley: University of California Press, 1985.

Bellah, R., and others. *The Good Society.* New York: Knopf, 1991.

Bennett, W. *To Reclaim a Legacy: A Report on the Humanities in Higher Education.* Washington, D.C.: National Endowment for the Humanities, 1984.

Bennis, W., and Nanus, B. *Leaders: The Strategies for Taking Charge.* New York: HarperCollins, 1986.

Bennis, W., and Slater, P. *The Temporary Society.* New York: HarperCollins, 1968.

Berger, P., and Luckmann, T. *Social Construction of Reality.* New York: Doubleday, 1967.

Bergquist, W. H. "Curricular Design." In A. W. Chickering, D. Halliburton, W. H. Bergquist, and J. Lindquist (eds.), *Developing the College Curriculum.* Washington, D.C.: Council of Independent Colleges, 1977.

Bergquist, W. H. *The Four Cultures of the Academy: Insights and Strategies for Improving Leadership in Collegiate Organizations.* San Francisco: Jossey-Bass, 1992.

Bergquist, W. H. *The Postmodern Organization: Mastering the Art of Irreversible Change.* San Francisco: Jossey-Bass, 1993.

Bergquist, W. H., and Armstrong, J. L. *Planning Effectively for Educational Quality: An Outcomes-Based Approach for Colleges Committed to Excellence.* San Francisco: Jossey-Bass, 1986.

Bergquist, W. H., Gould, R. A., and Greenberg, E. M. *Designing Undergraduate Education: A Systematic Guide.* San Francisco: Jossey-Bass, 1981.

Bergquist, W. H., Betwee, J., Meuel, D., and *Building Strategic Relationships: How to Extend Your Organization's Reach Through Partnerships, Alliances, and Joint Ventures.* San Francisco: Jossey-Bass, 1995.

Bergquist, W. H., and Weiss, B. *Freedom: Narratives of Change in Hungary and Estonia.* San Francisco: Jossey-Bass, 1994.

Birnbaum, R. *How Colleges Work: The Cybernetics of Academic Organization and Leadership.* San Francisco: Jossey-Bass, 1988.

Blake, R. R., and Mouton, J. S. *Managerial Grid III.* Houston: Gulf, 1984.

Bledstein, B. *The Cult of Professionalism.* New York: Norton, 1976.

Bloom, A. D. *The Closing of the American Mind.* New York: Simon and Schuster, 1987.

Bogue, E. G., and Saunders, R. L. *The Evidence for Quality: Strengthening the Tests of Academic and Administrative Effectiveness.* San Francisco: Jossey-Bass, 1992.

Boulding, K. "Religious Foundations of Economic Progress." *Harvard Business Review,* 1952, *30,* 33–40.

Boulding, K. "Intersects: The Peculiar Organizations." In K. Bursk and the Conference Board (eds.), *Challenge to Leadership: Managing in a Changing World.* New York: Free Press, 1973.

Briggs, J., and Peat, F. D. *Turbulent Mirror*. New York: HarperCollins, 1989.

Brint, S., and Karabel, J. "American Education, Meritocratic Ideology, and the Legitimation of Inequality: The Community College and the Problem of American Exceptionalism." *Higher Education*, 1989, *18*(6), 725–735.

Cadwallader, M. Videotape, Evergreen State College Archives, 1974.

Carnegie Foundation for the Advancement of Teaching. *Campus Life: In Search of Community*. Princeton, N.J.: Princeton University Press, 1990a.

Carnegie Foundation for the Advancement of Teaching. "Native Americans and Higher Education: New Mood of Optimism." *Change*, 1990b, *22*(1), 27–30.

Carothers, R. "Tripping on the Tongue: Translating Quality for the Academy." *AAHE Bulletin*, 1992, *45*, 6–10.

Clark, B. *The Distinctive College: Antioch, Reed, and Swarthmore*. Hawthorne, N.Y.: Aldine, 1970.

Clegg, S. *Modern Organizations: Organizational Studies in the Postmodern World*. Newbury Park, Calif.: Sage, 1990.

Cleveland, H. "Information as a Resource." *Futurist*, Dec. 1982, pp. 34–39.

Cohen, M., and Marsh, J. *Leadership and Ambiguity: The American College President*. New York: McGraw-Hill, 1974.

"College Entrance Rates for Recent High School Graduates Reached Record Levels in 1991—Except for Men and Blacks." *Postsecondary Education Opportunity*, July 1992, pp. 1–4.

Crosby, P. *Quality Is Free*. New York: New American Library, 1979.

Cross, K. P. "Involving Faculty in TQM." *AACC Journal*, 1993, *64*(4) 15–20.

Dews, P. *Logics of Disintegration*. New York: Verso, 1987.

"Disparities in Higher Education Opportunity Across Family Income Levels Were Huge and Growing in 1991." *Postsecondary Education Opportunity*, Mar. 1993, pp. 1–6.

Dressel, P. (ed.). *The New Colleges: Toward an Appraisal*. Chicago: American College Testing Program and the American Association for Higher Education, 1971.

Drucker, P. *The New Realities*. New York: HarperCollins, 1989.

Eble, K. E. *The Aims of College Teaching*. San Francisco: Jossey-Bass, 1983.

Eisler, R. *The Chalice and the Blade*. San Francisco: HarperCollins, 1987.

Evergreen State College. *Reaccreditation Report: Constancy and Change: A Self-Study Report for the Northwest Association of Schools and Colleges*. Olympia, Wash.: Evergreen State College, 1989.

"Family Income Backgrounds Continue to Determine Chances for Baccalaureate Degree in 1992." *Postsecondary Education Opportunity*, Sept. 1993, pp. 1–7.

Fiedler, F. *A Theory of Leadership Effectiveness*. New York: McGraw-Hill, 1967.

Fisher, E. "Sharing and Subordination: Approximating the Egalitarian Ideal."

Unpublished doctoral dissertation, Wright Institute, Berkeley, Calif., 1982.

Foucault, M. *Madness and Civilization*. New York: Random House, 1965.

Gabelnick, F., MacGregor, J., Matthews, R. S., and Smith, B. L. *Learning Communities: Creating Connections Among Students, Faculty, and Disciplines*. San Francisco: Jossey-Bass, 1990.

Garvin, D. A. *Managing Quality: The Strategic and Competitive Edge*. New York: Free Press, 1988.

Gergen, K. *The Saturated Self*. New York: Basic Books, 1991.

Gill, J. I. "Enrollment Limits: A Response to Quality and Financial Concerns in Higher Education." Paper presented to the Association for Institutional Research, San Francisco, May 1991.

Gilligan, C. *In a Different Voice*. Cambridge, Mass.: Harvard University Press, 1982.

Gleick, J. *Chaos: Making a New Science*. New York: Viking Penguin, 1987.

Greenleaf, R. *The Servant as Leader*. Peterborough, N.H.: Windy Row Press, 1970.

Gross, B. *Friendly Fascism*. Boston: South End Press, 1980.

"Growth in College Enrollment Rates During 1980s Limited to Americans Under Age 25." *Postsecondary Education Opportunity*, June 1992, pp. 1–5.

Hall, J. *Access Through Innovation: New Colleges for New Students*. New York: American Council on Education/Macmillan, 1991.

Hansen, W., and Stampen, J. "The Financial Squeeze on Higher Education Institutions and Students: Balancing Quality and Access in the Financing of Higher Education." *Journal of Education Finance*, 1989, 15, 3–20.

Hershey, P., and Blanchard, K. *The Management of Organizational Behavior*. (3rd ed.) Englewood Cliffs, N.J.: Prentice Hall, 1977.

Herzberg, F. *Work and the Nature of Man*. San Diego, Calif.: Harcourt, 1966.

Hesbergh, T. *The Learning Society: A Report of the Study on Continuing Education and the Future*. Notre Dame, Ind.: University of Notre Dame, 1970.

Hochschild, A. *The Managed Heart*. Berkeley: University of California Press, 1983.

Huyssen, A. *After the Great Divide*. Bloomington: Indiana University Press, 1987.

Jacobs, N. "Nontraditional Students: The New Ecology of the Classroom." *Educational Forum*, 1989, 53, 329–336.

Jameson, F. *Postmodernism, or the Cultural Logic of Late Capitalism*. Durham, N.C.: Duke University Press, 1991.

Jencks, C. *Inequality*. New York: Basic Books, 1972.

Jencks, C., and Riesman, D. *The Academic Revolution*. Chicago: University of Chicago Press, 1968.

Kanter, R. M. *The Change Masters*. New York: Simon & Schuster, 1983.

Karen, D. "Toward a Political-Organizational Model of Gatekeeping: The Case of Elite Colleges." *Sociology of Education*, 1990, 63, 227–240.

Kerr, C. *The Uses of the University*. Cambridge, Mass.: Harvard University Press, 1963.

Kerr, C. "Higher Education Cannot Escape History." In L. W. Jones and F. A. Nowotny (eds.), *An Agenda for the New Decade*. New Directions for Higher Education, no. 70. San Francisco: Jossey-Bass, 1990.

Kerr, C. "The New Race to Be Harvard or Berkeley or Stanford." *Change*, 1991, *23*(3), 8–15.

Kets de Vries, M.F.R. *The Irrational Executive*. New York: International Universities Press, 1984.

Kets de Vries, M.F.R., and Miller, D. *The Neurotic Organization: Diagnosing and Changing Counterproductive Styles of Management*. San Francisco: Jossey-Bass, 1984.

Kingston, P., and Lewis, L. (eds.). *The High-Status Track: Studies of Elite Schools and Stratification*. Albany: State University of New York Press, 1990.

Knefelkamp, L., Widick, C., and Parker, C. A. (eds.). *Applying New Developmental Findings*. New Directions for Student Services, no. 4. San Francisco: Jossey-Bass, 1978.

Kuhn, T. *The Structure of Scientific Revolutions*. Chicago: University of Chicago Press, 1962.

Lasch, C. *The Minimal Self: Psychic Survival in Troubled Times*. New York: Norton, 1984.

Lawler, E. E., III. *High Involvement Management: Participative Strategies for Improving Organizational Performance*. San Francisco: Jossey-Bass, 1986.

Lawrence, P. R., and Lorsch, J. *Organization and Environment*. Cambridge, Mass.: Harvard Business School, 1967.

Levine, A. *Why Innovation Fails*. Albany: State University of New York Press, 1980.

Levine, A., and Associates. *Shaping Higher Education's Future: Demographic Realities and Opportunities, 1990–2000*. San Francisco: Jossey-Bass, 1989.

Lewis, G. "Trends in Student Aid, 1963–64 to 1988–89." *Research in Higher Education*, 1989, *30*, 547–561.

Lewis, L., and Kingston, P. "The Best, the Brightest, and the Most Affluent: Undergraduates at Elite Institutions." *Academe*, 1989, *75*, 28–33.

Lindquist, J. *Strategies for Change*. Washington, D.C.: Council of Independent Colleges, 1978.

Loye, D., and Eisler, R. "Chaos and Transformation: Implications of Nonequilibrium Theory for Social Science and Society." *Behavioral Science*, 1987, *32*, 53–65.

Lyotard, J. *The Postmodern Condition*. Minneapolis: University of Minnesota Press, 1984.

MacDonald, G. (ed.). *Five Experimental Colleges*. New York: HarperCollins, 1973.

MacGregor, J. Intellectual Development of Students in Learning Community Programs, 1986–1987. Washington Center Occasional Paper no. 1.

Olympia: Washington Center for Improving the Quality of Undergraduate Education, Evergreen State University, 1987.

MacGregor, J. "What Differences Do Learning Communities Make?" *Washington Center News*, 1991, 6, 4–9.

McPherson, M., and Schapiro, M. "How Well Does It Work?" *Change*, 1991, *23*, 16–22.

Marchese, T. "Bitting, Bargains, Seatwork, and Finishers." *Change*, 1985, *17*(3), 6–7.

Marchese, T. "Regional Accreditation." *Change*, 1991, *23*(3), 4.

Marchese, T. "AAHE and TQM (. . . Make That 'CQI')." *AAHE Bulletin*, 1992a, *45*, 11.

Marchese, T. "Getting a Handle on TQM." *Change*, 1992b, *24*, 4.

Martin, G. "Encounter with Education: Impact of an Alternative College on Student Development." Unpublished doctoral dissertation. Teachers College, Columbia University, 1982.

Martin, R. *Conformity: Standards and Change in Higher Education*. San Francisco: Jossey-Bass, 1969.

Martin, W. "Mission: A Statement of Identity and Direction." In J. Green, A. Levine, and Associates (eds.), *Opportunity and Adversity: How Colleges Can Succeed in Hard Times*. San Francisco: Jossey-Bass, 1985.

Mayhew, L. B. *Legacy of the Seventies: Experiment, Economy, Equality, and Expediency in American Higher Education*. San Francisco: Jossey-Bass, 1978.

Mayhew, L. B., Ford, P. J., and Hubbard, D. L. *The Quest for Quality: Challenge for Undergraduate Education in the 1990s*. San Francisco: Jossey-Bass, 1990.

Miles, M. "On Temporary Systems." In M. Miles (ed.), *Innovation in Education*. New York: Teachers College Press, 1964.

Moll, R. *The Public Ivys*. New York: Viking Penguin, 1986.

Nason, J. "Presidents and Governing Boards." In P. Altbach and R. Berdahl (eds.), *Higher Education in American Society*. Buffalo, N.Y.: Prometheus Books, 1981.

National Commission on Responsibilities for Financing Postsecondary Education. *Making College Affordable Again: Final Report*. Washington, D.C.: National Commission on Responsibilities for Financing Postsecondary Education, 1993.

National Institute of Education. *Involvement in Learning: Realizing the Potential of American Higher Education*. Washington, D.C.: National Institute of Education, 1984.

Newman, F., and others. *Report on Higher Education*. Washington, D.C.: U.S. Department of Health, Education and Welfare, 1971.

Nielsen, N. "Responding to the New Student Diversity." *Community, Technical and Junior College Journal*, 1991, *61*, 45–48.

"No Progress for Blacks and Hispanics on Equity in 1992." *Postsecondary Education Opportunity*, Feb. 1993, pp. 1–5.

O'Brien, E. "American Indians in Higher Education." *Research Briefs*, 1992, 3(3).

Odell, M., and Mock, J. (eds.). *A Crucial Agenda: Making Colleges and Universities Work Better for Minority Students*. Boulder, Colo.: Western Interstate Commission for Higher Education, 1989.

Office of Educational Research and Improvement. *Trends in Racial/Ethnic Enrollment in Higher Education, Fall 1978 Through Fall 1988: Survey Report*. Washington, D.C.: U.S. Department of Education, 1990.

Orfield, G. "Public Policy and College Opportunity." *American Journal of Education*, 1990, 98, 317–350.

O'Toole, J. *Work, Learning, and the American Future*. San Francisco: Jossey-Bass, 1977.

Palmer, P. *The Active Life*. San Francisco: HarperCollins, 1990.

Parsons, T. *The Social System*. New York: Free Press, 1951.

Parsons, T., and Bales, R. *Family, Socialization, and Interaction Process*. New York: Free Press, 1955.

Peck, R. D. *Future Focusing: An Alternative to Long-Range Planning*. Washington, D.C.: Council of Independent Colleges, 1985.

Perry, W. *Form of Intellectual and Ethical Development in the College Years: A Scheme*. Austin, Texas: Holt, Rinehart and Winston, 1970.

Peters, T. J. *Thriving on Chaos*. New York: HarperCollins, 1987.

Polak, F. *Image of the Future*. San Francisco: Jossey-Bass/Elsevier, 1972.

Prigogine, I., and Stengers, I. *Order out of Chaos*. New York: Bantam Books, 1984.

Quehl, G. H. "The Inner World of Leadership." Unpublished essay, Orinda, Calif., 1991.

Rice, E. "Recent Research on Adults and Careers: Implications for Equity, Planning, and Renewal." Unpublished manuscript. Department of Sociology, University of the Pacific, 1980.

Riesman, D., and Fuller, S. "Leaders: President Who Make a Difference." In J. Green, A. Levine, and Associates (eds.), *Opportunity and Adversity: How Colleges Can Succeed in Hard Times*. San Francisco: Jossey-Bass, 1985.

Riesman, D., and Grant, G. *The Perpetual Dream: Reform and Experiment in the American College*. Chicago: University of Chicago Press, 1978.

Riker, H. "Residential Learning." In A. W. Chickering and Associates (eds.), *The Modern American College: Responding to the New Realities of Diverse Students and a Changing Society*. San Francisco: Jossey-Bass, 1981.

Rose, D., and Sorensen, R. "Federal Student Financial Aid Awards as Subsidies for Higher Education: What Kinds of Institutions Are We Supporting?" *Research in Higher Education*, 1991, 32, 525–538.

Rossman, M. *On Learning and Social Change*. Berkeley, Calif.: Heyday Books, 1984.

Rudolph, F. *The American College and University: A History*. New York: Random House, 1962.

Rudolph, F. "The Power of Professors: The Impact of Specialization and Professionalism on the Curriculum." *Change*, 1984, *16*(4), 13–17.

Rudolph, F. "A Historical Look at Institutional Success in Hard Times." In J. Green, A. Levine, and Associates (eds.), *Opportunity and Adversity: How Colleges Can Succeed in Hard Times*. San Francisco: Jossey-Bass, 1985.

Sanford, N. "And a Time to Integrate." Charter Day address, Texas Tech, Feb. 10, 1973.

Sanford, N. *Learning After College*. Berkeley, Calif.: Montaigne Press, 1980.

Sanford, N. "Foreword." In A. W. Chickering and Associates (eds.)., *The Modern American College: Responding to the New Realities of Diverse Students and a Changing Society*. San Francisco: Jossey-Bass, 1981.

Schein, E. H. *Career Dynamics*. Reading, Mass.: Addison-Wesley, 1978.

Schein, E. H. *Organizational Psychology*. (3rd ed.) Englewood Cliffs, N.J.: Prentice Hall, 1980.

Schön, D. A. *Beyond the Stable State*. New York: Random House, 1971.

Schön, D. A. *The Reflective Practitioner: How Professionals Think in Action*. New York: Basic Books, 1983.

Schön, D. A. *Educating the Reflective Practitioner: Toward a New Design for Teaching and Learning in the Professions*. San Francisco: Jossey-Bass, 1987.

Schumacher, E. G. *Small Is Beautiful*. New York: HarperCollins, 1973.

Senge, P. *The Fifth Discipline*. New York: Doubleday, 1990.

Sennett, R. *Authority*. New York: Random House, 1981.

Seymour, D. "TQM on Campus: What the Pioneers Are Finding." *AAHE Bulletin*, 1991, *44*, 10–13.

Sherr, L. A., and Teeter, D. J. (eds.). *Total Quality Management in Higher Education*. New Directions for Institutional Research, no. 71. San Francisco: Jossey-Bass, 1991.

"Shifting Responsibilities for Financing Higher Education from Government to Individuals." *Postsecondary Education Opportunity*, Jan. 1994, pp. 7–11.

Skinner, E., and Richardson, R. C., Jr. "Resolving Access/Quality Tensions: Minority Participation and Achievement in Higher Education." Paper presented to the Association for the Study of Higher Education, St. Louis, Mo., Nov. 1988.

Smith, B. L. "The Washington Center: A Grassroots Approach to Faculty Development and Curricular Reform." *To Improve the Academy*, Oct. 1988, p. 165.

Smith, B. L. "Taking Structure Seriously." *Liberal Education*, Mar.-Apr. 1991, pp. 42–48.

Smith, B. L. "Creating Community in Difficult Places." *Liberal Education*, 1994a, pp. 32–39.

Smith, B. L. "Team Teaching Methods." In K. Prichard and R. M. Sawyer (eds.), *Handbook of College Teaching*. Westport, Conn.: Greenwood Press, 1994b.

Spanbauer, S. *A Quality System for Education*. Milwaukee: ASQC Quality Press, 1992.

Tawney, R. H. *The Acquisitive Society*. London: Collins, 1921.

Toffler, A. *Future Shock*. New York: Bantam Books, 1971.

Toffler, A. *The Third Wave*. New York: Morrow, 1980.

Tommerup, P. "Teaching and Learning at Evergreen: An Ethnographic Study." Unpublished doctoral dissertation. University of California, Los Angeles, 1993.

Tussman, J. *Experiment at Berkeley*. New York: Oxford University Press, 1969.

Tussman, J. *A Venture in Educational Reform: A Partial View*. Berkeley: Center for Studies in Higher Education, University of California, 1988.

Vaill, P. B. *Managing as a Performing Art: New Ideas for a World of Chaotic Change*. San Francisco: Jossey-Bass, 1989.

Vaughan, G. B. "Maintaining Open Access and Comprehensiveness." In D. A. Puryear and G. B. Vaughan (eds.), *Maintaining Institutional Integrity*. New Directions for Community Colleges, no. 52. San Francisco: Jossey-Bass, 1985.

Vroom, V. H., and Yetton, P. W. *Leadership and Decision Making*. Pittsburgh: University of Pittsburgh Press, 1973.

Waldrop, M. *Complexity: The Emerging Science at the Edge of Order and Chaos*. New York: Simon & Schuster, 1992.

Watson, G., and Johnson, D. *Social Psychology: Issues and Insights*. (2nd ed.) Philadelphia: HarperCollins, 1972.

Weber, M. *The Theory of Social and Economic Organization*. New York: Free Press, 1947.

Weber, M. *The Protestant Ethic and the Spirit of Capitalism*. New York: Scribner, 1958.

Whittington, M. "TQM at Penn." *AAHE Bulletin*, 1992, *45*, 3–5.

Winston, R. B. Jr., and Associates. *Developmental Academic Advising*. San Francisco: Jossey-Bass, 1984.

Woodward, J. *Management and Technology*. London: HMSO, 1958.

Zaleznick, A. *The Managerial Mystique*. New York: HarperCollins, 1989.

Zaleznick, A., and Kets de Vries, M.F.R. *Power and the Corporate Mind*. Chicago: Bonus Books, 1985.

Index